In Praise of *Renewing*

"As a country, and as individuals, we stand at a crossroads-to continue on a path to godlessness, or to return to the way of righteousness. In his powerful new book, **Renewing the Soul of America**, Chuck Crismier shows us how we can make decisions that enable us to reclaim our destiny..."

Bill Bright, Founder
Campus Crusade for Christ International

"What will happen to America and to the world if the people of this generation rediscover our spiritual heritage and commit their lives and the life of this nation to it? Chuck Crismier tells us in **Renewing the Soul of America** what can be done if we have the courage to make the right decisions."

Pat Robertson, CEO and Chairman of the board
The Christian Broadcasting Network, Inc.

"Crismier's call for repentance, racial reconciliation, and revival in the Christian community is extremely timely and important, resonating strongly with Promise Keepers' call for a return to genuine moral integrity, courageous faith, and unity in the Church!"

Bill McCartney, Founder and President
Promise Keepers

"Chuck probes the heart and conscience of our nation with a rare combination of insight, directness, urgency and compassion. This message desperately needs to be heard and heeded before it is too late."

Nancy Leigh DeMoss, author and broadcaster

"With an insightful grasp on the history of our nation's founding, added to a deep understanding of the judgment God has imposed upon nations outside of His holy will, Chuck Crismier clearly and crisply enunciates the choices facing not only America, but Americans in this dangerous period of our God-blessed, but God-warned country."

D. James Kennedy
Coral Ridge Ministries

"...needs to be read by every American who is concerned about the future of our great nation."

Peter Marshall, Author
The Light and the Glory

"...a prophet for our time, sharing the road map for renewal..."

Tom Phillips, Vice President
Billy Graham Evang. Assoc.

"...calling us to foundational virtues without which America will not survive as a nation."

John Dawson
Founder, Int'l. Reconciliation Coalition
Author, Healing America's Wounds

"If each of us acts on what Chuck says here, there is hope."

Pierre Bynum
Editor, The Capitol Hill Prayer Alert

"A must read...highly personal and deeply moving...."

James G. Floor
President, InterNet Associates

"Charles Crismier has put his finger on the cancer that is corrupting America."

Elmer L. Towns
Dean, School of Religion, Liberty University

"...provides awesome insight into God's prescription for us to finally experience a **Renewing the Soul of America**."

Evelyn Christenson
Founder, United Prayer Ministry

"It would be glorious if every spiritual leader in America could read this book."

Dr. Adrian Rogers, Pastor, Tennessee

"...words that stir our souls...a message for our time."

Mike McManus, Syndicated Columnist
Founder, Marriage Savers

"...neither the problem nor the solution are to be found in Washington. Chuck Crismier understands that."

Cal Thomas, Syndicated Columnist
Co-Author, Blinded By Might

"...a gold mine of perspectives on America's God-given purpose..."

David Bryant
President, Concerts of Prayer Inernational

"Chuck makes the point...without virtue there can be no liberty."

Marvin Olasky
Editor, WORLD *Magazine*

"I encourage all who love God and our nation to read this book...in order to achieve our God-given destiny."

Dr. John Perkins
Founder, Christian Community Devel. Assoc.

"This book will inspire your soul, break your heart, and drive you to your knees."

Kent Humphreys
Chairman, American Health Diagnostics

"...the nation is nearing spiritual shipwreck. I pray that the Lord will use this book to turn up the light in America's lighthouse."

Dr. Paul Cedar, Chairman
Mission America Coalition

"...a resource for years to come...a perspective that is lost in today's generation."

Dr. Gene Getz, Host of Renewal

"Chuck Crismier has an intense passion to see spiritual revival sweep this country. I hope that same passion will be ignited in your heart as you read this book."

Lee Grady
Editor, Charisma

"...reminds us that the words, 'Righteousness exalteth a nation...' are as true for America today as for ancient Israel."

Chuck Smith Jr., Pastor, California

"...the time is now for spiritual and moral renewal."

Tim Clinton, President
Amer. Assoc. of Christian Counselors

"Passionate, prophetic, and right on time!"

Sid Roth, President, Messianic Vision

"...leads the reader to understand the times and know what must be done."

Jim Russell
President, the AMY Foundation

RENEWING the SOUL of AMERICA

Charles Crismier

elijah books

Richmond, Virginia

Renewing the Soul of America
ISBN 0-9718428-0-9
Copyright © 2002 by Charles Crismier

Published by Elijah Books
P. O. Box 70879
Richmond, Virginia 23255

04 05 06 07 08 09 10 / 10 9 8 7 6 5 4 3

CONTENTS

ACKNOWLEDGMENTS

I believe that a working faith is formed in the foundry of daily family living. Similarly, the character of a child is forged on the anvil of the child's father's knee and in the womb of his or her mother's tough, yet tender, love.

I want to give credit to this unexpected aspect of upbringing for even the capacity to conceive such a book as *Renewing the Soul of America*. But even more, I want to pay tribute to a mother and a father whose lives were dedicated to the service of God and who faithfully, through daily living, brought honor to their country.

I owe my appreciation for truth and respect for authority to my father's example of rock-solid faith and steadfast character. And I attribute my love for God and my perseverance in the face of imposing odds to my mother's faithful prayer and daily encouragement. Such a heritage is a rich treasure to me. It is a wealth unmatched by material substance, of which my parents have had little.

I owe a great debt of gratitude to my wife, Kathie, and our daughters Lisa, Cherise, and Nicole. My seemingly endless hours spent in thought and research challenged their endurance. Yet, my family shared ownership of the need for what was being conceived in a husband's mind and given life in a daddy's heart. For they, too, were finding it increasingly difficult to swim upstream against the current of "political correctness" and to stay afloat in the murky cesspool of moral relativism. Theirs was a personal sacrifice of a husband's attention and a father's time and affection, and they knew that their loss was an investment in the survival of the nation in which their children, our grandchildren, would be raised. I am most blessed by their love and affirming support.

I would be remiss, however, if I failed to honor my faithful secretaries, Trisha Smith and Nicole Akyeampong, whose concern for the moral and spiritual environment in which they would raise their children flamed my own passion for moral renewal and spiritual revival in the land. Their dedication through countless hours of typing and manuscript revisions on evenings and weekends reflects their conviction that this was more than just a book—it was an open letter from the heart, a passionate plea.

And finally, encouragement from Dave Meyer, John Van Diest, and Keith Provance have made the publication process meaningful.

My debt of gratitude and appreciation is exceeded only by my great desire that the words of this book take root in the minds and hearts of my countrymen and that God, by His grace, would "preserve us a nation" by Renewing the Soul of America.

Charles Crismier

Chapter 1

IF I COULD SPEAK

I WAS BUT A GLEAM in the eye of my father. He was attending a dinner party at the estate of Edouard de Laboulaye in Versailles, France. The year was 1865. Gathered were a group of Frenchmen, and Laboulaye began expounding excitedly on his favorite subject—the United States of America.

A TALE OF TWO NATIONS

France and the United States had each gone through a revolution at nearly the same time near the end of the 1700s. America had claimed her independence from Britain. Many, if not most, of the American colonists had preferred to remain loyal subjects of the British Crown, but abuses of power by King George III and the British Parliament's increasing taxation without representation finally turned the hearts of the American colonists to declare their independence. France had lent support to the American cause, especially by the hand of the celebrated Marquis de Lafayette.

The citizens of France had revolted against their own government just after the American Revolution. But the French Revolution was a much bloodier affair. The French had fought against and among themselves. The French monarchy was abolished. King Louis XVI and his Queen, Marie Antoinette, along with thousands of their followers, were beheaded under the blade of the guillotine. Then the revolutionaries themselves struggled for power and executed each other. The blade of the guillotine never seemed satisfied with the blood that flowed. That time became known as the "Reign of Terror." Naturally, the sympathies of many of the American colonists were for the French in their pursuit of liberty. Although some similarities existed between the two revolutions, great fear existed among the American sympathizers because there was something distinctly different about the two revolutions.

The French citizenry had been stirred and motivated by the writings and spirit of Voltaire and Rousseau, renowned philosophers of the day. It was the "Age of Enlightenment," or so they said. Frenchmen were being urged to repudiate all ties of society that might restrict or restrain—especially *faith* and *family*. "Enlightenment" thinking conveyed the idea that true freedom was liberation from God and from moral constraint, that there was no absolute truth, and that all truth was relative to the individual or group as they might enter into social compact together.

The American colonists also pursued freedom, but they saw true freedom as coming voluntarily under the authority of Almighty God and His commandments as the Great Ruler of Nations. They found that true liberty issued from voluntary submission to law based upon the Bible as the authoritative Word of God. They had grappled with "enlightenment" philosophy, and although many of them were enticed by it, most of the Americans largely rejected it.

As A Nation Thinketh

The American "experiment" in self-government had become an obvious success to the rest of the world. America experienced growth and excitement, and the nation had a clear sense of direction and purpose. France had not fared so well, and that, too, was fairly obvious. She was unable to establish a stable government and suffered continuous internal problems caused by a stunted sense of direction and purpose.

In the 1830s, the French "sociologist" Alexis de Tocqueville came to America to explore and study "the secret of her genius and power." Several years of careful observation brought de Tocqueville to the conclusion that "America is great because America is good." He had recorded his findings in his book *Democracy in America.* America's thinking had made a difference. Its philosophy of life had determined its direction. And its thinking had been based on a faith that defined the behavior of its citizens. America was liberty in action. So de Tocqueville recorded, "Not until I went into the churches of America and heard her pulpits aflame with righteousness did I understand the secret of her genius and power." The American vision was giving birth to the American dream. It was conceived in liberty, a special kind of liberty that carried her through a civil war that *all* of her people might enjoy the blessings of liberty. America had become a beacon to the world.

Conceived in Liberty

My father was an artist, a sculptor. At the age of thirty-one, he had become renowned as a builder of patriotic statues. As he sat with his friend Laboulaye following dinner in that Versailles palace, their conversation turned to the desire for a republican form of government in France. The French people felt a kinship as they watched American liberty blossom. As the men talked, Laboulaye suggested giving a giant statue to the United States to unite the two countries in the cause of liberty. As a result of their conversation, I was conceived in the mind of my father, Frederic Auguste Bartholdi, who had never even been to America.

In August 1871, my father set off on a trip across America to generate interest in my birth. He was amazed and nearly overwhelmed by the vastness of the land and the wonder of her beauty. After five months, he had spread word of his plans. His enthusiasm was never dampened, although no one offered to help pay for the project. And he named me before I was born: "Liberty Enlightening the World."

BIRTH OF A LADY

He determined that I should be a lady. I was to hold the torch of freedom high. But France was still in a state of political turmoil. Finally, in 1874, when the French Assembly completed a written constitution for the Third Republic, my father decided that the timing was right to present publicly to his countrymen his idea that France give a monument of liberty to the United States.

His goal was to raise $250,000 for my birth, which he had scheduled for July 4, 1876. Fund-raising was time consuming. He had built a four-foot model of a dignified lady draped in a classic Roman gown. Her face was grim in her determination to rise victorious over all forms of tyranny, holding high the torch of freedom, her sandal-clad feet having broken the chains of oppression. She wore a crown of seven spikes, representing the seven seas and the seven continents. And I saw what I was to become.

I do not have time to describe in detail all of the joys and sorrows that attended my birth. Gustave Eiffel, the famous engineer of Eiffel Tower fame, erected a steel framework. I was given a thin copper skin. The builders attempted to prevent galvanic corrosion of my skin by insulating my iron framework and supports from contact with it. Six hundred thousand rivets bound my skin to my skeleton. After my pedestal had been built in America, I was shipped in 214 crates to be assembled on site. On October 28, 1886, I was born on Bedloe's Island in New York Harbor amid much fanfare. At birth, I stood 305 feet, one inch from foundation to torch and weighed 225 tons.

GROWING PAINS

I was thrilled as I stood high over New York Harbor. I watched American merchants transport their goods to other nations. I reveled in the hustle and bustle of people and progress. I felt almost as if I stood watch over the handiwork of God himself as the nation recovered from the Civil War and prospered, seemingly in the favor of God and man across the world.

When I was born, many people rejoiced, but some of them jeered. Some people thought that perhaps I would be a pagan influence. But that was never the intent of my heart. I knew down deep that I was only a symbol and that true liberty was born not in the heart of man but in the heart of God. Clearly, man, made in the image of God and following Him, experienced that same spirit of liberty, for it was written, "Where the Spirit of the Lord is, there is liberty."[1]

I witnessed the fervent spirit of many Americans. They were by and large a God-fearing people. Clearly, they found their roots in the Bible. Although some of them did not espouse Christian faith, most of them did, and all of them were convinced that the only workable guidelines for life, business, and self-government were to be found in the Bible. The Bible was the basis for our laws, our families, and our society together.

In fact, just six years after I was born, our United States Supreme Court, in a case referred to as *The Church of the Holy Trinity vs. United States*, declared, ". . . this is a Christian nation."[2] And this America in which I was born was good—not perfect, but very good as nations go. It was a joy to be among the people. That the nation was blessed by the hand of God was beyond dispute. And the joy of that goodness and the prosperity that it brought caused me to glow from the inside. I just felt like radiating the light of that blessing across the seas and the continents, for there was great suffering and discontent elsewhere in the world. Although I was aware that I had a few skin problems and minor skeletal problems in those days, I felt good. It was good to be here.

THE LIGHT THAT SHINES

Someone has said that "beauty is only skin deep." But the beauty of America was not only what one could *see* but also what one could *feel*. It was as if it went to the core of its very being, to its heart. I felt the substance of its moral goodness in my heart. And I was not alone. It was as if America was the very essence of goodness, of life, of purity, and of nobility of mind and purpose. I felt that for myself. And as I stood daily to welcome those immigrants who followed my beacon to safe harbor on these shores, it was clear that I had become a symbol of not only liberty but also moral goodness and virtue. I believe that true liberty should breed virtue—and it did.

People flooded by me daily in ships from around the world. It was a never-ending procession. But they did not come to visit; they came to stay. They fled persecution, corruption, violence, and poverty. They yearned to be free and to experience the blessings of liberty.

America was a land of opportunity, a land of laws and not of men, a land where God presided as Lord over the affairs of men, and that fact was reflected in every aspect of our society. But we could hardly keep up with the teeming masses who followed the light of liberty. The attempt to do so was both agony and ecstasy. As my father had said when he named me, I was indeed "Liberty Enlightening the World."

A MOTHERING HAND

Interestingly, my role in symbolizing liberty was not yet clearly established. It takes time to become accepted and recognized. But when people need you, it is amazing what can happen to their thinking.

The world was becoming more intense. Storm clouds of war darkened the horizon. Suddenly, we found ourselves involved in "the war to end all wars"—World War I. Along with the rest of the American people, I was concerned. Although the battle was not raging on our shores, Americans experienced fear. We even had a surprise attack on a munitions facility just across the bay from where I stood. Those were real fireworks, and I was wounded in the explosions, but not seriously.

Our people needed a rallying point. War is stressful and demanding. There is no room for fear. It is a time not for selfish pursuits but for working together. Liberty was at stake. We had to pull together, not only for ourselves but also for peoples around the world. The world looked to us. Even Americans needed a symbol around which to rally. I held the torch of freedom high, and they began looking to me. I was not the source of freedom but only a symbol of it.

I was finally accepted in my American home. I stirred the hearts of my countrymen. I was no longer just a mother to tired immigrants but a source of encouragement to the entire nation. And they began calling me "The Statue of Liberty." I held high to all my mothering hand of freedom.

YEARS OF LEAN, YEARS OF PLENTY

The war was over. We thought that we had made the world "safe for democracy." But it was not long before we languished in a severe depression. We tried to hold our heads high while we stood in bread lines. By God's grace we recovered, but were confronted with a Second World War. It was tough. The price of freedom was not only vigilance but also blood—the blood of our young men. We learned that freedom is not free. We paid the price. We sacrificed. And we were proud to keep our honor clean as we set about helping rebuild the destruction around the world following our victory.

Victory is sweet, but prosperity in peace seems sweeter. I thrilled to see "swords beaten into plowshares." We began to feel good again. We prospered. While I rejoiced in the blessings of liberty that my countrymen enjoyed, I was beginning to feel a bit ignored. It had been years since I had received any real personal attention. Certainly, I had been available to aid in the cause of freedom as we fought, and sometimes it seemed as if I was even the center of attention, especially when my countrymen needed me as a symbol and needed my encouragement and strength.

But my skin was not doing well. I began feeling aches and pains throughout my support skeleton. I tried to ignore my own pains because there was no time, no energy, and no money for such maintenance and repair. But I was beginning to weaken. The stress of the harsh living environment was corroding my inner being. Yet my needs seemed to receive only token attention.

How could this be, I thought, *amid such prosperity? Surely there is sufficient time now to attend to my maintenance. We are no longer at war. Surely there are sufficient finances to keep me in repair.* A few people seemed concerned, but most people went on about their business. I tried not to worry or to think about the increasing feelings of weakness in my body. I felt it reaching increasingly into the very heart of my being. *And this is prosperity?* I thought.

LIKE MOTHER, LIKE DAUGHTER

My thoughts began to wander. With every pain I felt in my iron bones, I began to consider the well-being of the nation that I had served. With every cry of my inner being, I sensed a cry from the hearts of my countrymen. I had become like a mother to my countrymen. And as I looked at my tattered skin in the light reflecting from the waves of life crashing about me, I saw also the darkened countenance and pitted image of the faces of the daughters of America. And then I realized the truth: I am only a symbol; my countrymen are the substance.

And what was happening to me was also happening to them. They were being corroded from the inside out by the harsh environment of godless forces and humanistic philosophies that had torn the soul from the nation from which my father had come. They had left it weak and without the vitality of the spiritual awakening that had preserved her since the time of the Pilgrims and the Puritans. And I saw the devastating effect of corrosion of inward character in the faces and lives of the countrymen I had come to love. I was grieved. It was "like mother, like daughter."

Finally, some people began to take my plight seriously. When they took the time from their busy schedules, they discovered not only that my copper skin was in need of repair but also that severe corrosion in my foundation and framework threatened my very existence. I recalled the words of my father, Bartholdi. He had thought that I would stand the test of time, a beacon of liberty for thousands of years. I would never fall. I had thought the same of America. But if something did not happen soon, my days were numbered. So I worried for America.

LIBERTY OR DEATH

I was dying. That is a terrible thought. I could hardly face it, but it was true. Careless use and abuse had left me unprepared for the pressures and trials of a new century, a new millennium. Yet I wanted to live. I wanted to continue to stand tall, to hold the torch of freedom high for both the world and the American people.

I saw and felt the agony of body and spirit wracking the lives of my fellow Americans because it was my body, my spirit; I was but a symbol. Thoughts rushed through my mind. *How could this have happened? How could I, who was thought to be a timeless symbol, be in a life-and-death struggle? How could America, looked upon by her people and the world as a timeless bastion of freedom, be struggling with a cancerous corrosion of inner character and spirit that threatened her very existence?*

Yet I could not deny the truth. The carelessness of years of personal peace and affluence had allowed the very fiber of America's being, the substance of its soul, to be eaten way.

I turned away. It is hard to look at the ravages of cancer on a body. It is hard to accept the torn families, broken lives, violence, economic despair, and lack of a sense of direction, meaning, and purpose that had set in. But I saw it in the lives of my countrymen. And then I understood more clearly that indeed "the price of liberty is eternal vigilance."[3] When the price is not paid—the price of eternal vigilance—a much higher price will be paid, the ultimate price—*death*. I could not bear the thought.

RESTORING THE SYMBOL

Then it came to me: *They are going to restore me.* America is not going to let me die. My fellow citizens are not going to allow internal corrosion to eat away my substance. They are rallying to the cause. They say that it will be costly, but then that which is valuable is costly. Perhaps it would not have been so costly if they had attended faithfully to my needs. But then we cannot wish for what might have been. I am dying. It will take near-heroic measures to preserve me—and more than $250 million.

I also considered, *What will it take to preserve my nation? What will it take to renew its soul?* It might take billions of dollars. Yet it is really not a matter of dollars and cents, for my fellow citizens are already spending themselves silly. No, my nation does not need money. It needs mothers and fathers who are committed to train their children. It needs schoolteachers who live lives of principle and are not afraid to impart those principles. It needs husbands who love their wives and wives who respect and honor their husbands. It needs businesspeople who will not lie. It needs lawyers who triumph only in the truth. It needs public servants and not politicians. It needs pastors and priests who will not pander for popularity among their parishioners by trading God's timeless truth for the tawdry self-interest of self-help doctrines. It needs men and women of character, of courage, and of compassion. It needs a new you and a new me.

So I was ecstatic when leaders among my fellow citizens committed to restore me. The restoration was not to be "skin deep." I heard them say that they would renew, rebuild, and restore me from the inside out. And I hoped that they would do the same for my nation, the land that I love.

It took several years. My iron ribs were replaced or repaired. New protection was provided to prevent the terrible corrosion that had eaten away my inward parts. Care was taken to protect against those who would attack my inward being with dark and perverted messages of modern philosophy through graffiti on the walls of my mind. My foundations were secured, and my framework was rebuilt because its basic original design was good.

And after my inner substance was restored, my copper skin was cleaned and my blemishes were removed. I felt like a new woman. The work on the inside was reflected on the outside. I yearned for such a work for my America, but all I heard was the anguished cry of its people out of the pain of her decay. I was deeply grieved for my nation, desiring that it experience the same joy of restoration. But my fellow citizens seemed to have little interest. They seemed not to see the connection between my decay and theirs.

My crowning glory was the replacement of my beacon and the torch of freedom. I was nearly overwhelmed with emotion. With body and soul whole, my light of liberty once again shown even more brightly across the seas and continents of the world. Darkness had been creeping in. Moral decline and spiritual decay enshrouded my being with an ominous dusk that portended the twilight of liberty—and even of civilization itself.

One hundred years had brought me near death. But on October 28, 1986, as my beacon of virtue and liberty blazed forth gloriously with renewed intensity across the waters, darkness was dispelled. I stood tall once again, secure in the thought that the blessings of liberty and the light of freedom were assured to generations to come. But then I remembered painfully, *I am but a symbol.* My mind was wrenched! I cried out from within: *Which way, America? Which way will you go? This is my country, and I want to know. Which way, America, will you go?*

And I ask you, my fellow citizens, "Which way will you go?" I realized long ago that America is no greater than its people. Its faith is no greater than your faith. Its courage is no stronger than your courage. Its virtue is no purer than your virtue. Its principles are no firmer than your principles. Its vision is no clearer than your vision. Its foundation is no more secure than your foundation. Its heart is no more compassionate than your heart. And God's truth will march on only if it marches in your boots.

So which way, father, mother, husband, wife, businessman, politician, pastor, priest, will you go? Will you ignore your inner corrosion of mind and heart? Will you wink at the corruption of your character? Will you deny the cancer that ravages your soul? Will you pursue business as usual until your light is darkness and you have no more strength to stand? Or will you arise, rebuild, and once again restore the beacon of freedom and the virtues of true liberty in your life that the light and the glory of God, your Creator, will again be revealed in the life of *We the people?* If you would be restored, you must bow in repentance.

As Lady Liberty, I cry out to you, my fellow citizens, with impassioned heart, "Let the God who made and preserved us a nation renew your soul!" And to the great Ruler of Nations who governs in the affairs of men I plead:

> God bless America,
> Land that I love;
> Stand beside her,
> And guide her,
>
> Through the night
> With the Light
> From above;
>
> From the mountains,
> To the prairie,
> To the ocean
> White with foam,
>
> God bless America,
> My home, sweet home;
> God bless America,
> My home, sweet home.[4]

SOUL-STIRRING QUESTIONS FOR PERSONAL AND GROUP REFLECTION

1. What has the Statue of Liberty meant to you as an American?

2. What might motivate a foreigner like Frederic Bartholdi to want to expend such incredible time, talent, and energy to honor America with an immense statue shortly after our Civil War? What might he have seen in America that he did not see in France?

3. What moral or spiritual parallels to the internal decay of the Statue of Liberty have you seen in your own life over the last twenty years?

4. Do you believe that something has gone wrong in the life of our nation?

5. What observations have you made from your place as a citizen, student, mother, father, grandparent, etc., that cause you concern about our future?

6. Do you believe that your life and ways have contributed in any measure to America's moral and spiritual decline?

Chapter 2

A NATION AT RISK

IN HER RELATIVELY SHORT EXISTENCE, America has influenced the world for good as has no other nation in history. From a fledgling association of thirteen colonies struggling to get up and walk as a nation of one people to its position as the nation to which all eyes in the world turn, America has been blessed. One can scarcely indulge in even a brief review of its meteoric rise from the heroic bloodshed of the Revolutionary War to its position as leader among the powers of the earth without seeing the unmistakable hand of God upon the nation.

But America is at risk. Her foundations are cracking. And it appears the hand of God's protection is being withdrawn. The principles that made us great have become tarnished, and our moral fiber is corroded. We have been in turmoil from incessant infighting. We have become a nation in which everyone is a minority striving for "special interests." There is no "common sense." Despite the horror of terrorism, our enemy most to be feared is not from without, but is within. There is a vicious moral and spiritual war raging in the hearts and minds of Americans. Can we survive? Can America be saved? If so, how?

OUR CONSTITUTION WAS "SAVED"

As our Founding Fathers deliberated day after day in the seething heat of a Philadelphia summer to hammer out a constitution that would serve the emerging nation, they met with nerve-wracking frustration as delegates from the colonies sought to protect their "special interests." Tempers flared. Passions were inflamed. The task of achieving any consensus for a workable plan for the new government seemed doomed. Some delegates had already walked out. At that moment of despair and seeming hopelessness, Benjamin Franklin, the elder statesman, rose and addressed the president of the convention, George Washington, declaring:

Mr. President,

In this situation of this Assembly, groping as it were in the dark to find political truth, and scarce able to distinguish it when presented to us, how has it happened, Sir, that we have not hitherto once thought of humbly applying to the Father of lights to illuminate our understanding? In the beginning of the contest with Great Britain, when we were sensible of danger, we had daily prayer in this room for the Divine protection. Our prayers, Sir, were heard, and they were graciously answered. . . . And have we forgotten this powerful Friend? Or do we imagine we no longer need His assistance? I have lived, Sir, a long time, and the longer I live, the more convincing proofs I see of this truth—that God governs in the affairs of men.

Benjamin Franklin then went on to declare to that awesome assembly of the greatest minds in America, "If a sparrow cannot fall to the ground without His notice, is it probable that an empire can rise without His aid?"

Then he declared, "We have been assured, Sir, in the Sacred Writings, that except the Lord build the house, they labor in vain that build it."

The senior statesman then delivered his personal conviction concerning the future of the nation:

> I firmly believe that without His concurring aid, we shall succeed in this political building no better than the builders of Babel. We shall be divided by our little partial local interests; our projects will be confounded; and we ourselves shall become a reproach and a bye word down to future ages. . . . I therefore beg leave to move—that henceforth prayers imploring the assistance of Heaven, and its blessings on our deliberations, be held in this Assembly every morning before we proceed to business. . . .[5]

The Assembly of fifty-five of America's greatest intellectuals and leaders solemnly and humbly adopted Benjamin Franklin's motion, and each session thereafter was begun with prayer for God's guidance and wisdom. The effect on the Convention was nothing short of miraculous. The hand of Divine Providence was clearly revealed, as wisdom began to prevail over wrath and consensus over confusion. The delegates began to seek principle rather than personal position. A sense of order and direction emerged, resulting in the drafting and adoption of what leaders throughout the world have acknowledged as the greatest document ever crafted by the human mind. No constitution of any nation in the world has endured as has that seemingly Divinely inspired document. In the words of James Madison, the principal drafter of the Constitution and our fourth president, "Without the intervention of God there never would have been a Constitution."[6]

CHRISTIAN CONSENSUS AND AMERICA'S GREATNESS

The consensus of Christian faith as the foundation of America and its greatness is replete in virtually every fiber of the original fabric of the nation. All thirteen of the original state constitutions refer to Almighty God as the Author of liberty or declare reliance upon the hand and mercy of Providence. George Washington declared, "Of all the dispositions and habits that lead to political prosperity, religion and morality are indispensable supports. . . ."[7]

A generation after the Constitution was adopted, when the French political observer Alexis de Tocqueville came to these United States in the mid-1800s to study the success of the nation, he was greatly moved by what he found. He had observed how France had struggled after the French Revolution—enmeshed in the "Enlightenment," a secular humanist worldview. In America, he found a nearly universal belief in the principles of the Bible as the basis for law and life. He wrote in his book *Democracy in America*, "America is great because America is good. And if America ever ceases to be good, America will cease to be great."[8]

OUR PAST GIVES FOCUS TO OUR FUTURE

Woodrow Wilson, the twenty-eighth president of the United States of America, expounded to us as a people, "A nation which does not remember what it was yesterday does not know what it is today, nor what it is trying to do."[9]

George Washington, our founding president and the commander-in-chief of the American War for Independence, gave us a legacy worth remembering. Stated simply in his farewell address: "Reason and experience both forbid us to expect that National morality can prevail in exclusion of religious principle."[10]

That legacy was confirmed and at the same time reiterated when we officially adopted as our national motto "In God We Trust."

Our pledge of allegiance to the flag was officially changed in 1954 by an act of Congress, adding the words *one nation under God.* . . .[11]

But we, this last generation, have forgotten that Divine "Friend" upon whose power and guidance our forefathers relied. We have allowed the strident voices of a minority to convince us that our Creator should be dismissed from the halls of political debate, from the classrooms of our youth, from our decisions as a people, and from our conduct as individuals.

The shift from dependence upon our Maker to reliance upon ourselves has undermined the very foundations of this great American "house." The foundations are cracking, and America is clearly slipping off its foundation. Even secular observers now join in identifying the frightening picture before us. Witness the national headlines and commentaries that appeared just before the 1992 presidential election:

"How Our American Dream Unraveled"[12]
—*Newsweek,* March 2, 1992

"The Glooming of America—A Nation Down in the Dumps"[13]
—*Newsweek,* Jan. 13, 1992

". . . we believed that prosperity would create the Good Society. We were wrong."[14]
—*Newsweek,* March 2, 1992

"The Fraying of America"[15]
—*Time*, Feb. 3, 1992

"If America doesn't watch out, it is going to be judged as
finished by the world."[16]
—Associated Press, Jan. 21, 1992

"Voters are demanding in their leaders the personal virtues they
decreasingly demand of themselves."[17]
—*Time*, April 27, 1992

"We unwittingly adopted a view of human nature that assumed
spiritual needs could ultimately be satisfied with material
goods."[18]
—*Newsweek*, March 2, 1992

MIRROR-IMAGE REFLECTIONS

Just four years later, in the midst of the 1996 presidential campaign, the First Lady of the United States, a professed Methodist
and Christian, was discovered to have been consulting with a
New Age psychic in the White House, America's national house.[19]
Columnist Maureen Dowd lamented, "It seems sad, not only
about the first lady, but about the country. Why has America
developed this obsessive attention to self?"[20] What has happened
in the heart of a nation where First Ladies of the two leading political parties have in this last generation sought counsel from psy-
chics and astrologers rather than their Creator for personal and
national guidance?

The character issues that confronted the nation in 1992 turned to
open scandal by 1996. A nation that bristled at the Watergate
debacle in 1975 was too numb to respond to the multiple traumas
of Whitewatergate, Travelgate, Chinagate, and numerous other

breaches of public trust. "We are on scandal overload," observed political commentator William Safire when White House fund-raising scandals broke wide open. He asked rhetorically, "Will anything so old-fashioned as moral outrage ever make a come-back." He responded to his own question, "The fault lies in our-selves . . . we are benumbed."[21] Michael Kinsley, with characteristic American optimism, justified all of the scandals with his white-washing essay, "Everybody Does It," extending blanket absolution to the president and the people alike.[22]

Politics became unabashedly devoid of principle. "The polls have replaced judgment," noted *U.S. News and World Report.* "Polls have become for modern politicians and pundits what the oracle at Delphi was to the ancient Greeks. . . ." "Polls tell them everything except how to behave with integrity, judgment and honesty."[23]

U.S. News and World Report made observations that should have sent shock waves throughout the land, but we were too numb. "Never has the public felt so alienated from its leaders. Trust in the Federal Government has taken a nosedive from four decades ago when seventy-five percent of Americans said they had faith in the folks in Washington to do the right thing most of the time. Today, three out of four say they have no such faith. In fact, a third of those questioned in a recent Gallup poll say their *faith is so low they think the Federal Government poses 'an immediate threat to the rights and freedoms of ordinary citizens'*"[24] (emphasis added).

Then came the mother of all scandals: Presidential philander-ing with oral sex in the Oval Office coupled with notorious, in-your-face lying to the American people on national television; and obstruction of justice, all without repentance or resignation. We experienced the second presidential impeachment in the nation's history, yet we were unmoved. We saw, as a people, our collective reflection in the mirror of our president's life and, collectively convicted of moral debauchery as a people, we lacked the courage to convict him, declaring in false compassion, "He that is without sin cast the first stone."[25] And so the nation of laws became a nation of mere men, everyone doing that which was right in his own eyes. Deviancy was defined down to a national lowest "common denominator."

Yet, just a year later, the impeached president stood before a joint session of Congress and ludicrously declared in his January 2000 State of the Union Address, "We have built a new economy, and our economic revolution has been matched by a revival in the American spirit. My fellow Americans, the state of our union is as strong as it has ever been." It is precisely this characteristic state of denial of the moral and spiritual reality of our life and times from the church house to the White House which has resulted in what thoughtful observers call "a moral and spiritual disconnect." Pollster George Gallup, in his monthly *Emerging Trends,* described this gap as "the difference between the way we think of ourselves and the way we actually are."[26] Apparently, we really are getting the leaders we deserve. Our representatives are a mirror-image reflection of *We the People.*

WHAT IS WRONG WITH US?

In a gutsy editorial in *Time's* "The Looking Glass," political observer Jeff Greenfield gives us a serious look at our looking-glass image.

"What is Wrong With Us?" It is in the air we breathe. The things we do. The things we say. Our books. Our papers. Our theater. Our movies. Our radio and television. The way we behave. The values we fix. . . . We are, on average, rich beyond the dreams of kings of old. Yet something is not there that should be—something we once had.

Forty-one American newspapers and magazines reprinted those words. They were not the words of Jeff Greenfield but of *Cleveland Press* editor Lewis Seltzer—in 1952! Letters and phone calls flooded Seltzer's office, said Greenfield, to tell Seltzer that he had put his finger on our gravest crisis. If Seltzer's diagnosis was correct in 1952, what would it be today? Greenfield gives his own observation: "It is finally dawning on us that we may have made a Faustian bargain a half-century ago, swapping community and neighborhood and roots for the expectation of material abundance. . . ."[27] Perhaps *Time* distilled the diagnosis most profoundly and succinctly with its blatant front cover on April 5, 1993: "The Generation That Forgot God."[28]

WHERE LIES OUR HOPE?

George Gallup reports our own opinions about the devastating dilemma that threatens our nation's destiny. He concludes we are in a moral and spiritual crisis, with seventy-six percent of Americans believing that our moral values have weakened in the past twenty-five years. He notes that the public is "more concerned about morals today than at any time in the last 60 years."[29]

Neither politics nor terrorists created our moral and spiritual slide; neither can politics or eradication of terrorists correct it. Our politics, both liberal and conservative, reflect our moral and spiritual slide. For this reason, former Christian Coalition leaders Don Hodel and Randy Tate, with surprising candor, declared:

Even if every leader in this country from the White House to the school house shared our political goals, this nation still would not change. America cannot change until the hearts of the people change.[30]

It is clear. If we want to save this great American "house," we must repair and rebuild the foundations. But when a great house has become so decayed that even its foundations lie in ruin, it becomes necessary to go back to the original building plans to determine how that house was built. Where and how were the foundations established? What building materials were used?

Is there a message of hope in the midst of our horror? There is if we are willing to participate in *Renewing the Soul of America*. In the following chapter we inspect the "building plans" of America— the greatest national "house" in the history of mankind outside Israel. We must rediscover her original foundations.

"There is nothing short of a spiritual renewal and revival that will save us."

Dr. James Dobson
National Solemn Assembly, October 2002
Constitution Hall

Soul-Stirring Questions for Personal and Group Reflection

1. Why do you think our founding leaders prayed during the heat of the Revolutionary War but forgot to pray during the first six weeks of the Constitutional Convention?

2. What do you think Benjamin Franklin meant when he quoted the Bible to George Washington, saying, "Unless the Lord build the house, they labor in vain that build it"?

3. Do you believe that there is any significance to the fact that all thirteen of the original state constitutions refer to Almighty God as the Author of liberty or declare reliance upon the hand and mercy of Providence?

4. Do you agree with Alexis de Tocqueville that "America is great because America is good, and if America ever ceases to be good, America will cease to be great"? Why do you agree or disagree?

5. Why do you think George Washington declared, "Of all the dispositions and habits that lead to political prosperity, religion and morality are indispensable supports"?

6. Are religion and morality indispensable supports of your life? Are those supports in good condition or in decay?

A house with a crumbling foundation
will soon be a crumbling house.

Chapter 3

REMEMBERING OUR FOUNDATIONS

NO AMERICAN PRESIDENT HAS ENJOYED greater respect and honor for truth and integrity as viewed through the eye of history than Abraham Lincoln. President Lincoln clearly enunciated the source of American's blessing or that of any nation:

> It is the duty of nations, as well as of men, to own their dependence upon the overruling power of God and to recognize the sublime truth announced in the Holy Scriptures and proven by all history, that those nations only are blessed whose God is the Lord.[31]

John Adams, the second president of the United States, declared:

> Our Constitution was made only for a moral and religious people. It is wholly inadequate to the government of any other.

We have no government armed with power capable of contending with human passions unbridled by morality and religion.[32]

CONSEQUENCES OF UNDERMINED FOUNDATIONS

For just a brief moment, let us take a fleeting glimpse at what we have become as a nation. How has this great house slipped? It is a painful task, but we must look at the reflection of our souls because "America's future, your future, and the future of your children may depend on it."

James Patterson and Peter Kim, advertising executives of the respected J. Walter Thompson Agency in New York, set out to take the "moral pulse" of America in the 1990s. Using state-of-the-art research techniques, they conducted the largest poll of private morals ever undertaken to unearth the personal ethics, values, and beliefs of Americans of our time. Their findings are disclosed in their very insightful book, *The Day America Told the Truth* (1991). Following are illustrative excerpts of their findings.

"America has no leaders and, especially, no moral leadership."

"Our void in leadership—moral and otherwise—has reached a critical stage. We still want leadership; we just can't seem to find it."

"There is absolutely no moral consensus at all. . . ."

"Americans are making up their own rules, their own laws, their own moral codes."

"Only 13 percent of us believe in all of the Ten Commandments."

"Sixty percent of all Americans have been victims of a major crime. Fifty-eight percent of those people have been victimized twice."

"One in seven Americans has been sexually abused as a child."

"One in six Americans has been physically abused as a child."

"The number one cause of our business decline is low ethics by executives."

"While we still marry, we have lost faith in the institution of marriage."

"A majority of us will not take care of our parents in old age."

"Most Americans have no respect for what the law says."

"The Protestant ethic is long gone from today's American workplace."

"Every seventh person you pass on the street in America is carrying a weapon either on their person or in their car."

America is "the most violent country in the world."

"Children's [television] programming now averages twenty-five violent acts per hour."

"Whether we are adults or children, the sheer volume of the violence we witness is numbing." "This urge toward violent action is creating real epidemics in America—epidemics of violence."

"Lying has become an integral part of the American culture, a trait of the American character."

"We can no longer tell right from wrong. It raises fear and doubt, which often leads to depression."

"Americans have more of both freedom and doubt—and of depression too—than did any previous generation."[33]

Patterson and Kim conclude:

"Americans wrestle with these questions in what often amounts to a moral vacuum. The religious figures and scriptures that gave us rules for so many centuries, the political system that gave us our laws, all have lost their meaning in our moral imagination: We've become wishy-washy as a nation. Some would say we've lost our moral backbone."[34]

WHAT CAN WE DO?

A newspaper reporter attended a gathering where I spoke on the subject "Stand Up, America." In substance, I had conveyed much of the same information in that meeting, although in much more detail, as you have just read. That reporter called me at my office shortly afterward and asked, "What can we do to save America? What do you want us to do?"

Initially, I was puzzled by his question because the answer seemed obvious. As we chatted further, however, I learned quickly that the answer was not obvious to him, nor is it obvious to the majority of my fellow citizens. We have slipped so far off our foundations that we have lost sight of our vision for truths and principles that formerly defined our very identity as a nation and a people. Just as Woodrow Wilson warned, as Americans we no longer remember what we were yesterday; therefore, we do not know who we are today or even what we are trying to do.

Thomas Jefferson, author of our Declaration of Independence, gives us direction in answering this threshold question, "What can we do to save America?" His voice still speaks because the following words are inscribed on the Jefferson Memorial in our nation's Capitol:

"God who gave us life gave us liberty. Can the liberties of a nation be secure when we have removed a conviction that these liberties are the gift of God?"[35]

Jefferson is reminding America that if we want to continue to enjoy the liberties that our Founding Fathers secured for us at great cost, we must restore the conviction and acknowledge unashamedly that these liberties are the gift of God, not the gift of ourselves, and then conduct our national and individual lives accordingly. We must return to the foundational principles of the Bible—the instruction manual of the Almighty for His creatures and creation.

Noah Webster, author of the oldest dictionary in America and a leading voice in the early development of our nation, could not have set forth more clearly this essential element of our national prosperity. His statesmanship rings forth:

"The moral principles and precepts contained in the Scriptures ought to form the basis of all our civil constitutions and laws. All the miseries and evils which men suffer from vice, crime, ambition, injustice, oppression, slavery, and war proceed from their despising or neglecting the precepts contained in the Bible."[36]

Thomas Jefferson's words continue to reverberate: "Indeed I tremble for my country when I reflect that God is just, that His justice cannot sleep forever."[37]

I spent considerable time engaged with that newspaper reporter in discussion about where we are as a nation and about the critical need to rebuild our moral and spiritual foundations. "We must turn the tide of public sentiment," I told him. His response is important because it reflects the mind and thought of many Americans. He said, "Mr. Crismier, that's a tall order. That could take years, a decade, maybe a generation!"

I responded, "That's right! Rome was not built in a day, neither was it destroyed in a day."

We live in an "instant" society. We demand instant gratification and instant solutions. Our "button pushing" mentality is a modern version of the fairy waving the magic wand. But the most valuable things in life—things such as faith, character, integrity; things on which it is worthy of building one's life; things that are worthy on which to build or rebuild a nation—do not come instantly or by magic wands.

FROM THE PRINCIPLE TO THE PERSONAL

We cannot succeed if we do not begin. We must chart our course—a course to rebuild the moral and spiritual foundations of America. We must rebuild the American character. Begin today! Begin in your own life, in your family, wherever you are. Begin!

The short chapters that follow are intended to help us translate the basic need to rebuild the moral and spiritual foundations of America into practical, personal reality. It can be done! It will not be accomplished by the president, by Congress, or by any political process. It will be accomplished by you, by me, by your family, by my family, and by millions of Americans like you and me who love their country and pledge themselves to restore and preserve it.

THIS IS THE HOUR OF CRISIS!

Together, with God's help, we can change what "is" to "what should be." We can once again become a nation of vision, purpose, and character.

Together, with God's enabling power, we can **Save America.** We can "preserve us a nation." But time is short, and renewing the soul of America requires surrender to God's sovereign plans and purposes in our individual and national life.

If the foundations be destroyed, what can the righteous do?[38]

—*The Bible*

SOUL-STIRRING QUESTIONS FOR PERSONAL AND GROUP REFLECTION

1. Abraham Lincoln declared, "Those nations only are blessed whose God is the Lord." What do you think he meant? Why do you agree or disagree?

2. What is unique about American government that caused John Adams, our second president, to say, "Our Constitution was made for a moral and religious people. It is wholly inadequate to the government of any other"?

3. What thoughts passed through your mind as you read Patterson and Kim's findings on the state of American morals taken from their book *The Day America Told the Truth*?

4. Do you see any ways in which you have lost your moral backbone?

5. Where would you start to rebuild the moral and spiritual foundations of our nation?

Chapter 4

AMERICA'S SEARCH FOR LEADERS

THERE IS A NATIONAL CRY FOR leadership in America today. Why do we seem to be unable to find in this "enlightened" moment in our history men and women who challenge the hearts and minds of their fellow citizens? Why do we have so little sense of direction? Why is hope waning and despair increasing? Why have our latest national elections produced the lowest voter turnout in the history of the republic? Where have all the leaders gone? In the next few pages, we will look briefly at qualities and characteristics that make for effective leaders. Dare to see in the imagination of your own heart yourself being characterized by these qualities. But first, let us look once again to our Founding Fathers.

EXAMPLES FROM OUR FOUNDING FATHERS

After the American Revolution and about the time of the Constitutional Convention, around 1785–1789, the population of the thirteen colonies was approximately three million; that is nearly the size of the city (not the county) of Los Angeles today. Thomas Jefferson said of the fifty-five delegates who gathered at the Constitutional Convention in Philadelphia in 1789, "A more able assembly never sat in America."

Who today would make such an observation of any gathering of "leadership" in Los Angeles, New York, Washington, D.C., or even the entire nation today?

Although our Founding Fathers did not agree with each another on *every* issue, they had a comradeship of respect and a recognition of the qualities of leadership among them. Although they might not have manifested perfection in all of life's arenas, they were generally perceived to be worthy of honor.

I have examined the lives of these men who laid the foundations for this great nation to see what made them worthy of honor and respect, men who could not only lead but also establish a nation. Although each of them had his own weaknesses, as a group, they were examples of:

- vision
- principle
- truth
- virtue
- honor
- fidelity
- courage
- responsibility
- faith
- compassion
- integrity

Each was, in his own way, an ambassador for America, its good-ness, and its greatness. You, too, can and will become a leader and an ambassador as you begin to become or continue to be an example of these qualities.

TO BE A LEADER, I MUST FIRST BECOME A FOLLOWER

It is indeed strange that those who "reach" or "strive" for leadership find their path strewn with many sorrows and constantly risk public rebuke and censorship. We seldom genuinely respect such a "leader." Although such a person might gain temporary notoriety, he or she has no lasting, endearing memory in the hearts and minds of those who follow. Each one of us can think of such "leaders," whether in our businesses, churches, clubs, or government.

If a man is unwilling to submit to authority, he cannot rightfully expect others to submit responsibly to his authority. The insurgence of rebellion in the American culture has, therefore, severely affected our ability to produce genuine leaders. I cannot harbor a rebellious spirit and develop righteous leadership.

James Madison, our fourth president, also known as the "Father of the Constitution," alluded to this concept when he said, "Before any man can be considered as a member of Civil Society, he must be considered as a subject of the Governor of the Universe."[39]

Our growing refusal as a people to submit to the "Governor of the Universe" has manifested an upsurge of rebellion of spirit that has severely frustrated our ability to produce true leadership in this last generation. Consequently, we are experiencing widespread disillusionment among the American people, not only with those who purport to lead but also, in a "domino effect," with the institutions they purport to lead—whether in government, religion, education, or even law enforcement. Thus, for lack of trustworthy leadership, the framework of American society is threatening to collapse.

No life in history has ever produced more followers than that of Jesus Christ. He submitted to authority and thereby gained authority. The Bible says that Jesus first "humbled Himself and became obedient. . . ." The result was that God "highly exalted Him, giving Him a name that was above every name, that at the name of Jesus, every knee should bow in heaven and earth. . . ."[40]

The majority of our Founding Fathers similarly bowed their knee to the Almighty as the "Governor of the Universe" and were not ashamed to so declare it. The greatest nation on earth was born as a result, and those founders were exalted. We continue to reap their blessings today. Will you be a leader in America? Have you bowed your knee? If not, I urge you to take that first step. You will become a leader in your home, at the job, and in your community. For he who humbles himself before his Maker will be exalted.[41]

LEADERSHIP IS ACTING ON WHAT YOU BELIEVE

Leadership is acting on what you believe. After you have acted, those around you will ascribe to you the title of "leader."

The brave men who signed the Declaration of Independence— thereby pledging "their lives, their fortunes, and their sacred honor" to establish liberty and justice—did so not to perform a mere task but to carry out a principle, and for that they received the tribute of "leader," or "Founding Father."

If we want to Save America, we must act on what we believe.

LEADERSHIP IS NOT SOMETHING I HAVE BUT SOMETHING I DO

Leaders are grown, not born. Leadership can be developed. You can develop leadership. Yes, you can be a leader. The greatest leader is not one who can lead millions of people but one who can lead his own family.

America needs your leadership!

I honor the example of my father. Having come from simple stock and being bashful by nature and not endowed with much of this world's goods, he served for fifty years as pastor of small congregations across America, leading, encouraging, and guiding to preserve the "stuff of life"—true moral and spiritual values. At eighty-eight years of age, he continues to serve—now as the chaplain for a major hospital.

I give tribute to my father-in-law as well. As a railroad man and a blue-collar worker for all of his working years, he never saw himself as having that leadership "something" to offer. A few years ago, he moved to a small desert community, and it has been refreshing to see his life blossom with the leadership of serving in a small desert church.

TO BECOME A LEADER, BECOME A SERVANT

America was built on selfless service. Our ability to serve is rooted in our character, in the moral and spiritual fiber of our being, both individually and nationally. The moral and spiritual decay in our land has infected both our national character and our individual character, resulting in a perversion of true service. The principled motivation for "public service," which we admire in our Founding Fathers, has, in large measure, degenerated in this generation to "service" motivated by avarice and personal gain.

Service is the highest form of leadership! The greatest Leader in history tells us in the Scriptures, "He that is greatest among you shall be your servant."[42] Of the fifty-six men who subscribed their names to the Declaration of Independence, pledging their lives, their fortunes, and their sacred honor in service to their country, fourteen of them lost their lives in the cause, and most of them lost their fortunes, but none of them lost their honor through the eyes of history.

Undoubtedly, the most memorable words spoken by John Fitzgerald Kennedy, our thirty-fifth president, were these: "Ask not what your country can do for you; ask what you can do for your country."[43]

America needs leaders! Where can you serve? Find your niche today. America is depending on you.

A LEADER IS AN EXAMPLE

The wise Benjamin Franklin said, "None preaches better than the ant, and she says nothing." Many of us find it easier to "talk the talk rather than walk the walk." It seems easier to complain about the way things are than to do anything about it. It has become the great American pastime to accuse the president, bellyache about Congress, and chastise the governor. But where do *I* fit in? Where do *you* fit in? If I am unhappy about things or want change, can't I—*shouldn't* I—then set an example of what I expect?

Albert Schweitzer said, "Example is not the main thing in life; it is the only thing."[44] Seneca tells us, "Noble examples stir us up to noble actions"[45] Certainly we share a rich heritage of noble examples from our forefathers. They were examples of *personal responsibility, honesty, integrity, honor, fidelity, courage, faith,* and *vision.* Those examples stir us, encourage us, and, as Emerson said, "lift us to higher ground."[46]

A few years ago, an incident occurred that forever impressed upon me the significance of the voice of example in leadership. A man whom I had not seen for many years called me at my office and asked me to lunch. I had no clue as to his purpose other than renewal of friendship. After arriving at a local restaurant and having a few minutes of social banter with me, he suddenly changed the conversation. "Chuck," he said, "I have a serious personal problem and need to talk to someone I can trust." He continued, "I want to tell you why I have come to you." He then went on to relate a seemingly obscure incident that had occurred about seven years earlier.

We had been together with a group that was attending a very large seminar. We had broken for lunch and were returning for the afternoon session, walking briskly. As we approached the crosswalk at the intersection, the "Don't Walk" light appeared. My friend went on to remind me of the incident, saying, "You refused to cross against the light while the rest of us crossed." I had totally forgotten the incident, but he said, "I have never forgotten that. It made such an impression on me." I thought to myself, *Wow! Somebody is watching everything I do, hearing everything I say.*

But Somebody is watching everything *you* do as well and hearing what *you* say. The responsibility is awesome but real. It is the essence of leadership. Among those who are watching may be your spouse, your children, your coworkers, your neighbors, your parishioners, and your constituents.

Leadership is often established in the "little" things. It is destroyed by inconsistency and a double standard. An article appeared in the April 27, 1992, issue of *Time* magazine titled "In Praise of Mass Hypocrisy." The writer pointed out, "As voters we profess shock that our candidates should behave as we do. The paradox is striking. Voters are demanding in their leaders the personal virtues that they decreasingly demand of themselves. There is a word for the profession of virtue accompanied by practice of vice—hypocrisy."[47]

Lest I personally should have fallen into pride over doing something right, I was deeply grieved when not long after the lunch with my friend and his praise for my trustworthiness, I received another call from a fellow attorney and friend. He began the conversation by asking, "Chuck, how did you enjoy your jaywalk across Lake Avenue this afternoon?" I was embarrassed—not only because my friend had both seen my action and identified it for what it was, but also because it instantly recalled to my mind the previous incident in which I had done right and had been a source of uplift. I did not know that my attorney friend was driving by at that moment as I pondered whether or not to jaywalk. But eyes *were* watching. I grieved inwardly because of my own wrong choice but even more because of its potential impact on others.

Now you might say or be thinking, *That's ridiculous! People do that all the time,* or, *That's just a little thing. Let's get serious and talk about something important.*" But may I remind each of us, "It's the little foxes that spoil the vine."[48]

The leadership of America rests in my example. Example is nurtured or neutered in the soul. The leadership of America rests in your example, in the little things.

Virtue was once a keynote word describing the American character. Have we lost contact with its meaning? I am responsible for my example—and its consequences. It is my greatest, most enduring "ACT" of leadership.

If America's future depends on your example, what is America's future?

May God bless America through your example and mine.

Soul-Stirring Questions for Personal and Group Reflection

1. What qualities and characteristics do you believe make for good leadership?

2. What character qualities must a leader have for you to consider that person trustworthy? Does your life bear out those qualities?

3. What changes would have to take place in your life for your family and friends to consider your leadership trustworthy?

4. Have you done—or failed to do—anything in the past month that would make you upset if you knew that your pastor or president had done the same thing?

5. Did it bother you to read the illustration about jaywalking? Why or why not?

6. What message is your life, behavior, and attitude sending to your children and grandchildren?

7. Based upon your life example, what is America's future?

There is no national vision without personal vision.

Chapter 5

RESTORING THE AMERICAN VISION

VISION IS THE CHOICE TO see beyond today and the power to create tomorrow. It is available to every American.

Can you see beyond today? Have the pressures and intensity of life enshrouded you like a dense fog, causing you to focus daily on only those things that are immediately pressing about you?

Life has become increasingly intense in America, hasn't it? This generation has experienced more technological advances than the sum total of all earlier advances in history. Yet, amid these advances, we find ourselves engulfed by stress that threatens to destroy the very beings that technology purports to serve.

As a lawyer for many years, I have observed the gradual increase of stress and anxiety in both the lives of the people I have served and our American culture generally. I've seen it in the attitudes, hearts, and behavior of people toward each other:

of husbands to wives,
　　of wives to husbands,

of parents to children,
    of children to parents;

of neighbor to neighbor,
    of friend to friend,
        of employer to employee,
            of employee to employer;

of parishioner to his pastor, priest, rabbi;
    of pastor, priest, and rabbi to parishioner;
        of citizens to government,
            of government to citizens;

of an individual to himself or herself,
    of an individual to society,
        of society to an individual;

of an individual to the world,
    of the world to an individual,
        of an individual to his or her nation,
            of a nation to its people; and

of an individual to his or her God.

We have become increasingly "today"-oriented. At the same time, we have become increasingly "self"-oriented. The two most characteristic questions reflecting the "vision" of American society at this moment in our history are "What's in it for me?" and "What's it going to do for me today?"

In substance, we Americans have lost our ability to see beyond today. We have little or no vision for tomorrow. And we are reaping the agonizing consequences of lack of vision.

DEMISE OF THE AMERICAN DREAM

At its root, the demise of the "American Dream" has little to do with economics but everything to do with vision.

America is suffering. We all know it. We know it because we are suffering. We feel it. We see it. It seems to be everywhere.

Our national magazines feature headlines such as the following:

"How Our American Dream Unraveled"

"The Glooming of America—A Nation Down in the Dumps"

"The Fraying of America"

We cannot escape it. You cannot escape it. Our American Dream is, indeed, unraveling. We have been reluctant to admit it because the severity of our inward condition has been masked or camouflaged by our external prosperity.

LIFE WITHOUT VISION

In the midst of our national agony and frustration, we look for scapegoats. We point to the economy; education; crime; lack of leadership; and dishonesty in business, government, religion, and even law enforcement.

We think privately and aloud some of the following things:

If only the economy were stronger. . . .
If only we had more jobs. . . . If only we had more money for education. . . .
If only we had stronger penalties for crime. . . .

If only we had more honest politicians. . . .
     more honest business people. . . .
     more honest religious leaders. . . .
     more honest police officers. . . .
If only we had some real leadership. . . .

I have only one response. If we are morally and intellectually honest with ourselves, we should be asking, *If only we had not lost our vision. . . .*

My wife went through several years during which her eyes became clouded by cataracts. Simple tasks became more difficult. Enjoyment decreased. Frustration and irritation mounted. It was not pleasant. But thanks to laser surgery, clear vision was restored, and so was the quality of her life.

Life without vision in America is becoming increasingly unpleasant. The quality of life has diminished. We are becoming increasingly frustrated and irritated with daily life. Rage is invading every aspect of life. We need moral and spiritual laser surgery to restore our vision. My wife had to become sufficiently desperate in her lack of vision to seek out and submit to the surgery necessary to correct the problem. Are we sufficiently desperate to seek the surgery to clear our personal and national vision?

As Americans, we have learned to focus on the symptoms of our disease rather than on the disease itself. It is easier that way—at least for now. If I focus on the symptoms, I can cast the blame on the president, the governor, the school, the police department, the courts, the pastor, my parents, or the congressmen. I can absolve myself of responsibility. I can even raise money doing it.

Because we all absolve ourselves individually and collectively of responsibility, no one takes responsibility. If no one takes responsibility, the nation and the entire culture collapses from within. Demoralization, anger, and frustration breed more of the same. The nation crumples as a result of the vacuity of vision and lack of leadership.

THE SEARCH FOR LEADERSHIP

The most debilitating consequence of loss of vision is loss of leadership. There is no true leadership without vision. Aside from personal "example," vision is the single-most-important ingredient for genuine leadership. A nation that loses its vision loses its leadership. America has lost its vision and its leadership.

Perhaps we can now understand better why we face such a national malaise and cannot seem to get a sense of direction. As Patterson and Kim tell us in *The Day America Told the Truth,*

"America has no leaders and, especially, no moral leadership."[49]

"Our void in leadership—moral and otherwise—has reached a critical stage. We still want leadership; we just can't seem to find it."[50]

The unfortunate conclusion is that we will never see true leadership restored in America until we restore a vision for America. This fact should come as no surprise, however, for God himself has warned us in His Holy Word, "Where there is no vision, the people perish. . . ."[51]

HOW IS YOUR VISION?

America has been unique among nations. Our uniqueness was in our vision and our people. Abraham Lincoln declared that ours was a nation and a government "of the *people,* by the *people,* and for the *people.*"[52] This statement means that America's vision is not established or maintained by a king, dictator, or president, but by her people—by you and me.

America has not lost its vision solely because we have lacked leadership. Rather, America has lost its vision because you and I have lost our vision.

What was the American vision? What was it that enabled the early settlers to overcome seemingly insurmountable difficulties against odds that would totally deter the majority of us today? Why were they able to persevere? Did they have a cause? To what heritage of vision do we owe our dutiful respect and attention, both in appreciating the blessings of liberty that we enjoy and in seeking to restore our national sight? How did our vision become tainted? How did we develop the cataracts that now impair our vision?

THE AMERICAN VISION

French historian Francois Guizot asked James Russell Lowell, "How long will the American republic endure?" Lowell wisely replied, "As long as the ideas of the men who founded it continue to dominate."[53] So what were the ideas of our Founding Fathers? What was their vision for America?

You probably would not welcome an exhaustive discourse at this time on the entire scope of the vision of our Founding Fathers. Nor do I believe that such a thorough discussion is necessary for our purposes here. But we do need to understand where we have been to comprehend where we are going as a nation. Let's take a brief look back to the very words of our Founding Fathers—as found in their letters, speeches, and other documents—for a summary of the unusual vision they shared for America.

Christopher Columbus

Although Christopher Columbus was not actually a Founding Father of America, he has been credited, as an adventurer and explorer, for paving the way to the New World more than one hundred years before the first settlers arrived on the eastern seaboard. He was convinced that God had given him a special responsibility to carry the light of Christ to heathen lands. His own name, *Christopher,* meant literally "Christ-bearer," and he believed that the meaning of his name was additional confirmation of his call.

In his journal, Columbus quoted the book of Isaiah: *"Listen to me, O coastlands, and hearken you people from afar. The Lord called me from my mother's womb, from the body of my mother he named my name . . . I will give you as a light to the nations, that my salvation may reach to the end of the earth."*[54]

On each island where Columbus stopped, he instructed his men to erect a large wooden cross, which, he declared, was "a token of Jesus Christ our Lord, and in honor of the Christian faith."

Unfortunately, as with most men, greed, gold, and glory clouded his own vision, and he eventually lost sight of the very life impetus that inspired and led him. His gradual loss of vision had profound negative impact both on the motivations of those who would attempt to come to the New World for a century following and in the ultimate loss of his own mind and personal integrity.

William Brewster

As an elder among the Pilgrims, who, amid untold persecution, had separated themselves from the Church of England,

William Brewster gives poignant insight into the very heart and mind of those who would sail for America and settle at Plymouth Rock in 1620. In a letter to the treasurer of the Virginia Company seeking financial backing for their enterprise, Brewster set forth their reasons:

> We verily believe and trust the Lord is with us, unto Whom and Whose service we have given ourselves in many trials, and that He will graciously prosper our endeavors. . . .
>
> We are knit together as a body in a most strict and sacred bond and covenant of the Lord. . . .[55]

The Mayflower Compact

As the Pilgrims were preparing to land at Cape Cod on November 11, 1620, they drafted a simple compact that expressed their thoughts and intents for the new colony as to its purposes under God and its government with the consent of the governed— the cornerstone of the American democratic republic.

> In the name of God, amen. We whose names are under- written. . . .
>
> Having undertaken, for the glory of God and advancement of the Christian Faith and honor of our King and country, a voyage to plant the first colony in the northern parts of Virginia, do by these presents solemnly and mutually in the presence of God and one another, covenant and combine our- selves into a civil body politic. . . .[56]

William Bradford

William Bradford, governor of the Plymouth colony from the time of the Pilgrims' landing on these shores and for nearly thirty years thereafter, reflected on their labors and on their implementation of their original vision: "As one small candle may light a thousand, so the light kindled here has shown unto many, yea in some sort to our whole nation. . . ."[57]

John Winthrop

John Winthrop, an attorney and Cambridge graduate, was a leader of the Puritan movement in England. His godly example, practical wisdom, and servant's spirit placed him in natural leadership of the Puritans as they embarked to establish the colony at Salem.

Before the Puritans set foot on shore, Winthrop penned the following clear vision for the colony:

> We are a company, professing ourselves fellow members of Christ, we ought to account ourselves knit together by this bond of love. . . .
>
> Thus stands the cause between God and us: we are entered into covenant with Him for this work. We have taken out a Commission; the Lord hath given us leave to draw our own articles. . . . If the Lord shall please to hear us, and bring us in peace to the place we desire, then hath He ratified this Covenant and sealed our Commission. . . . But if we neglect the observance of these Articles . . . the Lord will surely break out in wrath against us.[58]

Winthrop understood that vision was useless without corresponding action. He also knew that vision must be translated in the example of godly leadership.

Winthrop further sharpened his vision for the Puritan colony, saying that the colony would stand as an example for others who followed. "The Lord make us like New England," he declared, adding, ". . . we must consider that we shall be as a City upon a Hill. . . ."[59]

So great was the impact of John Winthrop on not only the Puritan colony but also on the heart of the developing nation that at least one nineteenth-century historian ranked him second only to George Washington among the Founding Fathers.[60] Interestingly, we now see a resurgence of interest among both secular and religious thinkers and writers suggesting that the only real hope for America is to restore the vision of John Winthrop.[61] For this reason, the full text of Winthrop's inspiring vision is provided in the closing pages of this book.

George Washington

Leaders of the colonies urged George Washington, a gentleman farmer from Virginia, to become Commander-in-Chief of the Continental Army in our nation's fight for independence. After a bitter but victorious struggle with Great Britain, he was conscripted to chair the Constitutional Convention. So great was his respect and honor that he was said to be "first in the hearts of his countrymen."

As the first president of the United States of America under the Constitution, George Washington was keenly aware of the hand of God in establishing and preserving the new nation:

No people can be bound to acknowledge and adore the invisible hand, which conducts the Affairs of men more than the People of the United States. Every step, by which they have advanced to the character of an independent nation, seems to have been distinguished by some token of a providential agency.[62]

Washington acknowledged the responsibility of the nation and its leadership to act only under the overruling authority of God:

Whereas it is the duty of nations to acknowledge the Providence of Almighty God, to obey His will, to be grateful for his benefits, to humbly implore His protection and favor. . . .[63]

He understood and openly acknowledged before those who elected him to leadership that religious faith was a given essential to the health and prosperity of the nation and that they were so intertwined in the fabric of America as to be inseparable.

Of all the dispositions and habits which lead to political prosperity, Religion and morality are indispensable supports.[64]

Let us with caution indulge the supposition, that morality can be maintained without religion. Whatever may be conceded to the influence of refined education . . . forbid us to expect that National morality can prevail in exclusion of religious principle.[65]

In a farewell letter circulated to the governors of the thirteen states, Washington reaffirmed the covenant relationship of the American people to God and therefore of the people to each other.

Almighty God; We make our earnest prayer that Thou wilt keep the United States in Thy Holy protection; and Thou wilt incline the hearts of the citizens to cultivate a spirit of subordination and obedience to government; and entertain a brotherly affection and love for one another and for their fellow citizens of the United States at large.

And finally that Thou wilt most graciously be pleased to dispose us all to do justice, to love mercy, and to demean ourselves with that charity, humility, and pacific temper of mind which were the characteristics of the Divine Author of our blessed religion, and without a humble imitation of whose example in these things we can never hope to be a happy nation. Grant our supplication, we beseech Thee, through Jesus Christ our Lord. Amen.

Benjamin Franklin

As the eldest statesman of the Constitutional Convention, Benjamin Franklin was highly respected throughout the original thirteen states for his wisdom. After nearly five weeks of bickering and fighting among the fifty-five delegates, the vision for the rising nation and its spiritual moorings had become shrouded in clouds of human passion. When all hope of achieving a unifying constitution seemed lost, Benjamin Franklin stood and, addressing President Washington, directed the attention of the delegates in that great assembly to the God who had graciously protected the fledgling nation against staggering odds and whom they had ignored during weeks of deliberations.

> "Have we now forgotten this powerful Friend? Or do we imagine we no longer need His assistance? . . . The longer I live, the more convincing proofs I see of this truth—that God governs in the affairs of men.[66]

By his bold, yet humble statesmanship, Franklin renewed the minds and hearts of his fellow citizens to the well-recognized covenant relationship that the nation had enjoyed with Almighty God—the Hand of Providence. And upon their official recognition of that relationship by beginning each day's deliberations thereafter with prayerful thanks and supplications for wisdom and guidance, God met His part of that covenant by bringing peace, wisdom, and a quality of thought that gave birth to the most effective national constitution ever drafted in the history of the world.

Franklin further expressed his vision for the relationship between freedom and the national character by declaring, "Only a virtuous people are capable of freedom."[67]

John Adams

John Adams, second president of the United States, continued the clear expression of the national vision and of the inextricable link between faith and freedom as conceived in the fabric of what is America: "Our Constitution was made only for a moral and religious people. It is wholly inadequate to the government of any other."[68]

Thomas Jefferson

Thomas Jefferson, our third president, saw the signposts of slippage from the national vision. He knew the pride and selfishness of men's hearts and the threat that those presented to the covenant between the people and their God and to the covenant between "We the people." He declared, "God who gave us life gave us liberty." He then issued a warning to echo down through every succeeding generation of Americans:

> Can the liberties of a nation be secure when we have removed a conviction that these liberties are the gift of God? Indeed I tremble for my country when I reflect that God is just, that His justice cannot sleep forever.[69]

Impaired Vision

Many people indeed are trembling in the land of the stars and stripes in the wake of the aimless, purposeless foundering of a ship of state that wallows in the consequences of impaired vision—without having even a sense of leadership at the helm. Could it be that God's justice can no longer sleep? Could it be that we have repudiated the very fountain of our national prosperity or the wellspring of the American character?

Have we developed cataracts in the American vision? Have we become blinded by generations of personal peace and affluence unparalleled in the history of the world so that we can no longer see or discern the more fundamental issues of life itself—faith, truth, integrity, courage, and compassion? If so, what can we do to restore vision in the land?

Only You Can Restore Vision

Only *you*, with God's help, can restore vision. The president cannot do it. Another candidate promising grandiose remedies and pandering to our pet concerns or private needs cannot accomplish the task. We must knuckle under and face the truth. It will require changes in our lives, in our values, in the way we think, in the way we raise our children, in the way we spend our money and time—in our *hearts*. It will require "I" surgery.

We can and must make repairs and rebuild the foundations of our personal lives as Americans in our families, businesses, churches, and government. But vision comes first. Without vision, we will become lost and even more frustrated in our efforts to remedy, repair, and rebuild.

How You Can Restore Vision

There are three basic ways by which you can restore vision in America. Each of them begins with you and me as individuals and with our families.

First, I Must Personally Remember the American Vision. Abraham Lincoln, at a moment of deep national crisis in a civil war that threatened to destroy the nation, found himself in a very lonely place in the White House. It is always lonely when leadership is required and vision is clouded or absent. At the desperate moment in our history when he was drafting his Gettysburg Address, he reached back to a time when vision was clear as expressed in the lives of our Founding Fathers and in their writings, which endure as our most precious heritage.

Lincoln distilled from those lives and writings that gave birth to the new nation an unmistakable truth and building block—the cornerstone of the American vision. He then re-declared on the battlefield of Gettysburg the truth that would restore and hold the vision of America for the century that followed:

This Nation, under God, shall have a new birth of freedom. . . .[70]

My fellow Americans, voluntarily and humbly declaring our nation to be "under God," and then acting accordingly, is the sole and solitary prerequisite to restoring the American vision. New, believable, visionary leadership will then emerge. But America will never be "under God" unless you and I are under God. To place ourselves under God, we must choose to adopt God's ways, God's plans, and God's purposes as expressed in the Bible. We must repent or turn from our own pride, our rebellious ways, and our selfish ambitions and choose to humble ourselves under God's hand; and that step must begin with those who profess to be Christians.

The Scriptures tell us that if we will humble ourselves, the Almighty will exalt us; but if we exalt ourselves, we will be abased. Unfortunately, we are becoming more "abased" by the day. What we must do is clear, and what we do, we must do quickly.

Our forefathers knew that we would need to keep the vision ever before our eyes. The vision is declared from, and is inscribed on, every monument in our nation's capital.

In the Capitol Building:

Preserve me, O God: for in thee do I put my trust.—Psalm 16:1

In the Supreme Court:

The Ten Commandments are inscribed over the head of the Chief Justice.

In the Library of Congress:

What doth the Lord require of thee, but to do justly, and to love mercy, and to walk humbly with thy God?—Micah 6:8

In the Lincoln Memorial:

As was said 3,000 years ago, so it must still be said, The judgments of the Lord are true and righteous altogether.

In the Jefferson Memorial:

Can the liberties of a nation be secure when we have removed the conviction that these liberties are the gift of God?

In the Congressional Building:

In God we Trust.

May I ask you a personal question? Have you inscribed the American vision of a covenant relationship with God on the tablets of your own heart and mind? If not, do it today—for your sake, for your country's sake, and for the sake of your children.

Second, I Must Teach My Children the American Vision. *Forbes* magazine has been a foremost business publication in the

American scene since 1917. Its seventy-fifth anniversary issue was dedicated to analyzing and responding to the grave sense of despair and anger in the land.

It declared, "It isn't the economic system that needs fixing. It's our value system."[71] Among the numerous articles in this issue from America's scholars and writers dedicated to exploring the nation's demoralized condition are the following quotations from a single article:

Every parent in America knows that we're not doing a very good job of communicating to our children what America is and has been.[72]

We do not teach it as a society and we teach it insufficiently in our schools.[73]

Instead:

We teach the culture of resentment, of grievance, of victimization.[74]

We are certainly demoralizing our children. . . .[75]

In 1939, we could tell we were beginning to lose God—banishing him from the scene. . . .[76]

And it is a terrible thing when people lose God.[77]

I don't think it is unconnected to the [baby] boomers' predicament that as a country we were losing God just as they were being born.[78]

It has been said that our children are a message we send to a world we will never see. What kind of a message are you and I sending through our children? What message have we failed to send?

If America's future depends on the vision for America that you have instilled in your children or grandchildren, what is America's future? We are writing America's future with every opportunity that we fail to seize to instruct and guide the young lives entrusted to our care. We are writing that future when we fail to teach them about the utter dependence of our Founding Fathers on God's personal guidance and direction both in their personal lives and in the building of the nation. Yes, we teach even when we fail to teach.

Teach your children well. America cannot survive another visionless generation.

Third, I Must Live the American Vision. No one would deny the awesome truth that "actions speak louder than words." Yet we all find ourselves conducting our lives hypocritically at one time or another. We can make excuses and conjure every reason under the sun why we should be relieved of conforming to the standard of our verbal protestations of principle. But—over time—a telling story emerges from our behavior and attitude. We could call it a "life message."

So what is your "life message"? What message does your behavior, your attitude, send to your children and grandchildren? What are we teaching them? What are we teaching them about what it really means to be an American? Is what I am really teaching them the same message that I want to leave them?

What is the future of America based upon my example? Do I want to face such a future? Do I want my children to face such a future? Most of us have been more concerned about living the American dream than living the American vision.

Regardless of whether we like it, our daily choices, decisions, behavior, and attitudes are defining or redefining the American vision for tomorrow. We are in crisis today because of our example yesterday—not just my example, not just the president's example, or Congress's—but *your* example too.

Become an example of the American vision. And may God, through you, bless the America that your children will inherit. As the Scriptures declare, "Blessed is the nation whose God is the Lord."[79]

SOUL-STIRRING QUESTIONS FOR PERSONAL AND GROUP REFLECTION

1. The Bible tells us, "Where there is no vision, the people perish." What do you think that means?

2. We have all heard of the "American Dream," but how would you describe the "American Vision"?

3. What common thread, other than a pursuit of liberty, seems to bind the early founders of our nation together in one fabric of mind and heart?

4. What vision drives your life, giving it meaning and a sense of purpose from day to day?

5. Do you see any significance in the fact that Bible quotations are engraved prominently on so many of our national government buildings and monuments? What does it reflect of our past? How do these quotations measure our nation today? What influence might they have in defining our future?

6. What message is your life, behavior, and attitude sending to your children and grandchildren?

7. Based upon your life example, what is America's future?

I must sow what I should sow if
I would reap what I should reap.

Chapter 6

A MATTER OF PRINCIPLE

PRINCIPLES ARE LIKE SEEDS. If you don't plant them, use them, and live by them, they tend to blow away amid the winds and storms of everyday living.

PRINCIPLES ARE FOR LIVING

As a lawyer for two decades, I have had both the pain and the pleasure of working in the lives of thousands of individuals and families. I have seen my clients sometimes in their joys but usually in their sorrows. If there has been any common thread in their lives, it has been this—that a life or a family without vision is usually a life or a family without principles—and without principles, there is confusion, pain, heartache, and destruction. This point is true for professing Christians and non-Christians alike.

America's sage, Benjamin Franklin, reflected, "If principle is good for anything, it is worth living up to."

WHAT ARE PRINCIPLES?

So, what are principles? How would I recognize a principle if I saw one? What are they for? How do they develop? What are the consequences of straying from principle? How can I become an example of principle in action? Let's explore the answers to these questions because our answers to these questions will guide us to restoring the American vision and our souls.

PRINCIPLES ARE SIGNPOSTS

Can you imagine traveling for any considerable distance down a highway without having a signpost to give some assurance that you are headed in the right direction?

I remember taking a trip with my family several years ago in a different area of the country. As we drove along, we began to realize that there were far fewer signs and indicators along the freeways in that locale than we were accustomed to in our area of the country. There was little warning of imminent exits. Traffic was moving along at a vigorous clip and was unforgiving. We became increasingly frustrated as we searched for proper off-ramps to reach our intended destinations. It was apparent that the stress level in our vehicle was mounting and emotions became frayed.

Principles are life's signposts. They point the way, give direction, promote order, prevent confusion, and provide a sense of purpose. Where the signposts of principle are absent or ignored, great frustration results.

How Can I Know a Principle When I See One?

A principle, like a road sign, normally will head you in a particular direction or give a specific life instruction. Principles can be broad or specific; they can give general direction or precise direction. They can also be "good" or "bad." Occasionally, I have come across a road sign that gives incorrect or imprecise direction. You might have experienced the frustration of such "bad" road signs in your travels. They can lead to time-wasting detours and even prevent us from reaching our destination.

A "good" principle normally can be determined by how closely it matches the following standards:

Is it true in almost every situation?

Has it stood the test of time?

Is it something that I would want my neighbor to practice?

Is it consistent with the plan of our Founding Fathers?

Is it consistent in all respects with the plan of the Creator of all men as found in the Bible?

Failure of any questioned principle to meet these tests, especially the last one, should cause me to discard it for my life and that of my nation.

How Have We Strayed From Principle?

Unfortunately, many of us have mistaken *pragmatism* for *principle.* We have discarded the time-honored tests for principle upon which was established the greatest nation in history, and in their place we have substituted the tests of pragmatism: Is it expedient? Does it work for me? Does it work for me today? Which way is the "wind blowing" in my community, my school, my work, my church, my culture? What do the polls say?

But in following the wind, we have reaped the whirlwind as a nation. We have ignored the principles of the ages in favor of the expedients of the hour.

THE CONSEQUENCES OF PRAGMATISM

America is in crisis! We began this book with those four words, and with those four words we define the consequences reaped from sowing seeds of pragmatism rather than principle. We have sown these seeds of expediency individually, as families, as businesses, as churches, as communities, and as a nation.

How did this happen? How could it happen? Thomas Jefferson warned us, "Eternal vigilance is the price of liberty."[80] We have become slack. We went to sleep at our watch post over the last sixty years. We have not fallen into decay overnight. The blocks of our foundation have been eroded one at a time. It happened when we departed from measuring ourselves and our decisions, both individually and as a nation, by the yardstick of "principles" when:

- we decided to turn over the care of the needy to the government rather than accept the responsibility ourselves;

- we decided to report only a portion of our actual income on our last tax return;

- we decided to ask for a "cash" payment rather than a check so we wouldn't have to report it;

- we decided to claim damage to our car that preexisted an automobile accident so we could get insurance money to repair it;

- we decided to cheat on our spouse;

- we decided to "call in sick" to our employer when we wanted to go shopping or take a vacation;

- we made personal calls on the boss's time and tab;

- we fed our child from our plate on the "all-you-can-eat" salad bar;

- we loaded up our credit cards with purchases for which we couldn't afford to pay;

- we printed more money to pay the national debt;

- we eliminated prayer and the Bible from our public education; and

- we stopped Sabbath observance in the land.

Consequences inevitably follow such choices. Let us look briefly at the cultural and social consequences that have devastated America as a result of our drift from principle to pragmatism during the last sixty years.

- We have a national debt of nearly four trillion dollars.

- We have a divorce rate that has more than tripled.

- We have crime that has escalated to the point that law enforcement is no longer capable of keeping up.

- We have an illegitimacy rate that has soared.

- We have AIDS that threatens to kill millions of people and consume billions of dollars of money and resources.

- We have homelessness as a national plague.

- We have truth that has become extinct.

- We have greater wealth but more poverty of spirit.

- We have more counselors yet rampant depression.

- We have lost our sense of community.

- We have drugs and alcohol to deaden the reality of our choices.

We are not getting better. Education has not helped. We have never had so much "education." Education without principles, morals, and values is not education—it is foolishness and self-deception. We have no signposts or road signs, and we have lost direction. Let us look more closely at the connection between principles and moral order.

PRINCIPLES, MORALITY, AND AMERICAN SOCIETY

Morality describes the good and beneficial behavior of individuals and society in response to true principles. Immorality describes behavior outside of principle. Immorality results from the loss of principle in the fabric of the life of an individual, a culture, or a nation. If a society and its members do not respect, adhere to, and enforce guiding principles, everyone gradually drifts to doing that which is "right" in his or her own eyes. Chaos is the inevitable result. It should, therefore, come as no surprise that in the closing days of the "American Century," all three of

America's major new magazines emblazoned the word "chaos" on their front covers.

The famous writer, philosopher, and theologian of the last generation, C. S. Lewis, spoke clearly of the role of moral principles in a society. He observed:

> In reality, moral rules are directions for running the human machine. Every moral rule is there to prevent a breakdown, or a strain, or a friction, in running that machine. That is why these rules at first seem to be constantly interfering with our natural inclinations.[81]

We cannot avoid moral principles or moral laws—we can only ignore them. If we ignore them, we reap the natural and practical consequences of our ignorance or rebellion in very tangible ways in our finances, bodies, families, society, and nation. Similarly, the mere fact that I do not know of, recognize, or choose to respect the law of gravity does not mean that I can jump from a plane at 30,000 feet and expect to cruise alongside it by stretching out my arms as if they were wings. If I have failed to educate myself in the law of gravity or have conceived of some counter-concept to deny its existence, I will most certainly soon receive a genuine education that bears an exceedingly high-priced tuition.

America is paying the "tuition" for an "education" in the consequences of defying principle and moral law. Perhaps you and your family are as well.

Theories change, but genuine principles and moral laws do not. As Lord Acton declared, "Opinions alter, manner changes, creeds rise and fall, but the moral law is written on the tables of eternity."[82]

Another writer, Alexis Carrel, cogently described the interrelationship of moral principle and the culture in these words:

Moral sense is more important than intelligence. When it disappears from a nation, the whole social structure slowly commences to crumble away. Christianity is not something that we need to lug along and carry. It should carry us, putting a lift and a buoyant spontaneity into life.[83]

VALUES AND PRINCIPLES TO SUSTAIN A NATION

According to Roy Disney, "It's not hard to make decisions when you know what your values are."[84]

Our problem in America, as we launch a new millennium, is that we have forfeited values and the principles that our Founding Fathers so carefully observed in laying the foundation for the nation. We then cry that we have no leadership or vision and bemoan the fact that no one seems to be able to make quality decisions.

Bear with me as we take another brief look at the viewpoint of our founders. George Washington, in his farewell address as our first president, reminded us:

Reason and experience both forbid us to expect that National morality can prevail in exclusion of religious principle.[85]

John Adams, our second president, continued to bring the same truth to our remembrance:

Our Constitution was made only for a moral and religious people. It is wholly inadequate to the government of any other.[86]

We have no government armed with power capable of contending with human passions unbridled by morality and religion.[87]

THE SOURCE OF MORAL PRINCIPLE

The oldest dictionary in America was written by the true father of American education, Noah Webster. Webster made abundantly and incontrovertibly clear where the Founding Fathers looked for the source of moral principle worthy to be the building blocks of a society and a nation. His words continue to speak to us today:

The moral principles and precepts contained in the Scriptures ought to form the basis of all our civil constitutions and laws. All the miseries and evils which men suffer from vice, crime, ambition, injustice, oppression, slavery, and war, proceed from their despising or neglecting the precepts contained in the Bible.[88]

HOW YOU CAN BECOME AN EXAMPLE OF PRINCIPLED LIVING

Someone has said, "If you don't stand for something, you'll fall for anything."[89]

Thomas Jefferson put it thus: "In matters of style, swim with the current; in matters of principle, stand like a rock."[90]

So let me ask you: Are you a man of principle? Are you a woman of principle? Are your "principles" rooted in your vacillating feelings of today, tomorrow, or yesterday; or are they the ageless, timeless, and unchangeable principles of your Creator? Viewpoint determines destiny.

Each of us must make a choice. Our choices are not without consequences. America is awaiting your courageous choice. Your children and grandchildren are waiting. Here are steps you can take.

FIRST: Make your decisions and govern your behavior based upon the timeless and proven principles given by God, your Creator, in the Bible. If you do not know them, search them out.

SECOND: Make decisions for behavior leading to virtue.

THIRD: Make decisions for behavior leading to truth and integrity.

FOURTH: Make decisions for behavior that you would value highly if done by your neighbor.

FIFTH: Make decisions for behavior that you would like to have your children and grandchildren emulate.

SIXTH: Make decisions for behavior that will lay the foundation for America's future. Vote your principles— not your pocketbook or "group-think."

The following word picture painted by Adam Woslever will help us as a nation and as men and women in this desperate hour as our ship of state lists precariously as a result of moral decay and is buffeted by the stormy winds of unprincipled living and its consequences:

Let us cling to our principles as the mariner clings to his last plank when night and tempest close about him.[91]

Soul-Stirring Questions for Personal and Group Reflection

1. What is the difference between *principle* and *pragmatism?*

2. Can you think of something you did or a decision you made recently that was based not on what was *right* but rather on what you thought might *work?*

3. George Washington, in his farewell address, warned the nation, "Reason and experience both forbid us to expect that National morality can prevail in exclusion of religious principle." Why is morality in the nation directly related to the religious principles of the people?

4. Based upon the staggering and dramatic changes in American morality in the past thirty years, with 78 percent of our citizens believing that we are in a severe moral crisis, what do you think is the true condition of the religious "principles" of Americans, including those who profess to be "Christian"?

5. Noah Webster, father of American education and author of our oldest dictionary, said, "All of the miseries and evils which men suffer, proceed from despising or neglecting the precepts contained in the Bible." Are there any areas where, upon close inspection, it is clear that you either despise or neglect biblical principles? What might those be? Do you see a similar pattern in the rest of the society?

6. There are six steps on the final page of chapter 6 to guide you in making principled decisions. Rate yourself on a scale of 1 to 10 on each step. Then average your results. Consider "10" to be the most favorable possible response.

If I would hear the truth, I must tell the truth.

Chapter 7

NOTHING BUT THE TRUTH

TRUTH HAS BEEN AN ESSENTIAL ingredient of the American character. Just as we have admired those who dared to venture out into uncharted waters and wildernesses in our early life as a nation, so we have admired those who have dared to tell the truth.

OF TRUTH AND CHERRY TREES

Most of us, in our early schooling, were clearly taught to see the link between our personal and national character for truthfulness through the simple boyhood story of George Washington and the cherry tree. As the story goes, George, as an adventurous and active young boy, cut down a cherry tree on the family compound. When his father inquired as to how the cherry tree disappeared, young George summoned his courage and announced, "I cannot tell a lie."

He then proceeded to "own up to" his father as to his deed in chopping down the cherry tree. Whether the story is true or merely folklore, I cannot say. But it conveys a simple, yet unmistakable message that:

- truth is valued,

- truth is important to pass on to our children, and

- truth in our leadership is an important part of our American heritage.

We can safely say that regardless of whether the "cherry tree" account is itself a genuine historical event, the principle of truth was a pillar in the life of our first president. Among his own maxims are these choice words:

I hope I shall always possess firmness and virtue enough to maintain what I consider the most enviable of all titles, the character of an "Honest Man."[92]

Several years ago, I had opportunity to speak at Washington's boyhood residence in Ferry Farm, Virginia. Imagine my grief, in celebrating our nation's independence, to report that a nation whose first president could not tell a lie is now unable to tell the truth.

MIRRORED IMAGES

A mirror is a very important tool that we normally use privately to assist us in determining how others see us publicly. Most people put great value on how they look and appear to others. We place mirrors in strategic locations so that we can test at appropriate moments the view we present to those with whom we come in contact. Most of us want to present, at least outwardly, a view and image that we desire others to believe about us. But how can we inspect the reflection of our inner man and character on those around us? What looking glass reveals the contents of our national soul?

OUR "LOOKING GLASS" SELF

If we had a choice, most of us would love to have a three-sided mirror arrangement to allow us to see ourselves more completely from different angles and viewpoints.

The secular "looking glass" of our society and nation is a three-sided mirror consisting of polls, politics, and publications. Let us glance for a few moments into each of these three mirrors to gain perspective into our national character for truth.

Publications

The front page of the October 5, 1992, issue of *Time* carries the headline, "Lying—Everybody's Doin' It—(Honest)." The lead article and cover story is titled "Lies, Lies, Lies." The byline asks, "Is anyone around here telling the truth?" The article then goes on to explore our perversion of truth in politics and in our personal lives, concluding, "Lies flourish . . . when people no longer understand, or agree on, the rules governing their behavior toward one another."[93]

Politics

The front page of the July 13, 1992, issue of *Newsweek* is headlined, "Sea of Lies." The lead article chronicles how leadership in the American armed forces covered up and deceived the American

NOTHING BUT THE TRUTH

people in the matter of an American warship that mistakenly shot down an Iranian airliner.[94] But then *Time* tells us in its October 5, 1992, issue, "The public may now assume lying on the part of its representatives because it expects them to lie."[95]

Why does the American public *expect* its representatives to lie? Because representatives are just that—they represent, mirror, or are representative of the people. According to a *Time/CNN* poll conducted in early fall 1992, 75 percent of Americans believe that less honesty exists in government than existed a decade ago.[96] That view is quite a statement because less than two decades ago we experienced what we then believed to be a "low" in political ethics in the great cover-up of "Watergate" and the narrow avoidance of impeachment by our then-president through voluntary resignation.

Therefore, it should come as no surprise that the forty-second president of the United States, elected in 1992, should be only the second of America's presidents to be impeached. It should also come as no surprise that he, being a "representative" of the people, could look the American people in the eye on national television and lie with impunity for proud and pragmatic purposes. It should prophesy warning to us as a people that the president whose term closed the twentieth century should have had to plea bargain his way out of prosecution and publicly admit his deception on his last day in office.

A study of the Statistical Abstracts of the United States for the period 1973 through 1985 shows a dramatic increase of 484 percent in federal prosecutions for corruption of public officials. If our representatives are indeed representative of American society, we stand indicted as a society. It is easy to say, "Down with the politicians" or "kick out the bums." But what will we get as replacements from the general cut of *We the people?* For that answer, we might turn to the polls.

Polls

In 1991, Patterson and Kim, advertising executives with the J. Walter Thompson Company, published a moral portrait of the American people titled *The Day America Told the Truth*. Their results quantify our personal ethics, values, and beliefs as a people based upon the largest survey of private morals ever undertaken in any country on earth. Their goal—to probe beneath the public position of Americans to see what we really believe. Chapter 4 of their book is titled "American Liars." These are strong words. They are offensive to our sensibility as to who we want others to think we are or what we wish we were. But Patterson and Kim's exhaustive research reveals that 91 percent of us lie regularly—"conscious, premeditated lies."[97] They conclude, "Lying has become a cultural trait in America. Lying is embedded in our national character."[98]

We are in national disgrace. What a demoralizing tribute to the lofty vision of our first president, George Washington, who had declared the most enviable of all titles to be "the character of an Honest Man." It is a defining moment that the nation whose first president could not tell a lie now cannot tell the truth.

How could a nation known throughout the world for its virtue up until the mid-1900s have turned so rapidly? One key may be found in the results of another poll done in 1990 by George Barna and summarized in his book *What Americans Believe*. Barna reports, "Most disheartening of all . . . is the discovery that two-thirds of adults agree that there is no such thing as absolute truth."[99] What is even more shocking is that "adults associated with mainline Protestant churches are more likely than all other adults to agree that there is no such thing as absolute truth (75 percent)."[100] Just ten years later, despite America's alleged "Search for the Sacred," Barna discloses that "two-thirds of born-again Christians contend that there is no absolute moral truth," that "three-quarters of all adults and more than four out of five teens do not believe there is absolute truth."[101]

This is truly unnerving. As Barna reports, "More than ever before we are witnessing the entrenchment of what some refer to as 'secular humanist' attitudes."[102] And it appears to be coming from many of the pulpits of America—from those who have been entrusted to tell us the truth. Some others may refer to such thinking as relativistic. But the life effect of such thinking is that "people are responsible only to themselves."[103] Patterson and Kim observe, "We no longer can tell right from wrong."[104]

SOCIAL CONSEQUENCES

What might we expect to see from a "breakdown of truth" in our lives? Might I suggest that it is exactly what we are now experiencing? We are seeing:

- distrust of all of our institutions, including
    government,
    law enforcement,
    religious leaders,
    business, and
    marriage;

- loss of leadership;

- fear, doubt, uncertainty, anxiety, and depression;

- crime;

- confusion;

- alienation of citizens from each other; and

- alienation from God and His blessing on our land.

WHAT IS TRUTH?

Truth has become of such little value in current society that it has become the subject of much jest. By way of illustration, not long ago I was preparing to speak to a particular group, and the master of ceremonies, as part of his introduction, and knowing that I was a lawyer, set forth the following scenario as the humor for the day:

> A man gathered his three trusted counselors about him— his psychologist, his accountant, and his lawyer—to pose to them a most profound question: "What is 1 + 1?" To which question the psychologist replied, "What do you feel it should be?" The accountant queried, "What do you need it to be?" And the lawyer, in "true" allegiance to his client, responded, "What can we make it to be?"

Pastors have now largely joined ranks with the psychologists, as feelings reign supreme over truth that undergirds faith.

This scenario, unfortunately, is the current perception of truth among our fellow Americans. But the wanderings of our thinking have not changed much over the last two thousand years. A crusty Roman governor named Pontius Pilate stood as judge of the land over Jesus Christ, who had been brought before him by the leaders of his day who valued power more than purity. The words of that governor will continue to ring throughout history, "What is truth?"[105]

As Americans, if we have any hope of restoring faith in our government, our marriages, our businesses—and ourselves—we must answer this question honestly. Truth must be what it is and ought to be, not what I want it to be.

TO TELL OR NOT TO TELL THE TRUTH; THAT IS THE QUESTION

To tell the truth, I must know the truth. In matters of fact or principle, only one truth exists. Truth about facts or principles has nothing to do with my feelings, goals, needs, or wants. It is what it is—truth.

Thomas Jefferson, our third president and the drafter of our Declaration of Independence, reflected, "Honesty is the first chapter in the book of wisdom."[106] According to Shakespeare, "No legacy is so rich as honesty."[107] To tell the truth, I must tell the truth.

There is a standard for truth. Without a standard there is no truth. Truth becomes whatever I want it to be, whatever suits my private purposes at a given moment. Truth can be measured or evaluated only against an objective standard. Our Founding Fathers held high the standard for truth—the Bible—as the expression of an all-knowing and loving Creator to His creation. It was their final authority. It was the foundation for freedom. Upon that standard, they founded this nation of freedom. Benjamin Franklin declared, "He who shall introduce into public affairs the principles of primitive Christianity will change the face of the world."[108]

Truth and freedom are inseparable. Our Founders embraced the words of Jesus Christ, "If you continue in my Word . . . you shall know the truth and the truth shall make you free."[109] Have you embraced the truth of your Creator? What truth do you embrace? Is it dependable? Can you build a life upon it? Can you rebuild a nation upon it? Do you even care?

A Commitment for Americans Who Care

When I served as a trial lawyer, every witness that I called to testify was required to give an oath (which I have changed from *oath* to *promise* to meet the objections of those who do not believe that it is appropriate to take an "oath"). The court reporter would address the witness and say:

> "Will you now stand before God, before your children and grandchildren, your spouse, your business associate, the IRS, your parishioners, and your fellow Americans and repeat after me:
>
> 'I do now solemnly promise to tell the truth, the whole truth, and nothing but the truth, so help me God.'"

The future of your children depends upon your commitment to truth. Your grandchildren will reap the blessing of your honesty—or the curse of your prevarication. A nation is looking to you—and to me. If you are telling the truth and living the truth in the *little* things, you will make a major impact in the *big* things. America's future is in your mouth—in your heart.

If I am not willing to report honestly my income and expenses at tax time, how can I expect my senator to report his? If I am not willing to return monies to a store clerk who gave me too much change, how can I expect a businessman not to "rip me off"? If I am not willing to be true to my wife, how can I expect her to be true to me? If I tell my employer that I'm sick and then go off and play golf or go to the mall, how can I expect my child not to cut school?

Do you care for your country? Do you care enough to tell and live the truth, the whole truth, and nothing but the truth? Your example of truthfulness is the key to restoring the glory, prosperity, and blessing of our land. It is also the key to renewing the soul of the nation. May God, through truth lived out in your life, bless America, and may His truth march on in your boots and mine.

SOUL-STIRRING QUESTIONS FOR PERSONAL AND GROUP REFLECTION

1. *Time* reported, "The public may now assume lying on the part of its representatives because it expects them to lie." Why do we expect our representatives to lie?

2. How did it make you feel about your country when you read Patterson and Kim's research findings that "91 percent of us lie regularly, conscious, premeditated lies"?

3. Do you agree with Patterson and Kim's conclusion that "Lying has become a cultural trait in America . . . embedded in our national character"? Why or why not?

4. What is truth?

5. Can truth exist without a standard by which to measure whether it is true?

6. Why would Benjamin Franklin, not known to be particularly religious, declare, "He who shall introduce into public affairs the principles of primitive Christianity will change the face of the world"?

7. Can you have trust without truth?

8. As you read this chapter, did you become aware of areas and actions in your life that have been untruthful? What could you do about it?

9. Would you be happy if your children, grandchildren, or even the entire nation were to model themselves after your example of truthfulness? Why or why not?

If I would have virtue, I must be virtuous;
if I would have morality, I must be moral;
if I would have goodness, I must be good.

Chapter 8

THE LAMP OF VIRTUE

A MAN, AS THE STORY is told, approached a woman and inquired whether she would sleep with a man other than her husband for a million dollars. After a brief hesitation, she stated that she would. The man then asked, "Would you do it for five dollars?" She replied, "No, what kind of woman do you think I am?" The man responded, "I already found out what kind of woman you are. I merely wanted to find your price."

It is said that 95 percent of humor is tragedy in retrospect. Regardless of whether this story is actually true or a mere illustration, it conveys with an element of humor the tragedy of the current moral decadence in American society.

VIRTUE AND THE AMERICAN IMAGE

When was the last time you heard someone use the word *virtue?* Have you ever used the word? Certainly the word *virtue* has lost its place in American parlance. It has become disfavored as a word because virtue is no longer considered something to be desired or preserved. Virtue became, like a virus, something to be avoided. Morally defined *virtue* was replaced by morally neutral *values.*

America, however, was once known as the land of virtue. Our national symbols frequently included the word *virtue.* Virtue was an essential ingredient of the American way of life. It was the element that bound us together. Daniel Webster stated in 1830, "Union we reached only by the discipline of our virtues in the severe school of adversity."[110] Virtue was a necessary part of true liberty and independence. For that reason, it was spoken in concert with *liberty* and *independence* in banners depicting all that was to define our aspirations for America.

WHAT IS VIRTUE?

Virtue is not a plague. Virtue is moral goodness. It is purity in heart, motivation, intention. It is morally sound behavior. Virtuous behavior is that which seeks the best for those around us. It is not self-serving but other serving. Virtue is the outward display of inward character.

The Statue of Liberty, which most of us still hold dear as a symbol of our nation, is a symbol of virtue, of moral goodness. Its sculptor envisioned it as a beacon to the world of America's liberty and virtue. The world felt and experienced an unusual "goodness" emanating from the American experiment. Its "goodness" was the fruit of the tree whose roots went deep into the soil of righteousness and right living which our early founders sought to plant on these shores.

A LIGHT OR ENLIGHTENMENT

The Statue of Liberty was envisioned and sculpted by a Frenchman, Frederic Bartholdi. His vision for this memorial to liberty was sown at about the time our Civil War was concluding. Six decades had passed since France had experienced its revolution near the time of the American Revolution. The French Revolution was a product of the "Age of Enlightenment." The "enlightenment" had severed man's freedom from its roots of religious faith and morality, turning liberty into license. The result in France was moral and political chaos. They yearned for a republican form of government and a constitution.

America, on the other hand, had experienced a tremendous surge of virtue, righteousness, and goodness that permeated every aspect of American culture. The Frenchman Alexis de Tocqueville, upon studying the "American experiment" just twenty-five years before the dream of the Statue of Liberty was born, concluded, "Not until I went into the churches of America and heard her pulpits aflame with righteousness did I understand the secret of her genius and power."[111]

America was blazing a "light" across the seas at the very time the Age of Enlightenment was resulting in moral decay and darkness in Europe.

A BEACON OF VIRTUE

The Statue of Liberty was dedicated October 28, 1886. The seven spikes in Liberty's crown represent the seven continents of the world and the seven seas. Inscribed on the tablet held in her hand is the date of our Declaration of Independence.

Bartholdi first conceived that the Statue would be a lighthouse, shedding a light across the sea from its crown. He titled it "Liberty Enlightening the World." Congress, in 1877, accepted the Statue as a "beacon," authorizing it to be administered by the Light-House Board. Later, the torch was resculpted and became a beacon as well, radiating the light of liberty and virtue as far as the eye could see.

A SYMBOL OF MORAL CHARACTER

By World War I, the Statue of Liberty had grown in the heart and soul of America to symbolize the moral character of America. After the flag, it became "our" symbol.

But the famous, beloved words of poet Emma Lazarus inscribed in bronze inside the Statue have now become tarnished and have an uncertain ring:

> Give me your tired, your poor,
> Your huddled masses yearning to breathe free,
> The wretched refuse of your teeming shore.
> Send these, the homeless, tempest-tost to me,
> I lift my lamp beside the golden door!

A LAMP GROWN DIM

The light of American liberty and virtue has grown very dim. America is quickly gaining a reputation throughout the world for vice rather than virtue.

The headline of the seventy-fifth anniversary edition (September 14, 1992) of America's premier business magazine, *Forbes*, read, "A De-moralized Society." The article, with illuminating brilliance, brings focus to the gravity of our national life. The following quotations from the article will help us see the issue simply and clearly:

". . . moral concepts, still more moral judgments, are understood to be somehow undemocratic and unseemly."

"We pride ourselves on being liberated from such retrograde Victorian notions."

"Today we have so completely rejected the Victorian ethos that we deliberately, systematically, divorce morality from public policy."

"In the current climate of moral relativism and skepticism, it is thought improper to impose any moral conditions or requirements. . . ."

"We are now confronting the consequences of this policy of moral 'neutrality.'"

"We are discovering that the economic and social aspects of these problems are inseparable from the moral and psychological ones."

"And having made the most determined effort to devise remedies that are 'value-free,' we find that these policies imperil the material, as well as the moral, well-being of their intended beneficiaries—and not only of individuals but of society as a whole."

". . . we have demoralized society itself."[112]

WHEN THE LIGHT OF VIRTUE DIMS

It is common knowledge that crime increases as darkness falls. With the dawn of light, misdeeds diminish. So it is that as the light of virtue and morality has been quenched by purposeful and systematic snuffing of the candles of individual and social values, we see crime and numerous other consequences of "darkness" flood in upon us.

If the problem were not so serious, it might seem almost humorous. It is difficult to comprehend how seemingly intelligent, adult Americans can have slipped so far as to, for all practical purposes, call black "white" and white "black." We call immorality "choices," and we call the pursuit of virtue "bigotry," "rightist," "extremist," and "fundamentalist." Folks, our lamp is going out. We are groping our way in the late dusk of American society. In the words of the musical duo Simon and Garfunkel, "The words of the prophets are written on the subway walls. . . ." They are "sounds of silence"[113]—moral silence.

THE SOUNDS OF SILENCE

Let us look into the darkening windows of American society for a glimpse of the consequences of our dismissing virtue as "old-fashioned" and embracing moral "neutrality" both individually and as a nation. Perhaps our best insight is found in *The Day America Told the Truth,* a 1991 summary of the massive research and investigation by two advertising executives on what Americans really believe and do.

- Sixty percent of Americans have been victims of crime at least once.

- Fifty-eight percent of Americans have been victimized twice or more.

- Twenty million crimes were committed against the "persons" of Americans in 1988 alone.

- More than 25,000 homicides occur in America each year now, more than in any other industrialized country.

- Only 30 percent of Americans are loyal to their companies.

- Twenty-five percent of Americans will compromise their beliefs to get ahead on the job. But 66 percent of high school seniors would lie to achieve an important business objective.

- Ninety-one percent of Americans lie regularly, telling conscious, premeditated lies.

- Two million two hundred thousand Americans believe that they have AIDS. Another seven million believe they are "high risk" for AIDS, but more than one-third would not tell their lovers.

- One out of every seven Americans—that is twenty-six million people—carries a weapon in their car or on their person.

- One third of Americans have contemplated suicide.

- The United States has twenty times more reported rapes than do Japan, England, and Spain.

- Children's television programming averages twenty-five violent acts per hour, up 50 percent from the early 1980s.

- Twenty percent of Americans lose their virginity before age thirteen.

- Sixty-one percent of Americans now 18–24 years of age lost their virginity by age sixteen.

- Thirty-one percent of all married Americans have had an affair. Sixty-two percent of those people think that there is nothing morally wrong with their affairs.

- More than 50 percent of Americans accept "living together" as an acceptable alternative to marriage.

- Ninety-two percent of sexually active Americans have had ten or more lovers.[114]

Friends, if these facts do not cause your American gut to wrench and your mind and heart to grasp out for pillars of personal and national morality and virtue to keep balance, we are without hope. As the secular writers of *The Day America Told the Truth* describe, "For a fistful of dollars, we found that Americans would do almost anything: lie, cheat, steal, murder, abandon their families, and change their religion."[115] The writers conclude,

> It's been said that an era comes to an end when its dreams are exhausted. America's dreams are wearing extremely thin— at least the kind of dreams that can sustain a great nation.[116]

VIRTUE IS NOT A FOUR-LETTER WORD

The most vocal elements of our society have these last forty years led us to believe that virtue is "out" and moral neutrality is "in." Many heroes have been branded with labels for speaking up for that which was right and honorable. Labels and characterizations mold us and make us feel that somehow we are not in the mainstream of society. Because mankind's greatest needs are to be loved and to be accepted, we have defaulted on virtue and standing for morality to avoid feeling rejected. We have been made to feel as if "virtue" were a four-letter word.

I have good news for you! To quote *Forbes* business magazine, September 14, 1992, "Liberal intellectuals have, in short, divorced themselves not only from conventional morality but also from those conventional people who still adhere to that morality."[117] "After decades of silence and denial, it is now finally respectable to speak of the need for 'traditional values'—moral values, family values, social values."[118] We must ". . . encourage a 'counter-counterculture' that will resist the now entrenched 'counterculture.'"[119] Because the word *values* is morally neutral, many influential thinkers now suggest, "Instead of talking about *family values*, everybody would be better off talking about *virtues.* . . ."[120]

LET US REBUILD AMERICAN VIRTUE

Here is wisdom. The French Nobel prize winner Alexis Carrel, who spent many years in America, stated, "Virtue roots us firmly in reality. A virtuous individual is like an engine in good working order. It is due to lack of virtue that the weaknesses and disorders of modern society are due."[121]

Like a prophet, George Washington, in his farewell address, warned the fledgling nation:

> Of all the dispositions and habits which lead to political prosperity, religion and morality are indispensable supports. Let us with caution indulge the supposition that morality can be maintained without religion. . . . Reason and experience both forbid us to expect that National morality can prevail in exclusion of religious principle."[122]

Forty years later, Alexis de Tocqueville, having come from France to observe the prosperity of America, noted, ". . . the religious aspect of the country was the first thing that struck my attention." "I do not know whether all Americans have a sincere faith in their religion—for who can search the human heart? But I am certain they hold it to be indispensable to the maintenance of republican institutions." ". . . it belongs to the whole nation and to every rank of society." "Christian morality is everywhere the same."

He went on to reflect on his 1840 observations,

> In the United States the sovereign authority is religious, and consequently hypocrisy must be common; but there is no country in the world where the Christian religion retains a greater influence over the souls of men than in America; and there can be no greater proof of its utility . . . than that its influence is powerfully felt over the most enlightened and free nation on earth.[123]

Virtue and morality require a base—a foundation. Genuine virtue and true morality do not change. They are rooted in the laws of nature and of nature's God.

Noah Webster, founder of American education, wrote, "The moral principles and precepts contained in the Scriptures ought to form the basis of all our civil constitutions and laws. All the miseries which men suffer from vice, crime, ambition, injustice, oppression, slavery, and war, proceed from their despising, neglecting the precepts contained in the Bible."[124]

VIRTUE BEGINS AT HOME

The April 27, 1992, issue of *Time* magazine included an essay by Charles Krauthammer titled "In Praise of Mass Hypocrisy." He states, ". . . as voters we profess shock that our candidates should behave as we do. . . . The paradox is striking: voters are demanding in their leaders the personal virtues that they decreasingly demand of themselves." He then declares, "There is a word for the profession of virtue accompanied by the practice of vice: hypocrisy."[125]

Virtues have morphed into values to camouflage our hypocrisy. Changing the terminology from *virtue* to *value* eliminates the stigma of a moral standard for behavior, thus seemingly freeing us to do what we *want* rather than what we *ought*. "It was not until the present century that morality became so thoroughly relativized and subjectivized that virtues ceased to be 'virtues' and became 'values,'" writes Gertrude Himmelfarb in *The De-Moralization of Society*.[126] Values float freely on the sea of relativity while virtues are anchored firmly in timeless truth, keeping us from cultural and behavioral shipwreck on the shoals of self-serving and ever-changing personal or poll-driven whim. Virtues are simple, yet sublime.

Virtue begins at home. It begins with the little things. It begins with not calling in "sick" at work when I want to go shopping. It means not having my secretary say, "He's not in," when I don't want to talk to someone. Give God a crack into your mind, your thoughts, and your inner being—your heart. What does He see? What do you see? What do your children see?

If you were to sell your character, would you get full retail, or would it go for a bargain-basement price? Would a jury of your peers find you to be a virtuous person beyond a reasonable doubt?

A new call and desire for virtue seems to be arising in the land—at least in the other guy. *Newsweek* even speaks of "The Politics of VIRTUE."[127] A nationwide poll by the *Los Angeles Times* revealed that 78 percent of Americans are "fed up" with America's moral decline. The most shocking realities, however, are that "only 11 percent believe their own behavior has contributed to our nation's moral problems" and "96 percent believe they are doing an excellent job teaching their children about morals and values."[128]

This striking disconnect between the virtues that we Americans *say* we desire in the nation in contrast to the radically different perception of our personal role in achieving a truly virtuous society caused *Newsweek* to comment,

> The real risk is that the Virtue movement will become just another example of what has become a leading American character trait: talking a good game.

> The true test of our character, in other words, will require more than applauding politicians and passing resolutions. In the end, it's not the laws we pass but the lives we lead.[129]

Alexis de Tocqueville warned us, "America is great because America is good, and if America ever ceases to be good, America will cease to be great." If America's future depends on your example of virtue and morality, what is America's future?

SOUL-STIRRING QUESTIONS FOR PERSONAL AND GROUP REFLECTION

1. What is virtue?

2. Why do you suppose the early banners depicting all that was America used the words *virtue, independence,* and *liberty* together?

3. How does it make you feel to know that America is gaining a worldwide reputation for *vice* rather than *virtue?*

4. What evidence do you see that America's lamp of virtue is flickering and nearly out?

5. How has our pursuit of the dollar affected our virtue? Has it affected yours?

6. Nobel Prize winner Alexis Carrel observed that the weaknesses and disorders of modern society are due to lack of virtue. In what way have the problems that trouble you resulted from your own lack of virtue?

7. The Bible says, "Add to your faith *virtue.*" What must you do to add virtue to your faith? Where would you start? When?

8. If America's future depends on your example of virtue and morality in things both large and small, what is America's future?

Chapter 9

OUR SACRED HONOR

THE GLORY OF AMERICAN LIBERTY was born in the light of American honor. July 4 is a day of national celebration for all Americans. On that day, one of mankind's greatest declarations was signed, announcing the birth of a nation that would change the world and make it a better place. As we revel in fireworks and hang out the Stars and Stripes each year, few of us are conscious of the high cost that purchased the liberty we enjoy.

On July 4, 1776, fifty-six courageous men gathered in the city of Philadelphia to affix their names to the Declaration of Independence. Most of them were Englishmen at heart. They anguished over the manner in which the mother country had so tyrannized the thirteen colonies. King George and the English Parliament seemed bent on making second-class citizens of the colonists and repressing them with taxation in which they had no representation. Basic God-given rights were being ignored, and the people were exploited.

Tensions were high! Explosive! Although most of the signers had been fundamentally loyal to the Crown, they were now convinced that "the laws of Nature and of Nature's God" required that they individually and collectively take a stand for human dignity and against tyranny.

They found "these truths to be self-evident, that all men are created equal, that they are endowed by their Creator with certain unalienable rights. . . ." To this end, they declared their independence from an earthly power, England, and declared their dependence upon a heavenly power—God himself.

The fifty-six signers of the Declaration of Independence were the business, professional, scientific, political, and spiritual leaders of their day. Many of them were very wealthy. Most of them were men of means. They had families. Many of them had position and fame. They were prominent and prosperous. And they realized that their declaration of principle could turn their prosperity to poverty. They also considered the grave reality that if they lost in their bid for freedom, they would, as convicted traitors, feel the jerk of a hangman's rope on their necks.

In this crucible of human drama, fifty-six men decided that liberty was more important than life, that principle was more important than prosperity. And they fixed their names boldly to the Declaration. We must now carefully and prayerfully reconsider the closing words of that Declaration:

> With a firm reliance on the protection of Divine Providence, we mutually pledge to each other our lives, our fortunes, and our sacred honor.

THE PRICE OF HONOR

Calvin Coolidge, a former president of the United States, made a piercing observation that each of us might well consider. He said,

"No person was ever honored for what he received. Honor has been the reward for what he gave."[130]

What did our Founding Fathers give in pledging their "sacred honor"? Of the fifty-six signers of the Declaration,

- five were captured by the British and tortured before they died;

- twelve had their homes sacked, occupied by the British, or burned;

- two lost their sons in the army;

- one had two sons who were captured;

- nine died in the war either from bullets or from the stresses.[131]

They considered their honor "sacred." That which is "sacred" is precious, worthy of preservation, worthy of protection. It is worth living for and therefore worth dying for.

On the day the Declaration of Independence was signed, John Adams declared to his wife, Abigail:

> I am well aware of the toil, and blood, and treasure that it will cost to maintain this declaration, and support and defend these states; yet, through all the gloom I can see the rays of light and glory. I can see that the end is worth all the means.[132]

His son, John Quincy Adams, also a president of our nation, reflected,

> Posterity—you will never know how much it has cost my generation to preserve your freedom. I hope you will make good use of it.[133]

SHALL THESE DEAD HAVE DIED IN VAIN?

Undoubtedly one of the most vocal spokesmen of the American Revolution was Patrick Henry. The drama of his "Give me liberty or give me death" is unforgettable to us even today—at least mentally. But I'm afraid that in our hearts we have little comprehension of its significance. It expressed a willingness to give all—yes, even his sacred honor—for the cause of God-given liberty.

Thomas Paine was also a vital spokesman during the American Revolution. Let us consider the following statement by him:

> What we obtain too cheaply, we esteem too lightly; it is dearness only that gives everything its value. Heaven knows how to put a price upon its goods, and it would be strange indeed if so celestial an article as freedom should not be highly rated.[134]

Thomas Jefferson expressed his concern similarly, crying out from his inward being, from his sacred honor,

> My God! how little do my countrymen know what precious blessings they are in possession of, and which no other people on earth enjoy.[135]

What do we make of such service, such sacrifice, such honor today? Do we reverence it? Do we respect its fruits? Do we honor our Founding Fathers' blood, their lives, their vision? Or has our freedom, our nation under God, taken short shrift in the face of our headlong pursuit of personal peace and affluence? Jefferson minced no words when he declared, "The price of liberty is eternal vigilance."[136] Are we paying the price? Or do we no longer value liberty and honor? Were the efforts of these men ultimately in vain?

AMERICA'S HALL OF FAME / SHAME

Honor springs from the well of moral living. Without moral virtue, the glory of honor recedes behind the glare of vice. The first king of Israel discovered this truth when he rendered only partial obedience to God's command to him. God had exalted him from obscurity to kingship. In his kingly pride, he decided that he would "do his own thing," believing that as long as he gave lip service and partial compliance to God's expectations, God would see things his way. But God was not impressed. He sent the prophet Samuel to King Saul with a biting message: *To obey is better than sacrifice, and to hearken than the fat of rams.*[137] King Saul lost the moral light that raised him to honor, and his glory faded to disgrace.

America stands in a similar position today. The God who gave us life gave us liberty. He inspired our Founding Fathers, instilling in them the moral and spiritual light that revealed the path and blazed the way for development of the government and the social fabric of a nation, the light of which has radiated to the entire world. That light produced a glory rooted in national virtue and honor. But as we have become proud and self-sufficient, we thought that we could ignore that Divine Friend and His plans for life and prosperous living. We agreed with the popular song that said, "I'll do it my way." And we have. But not without consequence. Our honor is tarnished, and with it our glory is turning to shame.

Chapter 6 of Patterson and Kim's *The Day America Told the Truth* is titled "The American Hall of Shame." In that chapter, the two advertising executives inspect the behavior of Americans as reflected from the mind and heart of Americans as we view ourselves. Their conclusion: America is in shame.[138]

What is especially frightening, though, is that we are even losing our sense of shame. We have seared our moral conscience. Chapter 12 of *The Day America Told the Truth* is titled "Infidelity: It's Rampant. . . ."[139] We are then told, "Almost one-third of all married Americans have had or are now having an affair."[140] "Today, the majority of Americans (62 percent) think that there is nothing morally wrong with the affairs they're having."[141]

So much for honor. Whatever happened to the Marine Corps motto, *"Semper Fidelis,"* always faithful? If I cannot be faithful to my spouse, how can I be faithful to my country? If I cannot be faithful to these people or institutions, to what am I faithful? Where is my honor? I cannot be faithful even to myself. Hence, the increasing wave of suicides and flocking to "shrinks" and "tea leaf" readers, even in the White House. Yet, our cars sport license plates declaring our "independence"–"Screw Guilt." Friend, we are losing our liberty because we are losing our honor.

FLICKERING EMBERS

As a public speaker and author, I have gathered resource books around me as "tools of the trade." Of particular interest to me have been books compiling thousands of quotations broken down into various subject categories. These tools enable me to probe very quickly the halls of history for the thoughts of both sages past and more current thinkers. I have used four such references for many years, but recently I acquired several more such sources that promised to be helpful. I opened my older volumes to the key word *honor* and quickly found a number of quotations in each. But when I searched the three new acquisitions, I was grieved that the word *honor* did not even appear. Each one of these new volumes seemed to have many more quotations than any of the old standbys, yet no *honor.* What was especially shocking is that one of the books purports to be a large collection of "American" quotations and the other two are collections of "religious" quotations—yet, none of them contained quotations about "honor."

Not only are we losing our honor in fact, but we are even being stripped of the memory of honor. We must put new kindling on the flickering embers of honor. It is a cold and selfish world, nation, family, and heart that is without honor. It is the ultimate demise of a civilized people—yes, even of the nation itself.

SO MUCH FOR HEROES

One of the saddest consequences of the demise of honor is the disappearance of heroes. America has been rich in heroes—men and women who stood for truth, who courageously did and spoke what was right. Names such as Washington, Adams, Lincoln, Revere, Nightingale, Jones, Carver, Crocket, Boone, Finney, King, Winthrop, Bradford, Moody, Sunday, and Graham dot the American memory. Their memory enriches our spirit and lifts us to higher ground.

But where have all of the heroes gone? We shifted from statesmen and courageous moral leaders to athletes and superstars of the entertainment world, most of whom have epitomized anything but sound moral fiber with which to feed our youth.[142] Even Superman is now dead.

According to a recent poll, 70 percent of Americans believe that no living heroes exist today. About the same number of people say that our children have no meaningful role models. Neither do we trust our leaders or institutions—not even ourselves.[143] As the ballad from the decade of the sixties croons, "When will we ever learn?" No power from without could do to us what we have done to ourselves. It has taken profound tragedy at the hands of terrorists to uncover the glow of heroism from the whole of our decayed national house.

AN AWAKENING CONSCIENCE

Historian Paul Johnson, writing in the seventieth anniversary edition of *Forbes*, America's leading business magazine, observes that we embraced a "secularized utopianism" in the twentieth century, believing "that society can be made comfortable, safe, healthy, and secure for all, irrespective of merit or effort, and that the agency of this process is the state." He concludes that this "secular utopia" has not and cannot be realized and that its pursuit has been at enormous cost to an entire generation. Americans, he thinks, still have a "strong, deep-rooted moral sense" and that the current severe troubling throughout our society is evidence of a "returning sense of wrongdoing"—an "awakened conscience."[144] Perhaps these are indeed the flickering embers. If so, where do we go from here?

IS THERE HONOR AMONG THIEVES?

Someone once said that there is honor among thieves. Such "honor," however, limited to a macro society of general lawlessness, does little to benefit society as a whole. Yet, in current American society we have multitudes of little bands of "thieves," little groups, clubs, families, businesses, even churches where we honor one another within the ranks for our various deeds of "service" but where our behavior and heart toward the citizens and society outside is often less than honorable. It is not that we *intend* to be dishonorable, we just are . . . because the disease has so pervasively infected us as a people.

So we cannot "bootstrap" honor. Honor comes from within. It issues from the inner character . . . from the heart . . . from our very soul. And honor is then bestowed by society back to one who has acted honorably from his heart. So what is the means whereby we can restore honor in our hearts and lives individually and as a nation? The answer is not "blowing in the wind"; neither is it more tragedy. It is simple and straightforward.

RESTORING THE ROOTS OF HONOR

Our Founding Fathers were nearly universal in their conviction as to the root of honor. They were convinced, as George Washington himself declared, that, "Of all the dispositions and habits which lead to political prosperity, Religion and morality are indispensable supports."[145]

They were also convinced that "national morality cannot prevail in exclusion of religious principle."[146]

But it was not religion in general that moved them. It was the Christian faith as expressed in the Bible—the Holy Scriptures. Noah Webster could not state this fundamental belief more clearly:

The moral principles and precepts contained in the Scriptures ought to form the basis of all our civil constitutions and laws. All the miseries and evils which men suffer from vice, crime, ambition, injustice, oppression, slavery, and war, proceed from their despising or *neglecting* the precepts contained in the Bible.[147]

This understanding of the Bible as the root of American morality, honor, and success carried forward one hundred fifty years as reflected by our presidents.

All the good from the Savior of the world is communicated through this Book; but for the Book we could not know right from wrong. All the things desirable to man are contained in it.[148]

—Abraham Lincoln

The foundations of our society and our government rest so much on the teachings of the Bible that it would be difficult to support them if faith in these teachings would cease to be practically universal in our country.[149]

—Calvin Coolidge

DESPISING OR NEGLECTING

As we have seen, Noah Webster made clear that all of the evils and miseries of men proceeded from either despising or neglecting the precepts contained in the Bible. Although some scorners apparently despise the Bible as the Word of God, most Americans, fortunately, would not yet be so proudly arrogant.

But that does not leave us with excuse. Most of us are guilty of what we believe to be "benign" neglect. We do not intend to neglect. We just do not specifically intend not to. We do not intend harm. We just blithely disregard potential consequences, or we figure that, "What I don't know won't hurt me." Some of us, like

Israel's first king, pride ourselves on our belief in the Bible, on how often we go to church, on what good things we are doing for God; but we selectively leave out those things that He requires of us that are inconvenient or inconsistent with our current agenda.

According to the Author's view of His Word, no neglect is "benign." He expects us to take heed, to hear, and to act accordingly. Honor will follow. One of the most noble, honorable, and classic films of our time was "Chariots of Fire." Eric Liddell, the young Olympian upon whose life the film was based, made in a moment of moral choice and crisis a personal decision by choosing God's way rather than yielding to the pressure of political power in his nation. He was a man of principle and honor. He was willing to sacrifice temporary personal pleasure and goals in favor of God's eternal plan and principles. And he was honored by both God and man. In his moment of decision, he sought direction from the Bible and relied upon God's promise: ". . . them that honor Me I will honor. . . ."[150]

If we would see the light and the glory of America return, we must restore her honor. That must begin in our hearts and not artificially built through the horrors of war, necessary as war might be. Woodrow Wilson's words advise us well: "The nation's honor is dearer than the nation's comfort; yes, than the nation's life itself."

But there is no national honor without individual honor, honor in your life and mine.

THE HONOR OF HUMILITY

Humility is the soil condition of the heart and character out of which honor grows and is manifested. The Scriptures advise, " . . . Before honor is humility."[151]

But the same passage warns, "Before destruction the heart of man is haughty."[152] God hates pride. So do most people. But God honors humility in a man, a woman, and a nation. He has promised, "Humble yourselves under the mighty hand of God, that He may exalt you in due time." [153] But He warns, ". . . the nation and kingdom that will not serve Thee shall perish."[154]

Humble service to God and our neighbor is the hallmark of honor.

HONOR OF SACRIFICE

George Sand said, "There is but one virtue—the eternal sacrifice of self."[155] O. P. Clifford stated similarly, "The altar of sacrifice is the touchstone of character."[156]

I would like to close this chapter by sharing thoughts from one of America's most honored and successful businessmen and entrepreneurs—J. C. Penney, founder of the J. C. Penney chain of department stores. The founding motto of the J. C. Penney Company was "Honor, Confidence, Service, and Cooperation."[157] Mr. Penney encourages and guides us with the following words in his autobiography, *Fifty Years With the Golden Rule:*

> As to our country, my faith in our America, in its people and in the "American way of life" is unwavering. Its founding I believe to have been divinely ordained, and God has a mighty mission for it among the nations of the world. It was founded in prayer, in faith, and in the heroic spirit of sacrifice. Lives of comparative ease might have been the lot of our forefathers in their own country had they been willing to surrender their convictions. They chose the "hard right," rather than the "easy wrong. . . ."[158]

As a nation, and as individuals, our fate will always be determined by our choice of the "hard right" or the "easy wrong."[159]

Every aspect of world condition today opens a way provocatively for applying Christian principles to living. Let us not be afraid: loving God, and our neighbors as ourselves, let us only believe. Being not afraid, and believing, let us choose for ourselves the "hard right." If individuals in sufficient number will pledge their part as men willing to follow the hard right, our America will be made safe for her own people and will stand as a beacon light of hope to this war-torn, war-weary world.[160]

My friend, will you join me in making that pledge? Regardless of the branch of the Armed Services in which you might have served, will you, in the words of the Marine Corps hymn, be "First to fight for right and freedom, and to keep our *honor* clean"?

I pray that you will, because America is depending on you. From our ancestors came our names; from our virtues comes our honor. Leave your children and your grandchildren a heritage of honor. And may God bless you accordingly.

SOUL-STIRRING QUESTIONS FOR PERSONAL AND GROUP REFLECTION

1. What is honor?

2. How is honor gained or lost?

3. Can true honor exist without moral virtue?

4. How does shame develop in an individual or a nation?

5. In what ways is honor linked to true liberty?

6. The Bible states, "Before honor is humility." If we are losing our honor as a nation, in what ways have *We the people* become proud rather than humble?

7. What is the condition of your honor? Are you a virtuous man or woman? What would your children or grandchildren say? What does your secretary or coworker think?

8. God said in the Bible, "Them that honor Me, I will honor." Based upon this standard, are you worthy of God's honor? Is our nation, *We the people*, worthy of His honor?

Chapter 10

SEMPER FI

NOWHERE IS HONOR BETTER EXEMPLIFIED than in fidelity. Fidelity is an essential ingredient of honor. Without fidelity, there is no honor. Yet, the very word *fidelity* has largely been lost from our culture, conversation, and character as Americans. It is now most frequently found as part of the names of our financial institutions, as in "Fidelity Federal Savings." But in our lives and conversation, fidelity has largely become a "lost art."

How is it I can become concerned with fidelity when it comes to my money but can take it or leave it when it comes to the more important issues of life—people, principles, and purpose? Perhaps when we can answer that question we will also be able to explain how we can sacrifice character when electing our politicians in favor of their economic promises. If character is not an issue *during* an election campaign, then I have no right to make it an issue *after* the election.

The life quality of fidelity—or the lack thereof—pervades every fiber of our personal and national character. It is interrelated with both our vices and our virtues. It lies at the root of both our honors and our horrors.

AMERICA'S CLASSIC CONTRAST

America's Hall of Honor

He was a graduate of Yale, Class of 1773, and he taught in a girls' school while preparing for the ministry. When news of the "shot heard 'round the world" at the Battle of Lexington and Concord reached him, he immediately enlisted in the Connecticut Rangers to fight the tyranny of the British. At a town meeting he declared, *"Liberty? Independence?* Are they to remain only words? Gentlemen, let us make them fighting words!"

General Washington desperately needed intelligence information about British intentions, and he gave that delicate assignment to the young captain. Disguised as a schoolmaster, the young officer infiltrated British lines, making sketches and taking notes in Latin. He was captured after taking the wrong boat on his way back to the American encampment, and he readily admitted his identity.

The following day, September 22, 1776, the British hanged the twenty-one-year-old captain without a trial. Witnesses sobbed, but the condemned soldier never lost his composure. As they put the noose around his neck, he declared, "I only regret that I have but one life to lose for my country."[161] The name of Nathan Hale has been immortalized in America's "Hall of Honor." He was true to himself, his conscience, and his country.

America's Hall of Shame

He was given high command in the Continental Army. Despite his courage and brilliance, his ego and flamboyant ways raised eyes of distrust among many of his colleagues. He staged elaborate banquets, rode in gaudy carriages, and caused many people to wonder how he could finance such lavish living. He also developed unusually close relationships with British sympathizers. When Congress acted to investigate his business deals, he retaliated by selling his services to the British.

Because of his military brilliance, General Washington offered him command of the left wing of the American Army, but he was granted command of West Point by his own specific request. He immediately took steps to turn over West Point—the gateway to the entire Hudson River region—to the British for a price. He sought full details on all secret agents working for the American command. But no real suspicion of his treachery ever entered the mind of General Washington or his other commanders.

On September 23, 1776, the day after Nathan Hale was hung, American militiamen captured a British agent. A search revealed that hidden in the agent's shoe were documents in the handwriting of the commander of West Point that would have set the stage for the British to divide the colonies. The conspiracy failed, and the traitorous American commander of West Point escaped.

He received a reward from the British as the price of his prostituted fidelity—£6,315 for himself and an annual pension of £500 for his wife. Offsetting his reward, however, was a future of disgrace. The name of Benedict Arnold is immortalized in America's "Hall of Shame." The rest of his life was tormented by the hatred of the Americans he had sold out and corroded by the scorn and distrust of the British who had bought him.[162]

WHAT IS YOUR PRICE?

Are you a Nathan Hale or a Benedict Arnold? Can you be bought? Are you true to yourself, your family, your conscience, your countrymen, and your God? Or have you sold out? Have you sold out in little ways? Maybe you did not commit treason against your country—maybe only against your family—maybe against your own conscience.

Someone once said, "Conscience is a sacred sanctuary where God alone may enter as judge."[163] Conscience reveals the little things. We know that "It is the little foxes that spoil the vine."[164] The American "vine" is being destroyed by little "foxes." That is true in the area of fidelity as it is in other areas. "Fidelity in small things is at the base of every great achievement,"[165] says Charles Wagner.

Cicero gives us insight into the wisdom of the ages in the following reflection:

Nothing is more noble, nothing more venerable, than fidelity. Faithfulness and truth are the most sacred excellences and endowments of the human mind.[166]

WHAT IN THE WORLD IS FIDELITY?

We may need to ask ourselves this question: What is *fidelity* anyway? Certainly, we do not use the word in common parlance anymore. But we do hear a familiar ring to its counterpart: *Infidelity.* Isn't it interesting that we should be more familiar with *infidelity* than with *fidelity*? Perhaps that is a commentary on where we are as a people and as a nation.

But we more commonly use some other terms that are relatives of fidelity, words such as *faithfulness, dependability, reliability, commitment, loyalty,* and *duty.* In the pages that follow, we will explore where we are in our individual and national "fidelity" and the practical impact on our American society and culture. We will inspect the fidelity chain throughout our relationships—fidelity to

family, children, spouses, institutions, and our fellow citizens—
and how they all relate to our fidelity to God.

FIDELITY TO THE FAMILY

Chapter 7 of George Gallup's book titled *Forecast 2000* is "The
Faltering Family." Because the "family" is generally considered to
be the "building block" of our society, perhaps we should begin
our exploration there with Gallup's opening paragraphs:

> In a recent Sunday school class in a Methodist Church in
> the Northeast, a group of eight- to ten-year-olds were in a
> deep discussion with their two teachers. When asked to
> choose which of ten stated possibilities they most feared hap-
> pening, their response was unanimous. All the children most
> dreaded a divorce between their parents.
>
> Later, as the teachers, a man and a woman in their late thir-
> ties, reflected on the lesson, they both agreed they'd been
> shocked at the response. When they were the same age as their
> students, they said the possibility of their parents being
> divorced never entered their heads. Yet in just one generation,
> children seemed to feel much less security in their family ties.[167]

In a poll of opinion leaders, says Gallup, "Thirty-three percent
of the responses listed decline of the family structure, divorce, and
other family-oriented concerns as one of the five major problems
facing the nation today."[168] Fifty percent of my legal practice for
eighteen years was in "family law" in the largest Family Law court
in the nation, the Los Angeles Superior Court. I am personally convinced that the breakdown of the family as a major threat to our
national health, strength, security, and integrity is second only to

the breakdown of truth, which we will examine as we conclude this chapter.

This chapter is not intended to be an exhaustive coverage of the subject of the family in American life. However, its importance is so basic and the consequences of its breakdown are so cataclysmic that we must look a little further. Consider the following facts.

* Today, one out of every two marriages ends in divorce.

* The rate of divorce has more than doubled in the last two decades.

* About 100,000 people over age fifty-five get divorced in the U.S. each year—usually initiated by men who reach retirement—and break marriages of thirty or more years' duration.

* In 1970, 71 percent of all adults were part of a married-couple family. By 1991, only 55 percent of adults were in married-couple families.

* Some demographers confidently predicted that a majority of American adults would be single by the year 2000.[169]

The year 2000 census revealed a virtual total breakdown of traditional moral values among U.S. citizens. The nuclear family, consisting of a married father and mother with children in the home, now comprises only 25 percent of the family units in our country.

So what is it that is driving the American family into oblivion? What forces are creating these frightening statistics? George Gallup cites four such forces:

• sexual morality,

• alternative lifestyles,

• economics, and

• feminist philosophy.[170]

If one looks closely, the conclusion is virtually inescapable that each of these forces or causes of family disintegration finds its root in lack of fidelity or lack of faithfulness. Lack of fidelity is infidelity.

Changes in sexual morality are rooted in infidelity. We are committed no longer to sex within the bond of marriage or to being true to our spouses during marriage. Chapter 12 of Patterson and Kim's *The Day America Told the Truth* is titled "Infidelity: It's Rampant . . ." They state the following statistics.

- Almost one-third of all married Americans (31 percent) have had an affair.[171]

- Sixty-two percent of Americans think that there is nothing wrong with the affairs they're having.[172]

Marital infidelity is not our only concern. We are also untrue to ourselves before marriage and untrue to our friends. Chapter 13 of *The Day America Told the Truth* is titled "The End of Childhood in America." It states the following findings.

* Twenty percent of kids lose their virginity before age thirteen.[173]

* Sixty-one percent of eighteen- to twenty-four-year-olds lost their virginity by the age of sixteen.[174]

The January 18, 1993, edition of *Newsweek* carries a front cover that declares, "AIDS and the Arts"—a Lost Generation."[175] AIDS has no cure. Because it is carried predominantly among homosexuals who practice what we are asked to call "an alternative lifestyle," not only is the family itself breached by homosexuality but also the entire family of the human race is threatened, the disease having now spread to heterosexual practitioners through blood or through their own infidelity.

Infidelity is killing us physically, spiritually, and socially. Infidelity—the failure to be faithful—is at its root selfishness.

Infidelity goes to the core of character. It reveals the true condition of our soul.

Infidelity—lack of fidelity—is often involved in women leaving the home to work. I want to be sensitive here, but not so sensitive that the issue is skirted politely. We need to search deeply into our hearts and motivations.

Husband, have you asked your wife to work instead of staying home with the kids because you want another car, a bigger house, or fancier vacations? If so, can you see selfish choices resulting in infidelity to your family and children?

Wife and mother, are you motivated to go to work because you "want to be where the action is," want to feel more important, expect to gain your self-worth from the job, or are trying to "improve" your standard of living?

Could it be that the long-range "standard of living" of your family and children will suffer for a choice that was really not truly necessary? Are we sacrificing long-term values for short-term gain? Are we being true? Are we being faithful? Am I telling myself the truth? Moms and dads, your family needs you more than your money.

In his book *The Future of the American Family*, George Barna, pollster and researcher, talks about what he calls "nouveau families." These "nouveau," or new, families are made up of various combinations of persons not related by blood or marriage, even including casual acquaintances—people who care about each other.[176] Young people increasingly define *family* as "the people who really care about me" rather than my parents and my siblings.[177] According to Barna, one of the principle causes of this trend toward redefining family is that people "believe the traditional family configurations have failed them personally."[178]

Why do an increasing number of people find it necessary to redefine the family? It is because of:

- child abuse,

- child molestation,

- latch-key children,

- divorce,

- "child care" instead of parent care,

- trust of the TV to parent,

- failure to spend personal time with our children,

- failure to spend personal time with our spouses,

- all work and no play,

- all play and no pray, and

- exalting my rights over my responsibilities.

It is family infidelity. It is lack of faithfulness to our calling as parents and spouses. Barna expresses the problem succinctly:

> . . . those who advocate such loose family ties often fail to grasp that successful families are successful largely because they offer safety, trust, and permanence. Once a family ceases to offer those protections, the atmosphere for love and intimacy is lost. Ultimately, the family falters because its members refuse to surrender some of their freedoms for the benefit of others.[179]

A Special Word to Fathers

Dr. James Dobson is widely known as "America's family advocate." As founder and president of the large nonprofit organization "Focus on the Family," he has spoken widely across America and conducts a daily radio broadcast in response to which he receives many thousands of letters monthly. In his book *Straight Talk to Men*, Dr. Dobson boldly states,

> If America is going to survive the incredible stresses and dangers it now faces, it will be because husbands and fathers again place their families at the highest level on their system of priorities. . . .[180]

> The Western world stands at a great crossroads in its history.[181]

> . . . our very survival as a people will depend on the presence or absence of masculine leadership in millions of homes.[182]

In reviewing the numerous letters that he receives, Dr. Dobson observes, "One of the most common letters I receive is sent by hundreds of women who ask the same question: 'My husband won't assume spiritual leadership in our family. He doesn't seem to be aware of my needs and the requirements of our children. How can I get his attention?'"[183]

Dr. Dobson strongly contends that "husbands hold the keys to the preservation of the family."[184] If we hold the keys, husbands, what have we done with them? Another writer has said that our real problem is "renegade males."[185] A renegade is one who "reneges." A man who "reneges" is one who is not faithful to his calling. He does not provide moral and spiritual leadership in the home. He is more concerned about his work, Monday-night football, the news, and anything and everything but what really counts. He has never seriously considered that his children follow his example, that the twig is being bent.

Fatherlessness is a plague of epic proportions in American society as a whole, but for black children it is "A World Without Fathers." The agonizing reality is that 80 percent of all black children under the age of sixteen do not live in a home with both parents. "Many black leaders rush to portray out-of-wedlock births as solely a problem of the entrenched underclass. But it's not. It cuts across economic lines, as 22 percent of never-married black women with income above $75,000 have children," ten times that among Caucasians.[186]

Fathers, we are America's first line of defense. We are also America's primary offense. We must straighten up our act, discipline ourselves to be faithful as "God's hand extended" to our children. We must love them, nurture them, pray with them and for them—and we must love their mother. Someone has said, "The greatest gift a father can give to his children is to love their mother."[187] "Fathering," says Ken Canfield of the National Center for Fathering, "may be your most important social, spiritual and physical contribution to the future of America."[188]

Dads, our children are waiting for us. America's future is in our hands. Because America's future is in your (and my) hands, what will America's future be? Will you be faithful? If you have not been faithful, will you go to your wife and children and ask their forgiveness for your failure? Will you then repent, turn, and become the man God created you to be? Fathers are the first hope for America's future. Will you dare to be a father in America?

CHILDREN—FIDELITY WAR CASUALTIES

In my law practice, I watched in agony as children were pulled and torn in the breakup of homes. I heard their desperate, heart-rending cries echo down the corridors of the courts. No matter how much we rationalize from the depths of our personal pain, children really do need a mother and a father—yes, in the same house. Barna, in *The Future of the American Family,* quotes a professor of cultural studies who predicts,

> I think we are just beginning to see the results of the devastation we sowed over the last twenty-five years. The deep scars laid on our children as a consequence of our narcissistic, driven way of life cannot be downplayed. For years to come, you will see the ramifications of a divorce-happy, single-parent society when you look at crime statistics, suicide rates, relational crises, moral ambiguity, and the widespread problems of self-esteem that manifest themselves in a myriad of public and private ways.[189]

Kids do pay a high price! Is it worth it? But we have barely scratched the surface of the impact of our lack of parental fidelity to our children. Child abuse is now rampant. Now that child abuse has been brought before the public eye in glaring technicolor, government and the courts have stepped in. As occurs whenever government steps in, there is overreaction. Because we have delegated excessive responsibility to government, government now becomes a significant threat to the family itself, stepping in under cover of the law to undermine the authority of parents. Social engineers with godless agendas seek to place the state in the role of the "ultimate parent."

Now we even have children divorcing their parents. How can this be? It is the fruit of the tree of infidelity. The Scriptures warn us that in the last days children will rise up against their parents.[190] It also admonishes us that a curse on our society is directly linked to whether the hearts of the fathers will be turned to the children and the hearts of the children to their fathers.[191] When will we break the cycle? Will you be the first? Will you vow that from this day forward you will be faithful in parenting your children? Will you adjust your priorities—your finances, your time, your energies? Can America depend on you? Can your children depend on you?

DUTY IS A FOUR-LETTER WORD

Duty is a word that is in disrepute. It fell into disfavor as rights became exalted over responsibility in our society. It has largely become "a four-letter word" in the American mind and consciousness. That result is consistent with the mortal blows that are being dealt to fidelity, because duty and fidelity are close relatives.

Someone has said, "Not liberty, but duty, is the condition of existence."[192] The trouble is that so many Americans who are standing up for their rights are falling down on their duties. When duty calls, some people are never at home. Generally speaking, duty is what we have come to expect of others. "A man never gets so confused in his thinking that he can't see the other fellow's duty."[193]

Our failure, as individuals, to be true and faithful to our fellow citizens and our God has resulted in severe economic crisis and near bankruptcy as a nation. We need some radical rethinking of some premises that we have come to accept as "givens." The following list of facts is food for thought.

* If we personally cared for our parents, we might not need Social Security.

* If we personally, or through our churches and clubs, cared for the hungry and the homeless in our neighborhood and helped the unemployed find work, we might not need welfare.

* If I, as an elected official, refused to vote "largess from the public treasury" and fill the "pork barrel" of special interests,

or to exceed funds in a balanced budget, we would not have a federal deficit.

* If we church members had truly tithed 10 percent of our after-tax income last year, $131 billion in additional resources would have been available to care for the needy who now depend upon the government for care.

A genuine sense of duty has a way of simplifying matters that loom excessively complex when I want to delegate my duty. These are but a few examples. We have created major problems for ourselves because of our collective refusal as individual Americans over the years to "do our duty." I include myself in this indictment. We have been unfaithful to our national call and purpose. We have mortgaged our future. Truly, *We the people* must act as "individuals"—not as a "government." We can no longer shirk our duty. Duty calls.

This issue is not new. In 1802, John Quincy Adams said that when you think of duty, "Think of your forefathers! Think of your posterity!"[194] In other words, duty and faithfulness must be reviewed continually and assessed in light of both our past and our future. In the words of Abraham Lincoln, ". . . let us to the end dare to do our duty as we understand it."[195]

"The duty to our neighbor is part of our duty to God."[196] It is not the government's duty. It is my duty. It is your duty. Let us come before our Maker for clarification of our duties. One thing He has made clear: "It is required of stewards that a man be found faithful."[197]

THE FIDELITY FULCRUM

The "fulcrum" is the point over which a lever is balanced. The position of the fulcrum determines whether the lever will be balanced, "all else being equal," as in a child's seesaw.

Fidelity to God's plans and design is the fulcrum over which the lever, or seesaw, of an individual's—or a nation's—life is balanced. If the fulcrum is out of balance, the seesaw is not in balance unless weight is added or adjustments are made to compensate. If the fulcrum is removed, no action is possible; the lever cannot move no matter how much weight is added.

That is a simple picture of our plight as a nation. God himself has established the fulcrum. He has declared and ordained plans whereby we can prosper as individuals, families, and a nation. But when we tamper with the fulcrum or attempt to relocate it to suit our desires, the lever of personal and national life does not balance. We then find ourselves trying to shore up one side or the other of life's seesaw to create balance. We do this by throwing tremendous quantities of time and money at our problems that result from our infidelity to the fulcrum.

Our Creator tried to make it simple. He stated in the Bible, "Let us hear the conclusion of the whole matter: Fear God, and keep his commandments: for this is the whole duty of man."[198]

The Mayflower Compact, signed as the Pilgrims were preparing to land on our eastern shore, clearly described the understanding of those "founding" fathers in coming to these shores.

> Having undertaken, for the glory of God and advancement of the Christian Faith and honor of our King and country, do by these presents solemnly and mutually in the presence of God and one another, covenant and combine ourselves into a civil body politic. . . .[199]

The Puritan colony under the governorship of a lawyer, John Winthrop, was established by a similar document titled "A Model of Christian Charity." It stated:

We are a company, professing ourselves fellow members of Christ, we ought to account ourselves knit together by this bond of love. . . .

Thus stands the cause between God and us: we are entered into covenant with Him for this work.[200]

These two colonies and their founders affected American society, government, and law more than any other influences. They set the direction, established the purpose, and provided the means for establishing the nation. Based upon those premises, this nation has become the greatest nation, not only in power but also for good, in the history of mankind.

Those founding principles were in the form of a covenant or promise.

FIRST: A covenant was declared between the founders and God himself to honor, respect, and obey God's laws and commands for prosperous living.

SECOND: A covenant was declared among the people to love, honor, care for, and respect one another as a reflection of God's love, care, and respect for them.

The Plymouth and Massachusetts Bay colonies set forth in good faith to honor those covenants. They developed laws based upon those covenants issuing straight from the Bible. Our current system of law is a by-product of their covenants. When they erred and violated those covenants, they sought God's forgiveness and repented, always seeking faithfully to preserve their covenant with God because they knew and had written into the founding document itself that if they were unfaithful to God's plan and call and to their observance of the covenant, ". . . the Lord will surely break out in wrath against us."[201]

As our Founding Fathers lean over the parapets of history to see the waywardness of the nation they "birthed," they must wrench in mortal terror for the wrath now being poured out upon us. Surely we do not have to repeat *ad nauseam* the dire social, economic, moral, and spiritual mess in which we find ourselves. Surely we are not so numb, so naive, so callous, or so blind that we cannot see the cause-and-effect relationship of our moral and spiritual rebellion against our Creator and our desperate national crises. We have breached the covenant. We have been unfaithful, and God cannot bless and prosper us.

UNDER GOD OR "UNDER THE GUN"

As a nation, we have always looked to and trusted that God would be faithful, that He would be true to His Word. We have expressed that confidence in many ways, including the following:

In our "Pledge of Allegiance," we declare ourselves to be "one nation *under God*, indivisible. . . ."

In "America the Beautiful," America's favorite patriotic song, we sing, "America, America, God shed His grace on thee. . . ."

In "My Country 'Tis of Thee," we sing, "Long may our land be bright, With freedom's holy light; Protect us by Thy might, Great God our king."

In our national anthem, "The Star-Spangled Banner," we declare, "And this be our motto, *In God Is Our Trust* . . ."

As both a nation and a people, we have not hesitated to express our trust and our confidence in God as the ruler of nations and the rewarder of those who diligently seek Him. One of the great gospel songs sung in our churches is "Great Is Thy Faithfulness." We know in our hearts that He is faithful. But we also know in our hearts that we are not faithful.

In his book *America's Only Hope*, Tony Evans, a vibrant black pastor from Dallas, Texas, boldly trumpets,

> . . . the problems we face in our society are the result of individuals, families, churches, and society at large making up new rules rather than following God's rules.[202]

Dr. Evans continues,

> We must realize the serious nature of our covenant with God. . . . when we fail to keep the terms of the covenant, it affects all other relationships as well."[203]

A CALL TO THE CHURCH

Although this book is a letter to America at large, I want to briefly but specifically address those readers who currently profess faith in Jesus Christ, the Christian church in America. Folks, we have left our first love. We have been prodigal in our ways. And we are accountable—not only to God but also to our nation. As the Apostle Peter announced in the New Testament, "The time is come that judgment must begin at the house of God."[204]

George Gallup, in a survey of business executives and the general public conducted for the *Wall Street Journal*, found "very little difference between the churched and the unchurched in terms of their general views on ethical matters, and also their practical ethical responses in various situations."[205]

That is a scathing indictment! What has happened to God's church in America since Alexis de Tocqueville declared in the first half of the nineteenth century, "Not until I went into the churches of America and heard her pulpits aflame with righteousness did I understand the secret of her genius and power"?[206] The simple answer is that our pulpits no longer flame with righteousness but offer a stew of psychology, pop-culture, and biblical platitudes.

Quoting Dr. Tony Evans once again, we look at our responsibility in the church:

> Since God is the source of the church's authority, He holds the church accountable to function according to His authority.[207]

> If the church operates apart from His authority, God says He will withdraw His presence, leaving it powerless.[208]

> Jesus is not smiling at the way we run our lives. He's not grinning at the way we run our homes. He's not happy about how we run our churches.[209]

> Pastors must be absolutely sure that they are proclaiming Jesus' message to His church.[210]

> As a pastor, I am also accountable for making sure God's people implement His message. . . .[211]

> Sermons are to declare the Word of God. . . .[212]

> God's Word cuts and prunes away. . . .[213]

> "Everyone in the church is accountable to abide by the terms of the covenant—the pastor, the elders, the deacons, the whole congregation.[214]

If the church is ever to fulfill its mission, it must hold God's people accountable to Him.[215]

We are accountable for our actions to the Lord of the church. . . .[216]

A CALL TO MY FELLOW AMERICANS

Today is the day of reckoning. Today is the moment of decision. We must individually humble ourselves, pray, and repent of our errant and arrogant ways so that we can once again be found faithful. And God will once again bless us.

An article in the seventy-fifth anniversary edition of *Forbes* magazine remorsefully states, "People don't have faith in America's future anymore."[217] Restoring faith requires restoring fidelity. Fidelity or faithfulness is a sure cure for infidelity.

The Marine Corps motto is *"Semper Fidelis*—Always Faithful." No Marine can forget that motto, at least mentally. Let us all restore faithfulness in America—in our private lives, in our jobs, in our churches, and in our families. Let it begin with you and me. In the words of a song, "May all who come behind us find us faithful."[218]

SOUL-STIRRING QUESTIONS FOR PERSONAL AND GROUP REFLECTION

1. How would you define *fidelity?*

2. Do I have a right to complain about character issues after an election if I refuse to make character an issue during the election campaign?

3. Why are we as a people more familiar with *infidelity* than with *fidelity?*

4. In what way is the exploding divorce rate, especially among Christians, one of the best measures of the condition of our national soul?

5. Someone has said, "The greatest gift a father can give to his children is to love their mother." Why is that true?

6. How has government interference in the family been caused by our lack of fidelity to the family?

7. Why do so many Americans stand up for their rights but fall down on their duties?

8. Forbes noted, "People don't have faith in America's future anymore." Do you agree or disagree? Why?

9. Benedict Arnold sold America's security secrets for a sum. Have you sold out any of your principles or become unfaithful to family, friends, an employer, God, or your nation for personal gain—for money, position, fame, success, pleasure, or personal peace? What was your price?

10. Will all who come behind you find you faithful?

Chapter 11

TAKE COURAGE

THE TORCH OF FREEDOM IS carried by the courageous living of men and women who dare to live a cut above the survival mentality of the masses. Such are men and women who choose the road of selfless service, who refuse to be sucked into the mire of despair about them. They relight the lamp of liberty for us when they speak, when they act, and when we reminisce about their heroic deeds.

Most of our historic examples are average people just like you and me. They are not men or women of rank or noble birth. They are regulars in the army of life. Because no one else can be expected to do it, you and I are called upon to take up the torch of freedom in our time. Let us, for our own encouragement, peek through the window of history at just a few profiles of courage from the annals of America's past.

PROFILES OF COURAGE

Molly Pitcher

On June 28, 1778, a hot battle broke out near the home of Mary Ludwig Hayes in Monmouth, New Jersey. Her husband, John, was a gunner. The thirty-four-year-old housewife helped the soldiers by drawing pitchers of water from a nearby spring. The soldiers began calling her "Molly Pitcher." When John Hayes fell, unable to man his cannon, Mary grabbed the rammer, reloaded, and began firing the cannon. In the process, a cannonball sailed between her legs, tearing away part of her petticoat. After the battle, General Washington called her "Sergeant Molly."[219]

Crispus Attucks

On a snowy March 5, 1770, Crispus Attucks led a group of men into the Boston town square. Twenty years earlier, Crispus had been a slave. He opposed the British rule and the threat to colonial freedom. British soldiers had knocked down a young boy, and Boston's citizens were outraged. Unarmed, Crispus and other colonists faced the armed British Redcoats. Suddenly, someone in the crowd threw a rock, and an order was shouted, "Fire!" Crispus Attucks and four other colonists were killed in what came to be known as "The Boston Massacre." The deaths of those five courageous men inspired the colonists and continues to ring the bell of freedom two centuries later.[220]

Francis Scott Key

During the War of 1812, Francis Scott Key, a lawyer in his early thirties, agreed to take the responsibility of seeking the release of Dr. William Beanes, who had been captured by the British in their invasion of Washington, D.C. The British had burned the White House, and President Madison and his wife, Dolly, had barely escaped.

Dr. Beanes was being held prisoner aboard a ship in the British fleet that was maneuvering in Chesapeake Bay to attack Baltimore. Francis Scott Key was taken out to the British fleet under a truce flag. After serious negotiations, the doctor's release was promised, but because of the British attack plan, Key and Beanes were detained aboard the British ship overnight while the British bombarded Fort McHenry.

Caught in the midst of the cannon fire, Key witnessed the vicious bombardment firsthand. His courageous act on behalf of the dear doctor, and his personal risk, put Key in a position to inspire the entire nation as he penned the words of our national anthem. The words of "The Star Spangled Banner" turned the hearts of a discouraged American people to victory in the War of 1812 and continue to stir the heart of every American today.[221]

Barbara Frietchie

When the advance troops of the Confederacy moved through Frederick, Maryland, in 1862, most of the citizens locked their homes and businesses and hauled in their Union flags. Not Barbara Frietchie. The ninety-seven-year-old widow defiantly went to the top of her house, leaned far out of her attic window, and waved the Stars and Stripes. Shots broke the flagstaff, but the indomitable Barbara Frietchie fetched the flag and continued to wave it. Her memory was preserved and honored by John Greenleaf Whittier in his poem "Barbara Frietchie," giving us lasting insight into the spark of courage that her courageous act brought at a time of national turmoil.[222]

CONCEIVED IN COURAGE

They left England reluctantly under great persecution. They were hounded, bullied, imprisoned on trumped-up charges, and driven underground—all because of their sincere desire to worship God according to the dictates of their conscience. They were labeled "Separatists" because they did not want to fall prey to the decay of English society. Their message was not "politically correct." They finally sought religious asylum in Holland, which cost them dearly.

A dozen years later, with their children worn by the lures of ungodly society in Holland and the bodies of the adults having wasted under almost unbearable toil, their spirits were sparked by the hope of establishing a society in the New World—America— where they could establish religious, social, and political freedom in a covenantal relationship with each other under God.

As they boarded the Mayflower to sail for these shores, they were not ignorant of the difficulties that lay ahead. They heard of the tremendous death rate in Virginia from starvation, of the savagery of the Indians, and the death rate at Jamestown. Yet, they also had a high calling and a firm purpose. With God's help and provision, they could make it.

Thus, the Pilgrims embarked on a journey of great courage and bravery that brought them to Plymouth Rock in 1620. We would not have become the nation of greatness and glory revealed by the last nearly four hundred years but for the courageous conviction in the hearts and minds of the Pilgrims and the Puritans.

William Bradford, a leader of the Pilgrim expedition and the governor of that colony for thirty years, expressed the tremendous depth of their hearts' resolve:

> It was answered that all great and honorable actions are accompanied with great difficulties, and must be enterprised and overcome with answerable courages. It was granted that the dangers were great, but not desperate, and the difficulties were many, but not invincible . . . and all of them, through the help of God, by fortitude and patience, might either be borne or overcome. Their ends were good and honorable . . . therefore, they might expect the blessing of God on their

proceeding; Yea, though they should lose their lives in this action, yet they might have comfort in the same, and their endeavors would be honorable.[223]

BORN IN BRAVERY

On July 4, 1776, the Declaration of Independence was adopted. As president of the Continental Congress, John Hancock signed the Declaration first, boldly and conspicuously. Knowing that he was laying his very life on the line, he declared, "There, I guess King George will be able to read that." The fifty-six patriots who affixed their names to that document of freedom declared solemnly but firmly, ". . . with a firm reliance on the protection of Divine Providence, we mutually pledge to each other our lives, our fortunes, and our sacred honor."

Samuel Adams, in writing to his wife of the momentous occasion, revealed his clear sense of courageous commitment:

> I am well aware of the toil, and blood, and treasure, that it will cost us to maintain this declaration. . . ." "I can see that the end is more than worth all the means, and that posterity will triumph in that day's transaction. . . ."[224]

On March 23, 1775, a few short months before the signing of the Declaration, Patrick Henry addressed the Virginia Convention with stirring words of courage and hope. We might give renewed consideration to his words amid the great struggle that we now face for survival as a nation. Listen to him thunder!

> We are not weak if we make a proper use of those means which the God of Nature has placed in our power. . . . Besides, Sir, we shall not fight our battles alone. There is a just God

who presides over the destinies of nations, who will raise up friends to fight our battles for us. The battle, Sir, is not to the strong alone; it is to the vigilant, the active, the brave.[225]

In his Phi Beta Kappa oration to Harvard University in 1953, Elmer Davis trumpeted a message we must hear: "This Republic was not established by cowards; and cowards will not preserve it."[226]

CONTRASTS IN COURAGE

The ship was sinking, a gaping hole in her hull. There was no hope of saving her. She would certainly make her resting place at the bottom of the sea. Passengers, alerted to the plight of the ship, scrambled frantically around the deck. Others remained in their cabins, unaware of their desperate doom.

The captain and the crew, however, sprang quickly into action. They began skillfully to maneuver the lifeboats into the churning sea. And then they made their way into the lifeboats, abandoning the doomed vessel—and her passengers.

Fortunately, the desperate plight of the sinking ship and her passengers reached the responsive ear of help from shore. Helicopters were dispatched, and, one by one, the stranded passengers were snatched from the jaws of certain death. After hours of the dramatic rescue effort, the last of the passengers having been saved, the ship slipped under the surface and out of sight.

Later, as viewers watched the rescue drama unfold on a television special, they were gripped by suspense as the trapped passengers waited as patiently as was humanly possible for their turn to escape the clutches of death. But the joy of heroic rescue was a mixed blessing for viewers as the pallor of the cowardice of the defecting captain and his crew hung over the story. The captain was arrested and prosecuted for abandoning his duty.

In contrast, one is immediately reminded of classical expressions of courage arising from the sea and our nation's past. "Don't give up the ship!" was the battle cry inscribed on the flag flown from Oliver Hazzard Perry's ship in the Battle of Lake Erie, September 10, 1813.[227] On September 13, 1779, John Paul Jones, captain of the *Bonhomme Richard,* engaged in battle the British frigate *Serapis* at point-blank range. After daringly sailing directly against the British vessel, he locked the vessels together. During the fight, two of his cannons exploded. When the British captain called for him to surrender, Jones responded, "Sir, I have not yet begun to fight!"[228]

While we revel in the daring and glory of such bravery and courage and debase the cowardice of the captain who abandons his ship, it is easy to mask and lose sight of more fundamental issues of courage that affect us right where we live. What do we do in our own homes? How do we behave in our communities? How do we preach in our pulpits? What is *my* courage quotient? Have I abandoned ship?

A HAUNTING QUESTION

What is my duty?

Courage arises from a perception of responsibility, from a sense of duty. The problem is that when duty calls, some people are never at home. The greater the number of people who are "not home" when duty calls, the more apparent becomes the lack of courage in our society.

Most of us remember the New York story emblazoned across the national news a few short years ago. The neighborhood echoed with screams. Clearly, a woman was in urgent need of help. The cry for help was heart-rending. But the terrified cry failed to rend any hearts that evening.

No, the cries did not go unheard. Many people were drawn to their windows to see what was happening. And view they did, but none of them saw fit to respond to the woman's desperate plight, although well they could have.

Her death did not occur instantly. There was warning. There was time. There was opportunity to act as the attacker pursued his victim. But the onlookers looked on, mesmerized as if watching just another bloody movie. After all, they were warm, safe, and cozy in their own homes and apartments. Why should they get involved? It did not affect them . . . at least not today. It wasn't their responsibility, was it? The deadly silence that followed gave loud testimony to the waning of courage in American society. A woman lay dead in the street. One might ask whether her death was due to the breach of duty of the onlookers to intervene or to the viciousness of her attacker. Whatever your view, it is evident that no bravery or courage lifted the American spirit that evening. The question remains, "What is my duty?"

THE CALL OF DUTY

Courage arises in response to the call of duty. But duty is no longer easily defined because we have done cultural violence to the sources from which duty flows.

Duty is defined in a much larger life context. It is defined first by the authorities in my life—parents, law enforcement personnel, government leaders, our civil institutions, the church, and God himself. To the extent that I step out from under any authority in my life, I lose my sense of duty that arises from that relationship. If I step out from under God's authority, either by direct decision or by my behavior over time, I lose my sense of the duties that emanate from that relationship.

As I shed my allegiance to legitimate authority, I claim increasing rights while shedding corresponding responsibility. The result is that I serve only myself and have no sense of obligation. Ultimately, even civil law itself becomes powerless to guide or establish my "bottom-line" duty, resulting in anarchy in which courage is redefined to mean the ultimate service to myself rather than the ultimate service to others.

When Patterson and Kim announced in their book *The Day America Told the Truth*, "You are the law in this country. Who says so? You do, pardner,"[229] they are decrying the very undermining of all authority that is gradually destroying our sense of duty. Courage pales into insignificance when not even the law will get my attention.

But for the seeds of courage to grow and prosper, another context is critical. That context is society itself. A *sense* of duty becomes the *call* of duty only if I perceive myself to be in a genuine, valuable relationship with those around me—my spouse, children, church, neighborhood, and even my country.

What happens if I lose that sense of value in the various levels of social and cultural relationship about me? What if the only thing that really matters is the material rather than the moral and spiritual values that require the investment of mind and heart with others and with my God? I become what sociologists and other astute observers are now calling an "economic man."

The "economic man" does not work to live but rather lives to work. He is not necessarily a workaholic, but he finds life's meaning in his work and the financial economy that he creates rather than in the relationships about him. Relationships serve his economy rather than his economy serving the relationships. And, in the process, he is increasingly alienated from both God and man. He is becoming "independent."

Such is the condition of American life today. To one degree or another, we have all been affected by it. We have become increasingly alienated from one another. In our desire to be independent, we have lost an essential dependence that is required for meaningful living. We are speeding rapidly toward the point at which we declare our independence from God and man. If we reach that point as a nation, we are doomed. If I reach that point as an individual citizen, I am, at best, most miserable. If you and I are on that path, we are dying a slow death. In such an environment of alienation and isolation, courage cannot take root.

"Alienation! Isolation! Individualism! Anarchism!" These are the "Door to Tyranny," warned Richard Halverson, chaplain of the United States Senate in his April 22, 1992, issue of *Perspective*.[230] Relationship and authority comprise the soil in which duty grows, producing the fruit of courage, which rises against tyranny of any sort. Yes, even the tyranny of crime and drugs in the streets of your city will succumb to the courage of neighbors and local citizens who see themselves bound in relationship with each other.

We can courageously make a difference together—in relationship with God and each other. We are in this together. Do we have what it takes? If not, can we get it back? Can we restore courage to the American soul?

THE AMERICAN BACKBONE

When the authors of *The Day America Told the Truth* inquired in their poll for what beliefs people would die, 48 percent said "none." Only 30 percent would be willing to die for God and their faith under any circumstances. Even fewer, 24 percent, would die for their country. The authors observed, "Americans . . . stand alone in a way unknown to any previous generation."[231] These, they say, are the "measure of Americans' alienation from the traditional authority of God and country."[232] Such is the observation of secular analysts. "We've become wishy-washy as a nation," they conclude. "Some would say that we've lost our moral backbone."[233]

RESTORING THE MORAL BACKBONE

The sage Goethe left us the following words, which are well worth our serious personal consideration:

Wealth lost, something lost;
Honor lost, much lost;
Courage lost, all lost.[234]

Courage is the backbone of moral character. When courage weakens, the back slumps. When courage leaves, the back is broken. The moral back of America is slumping seriously. Yet, the moral back of a nation is built upon the moral fiber of its people. No national morality exists without personal morality. And no national courage exists without personal courage. Unfortunately, much of what passes as courage these days is poured from a bottle, popped from a pill, or gleaned vicariously from a violent movie. As James Michaels observed in his article "Oh, Our Aching

Angst," published in *Forbes*, September 14, 1992, "It isn't the economic system that needs fixing . . . it's our value system."[235]

Courage is inextricably linked to all aspects of character and moral behavior. One can barely fathom leadership without courage. Is it any wonder that we languish for leadership? Consider honesty. Can honesty prevail in the absence of moral courage to deliver the truth? Or consider fidelity. Courage is required these days to resist the rising tide of infidelity in all areas of life. The simple truth is that courage links all of character and morality into a single operative body that enables a man or a woman to "take a stand."

TAKING A STAND

Are you willing to take a stand? If willing, are you ready to take a stand? Given the condition of your moral backbone, are you in any condition to take a stand? Or will the winds of social pressure, employment compromise, relational infidelity, selfish ambition, or the fear of loss of ministry funding or loss of constituent support topple your feeble moral frame? Do you even have something for which to stand? Is it worth standing for? Why or why not?

If you don't stand for something, you'll fall for anything. Be bold in that for which you stand, but be careful about that for which you fall.

In this world of "political correctness," it is dangerous to check the prevailing winds before determining your stand on any issue or matter. Morality is not determined by majority rule. Neither is truth established by the strident voice of a vocal minority whom we perceive to have the dollars we desire. If we have lost common sense, we cannot have a common consensus. We must be willing to search for and speak the truth—even if we must stand alone.

THE COURAGE OF CONSCIENCE

Courage is forged in the crucible of conscience. Where there is no conscience, courage languishes. Where the conscience is seared by violation or is twisted by political correctness, courage has a hollow and uncertain ring. "Conscience in the soul is the root of all true courage," reflected J. F. Clarke. "If a man would be brave, let him learn to obey his conscience."[236]

Where no conscience exists, the moral and spiritual fabric of life has become threadbare. If we wish to see a refreshing rise of courage in American life, business, politics, and the church, we must first reweave the moral and spiritual fabric of our society. That does not begin with my neighbor or my congressman; it begins with me.

As we head into the twenty-first century and a new millennium, the call of courage in our society is enough for more than a few good men. "When moral courage feels that it is in the right, there is no personal daring of which it is incapable," said Leigh Hunt.[237] Your courage quotient is a direct reflection of your conscience quotient.

So what is your conscience quotient?

William Bentley Bell, a constitutional attorney of renown, in his comments prefacing *In Search of a National Morality*, writes, "Moral courage [is] that most unfashionable virtue."[238] In the same collection of essays, Paul C. Vitz, professor of psychology at New York University, observes, "America has now reached the point where it permits almost everything and stands for almost nothing—except flabby relativism."[239]

For what do you stand? If it feels good, do you do it? If it suits your present need, do you modify your principles? If it threatens your financial flow, do you change your tune? If it threatens your electability, do you "turn tail"? Are you a man or a woman of principle? Do you exercise restraint in the face of your desires?

Don't answer too quickly.

Courage is not much needed to do what I want, but it is much needed to do what I ought. If I would see courage arise in America, I must break the paralysis of fear that renders me a moral wimp. It is a choice. Your and my choices will determine America's survival. In his "Farewell Address," George Washington rhetorically and yet prophetically asked, "Can it be, that Providence has not connected the permanent felicity of a Nation with its virtue?"[240]

THE CALL TO COURAGE

Slavery was not a new issue when our sixteenth president was sworn into office. It had been an issue of moral confrontation in the American mind and heart for a century. But it had been presented acutely to the American conscience by such spokesmen as the lawyer-turned-preacher Charles Finney in the years before 1860 in the confluence of moral and spiritual revival in the nation.

Slavery was not just a moral issue in the abstract. It permeated every aspect of the social and economic structure of an entire region within the nation. While its continued presence was unconscionable, its eradication was unpalatable to the entire South. There were no easy answers. There was no way to act on the issue or fail to act without making enemies.

Such was the heritage of Abraham Lincoln at his inauguration. His Emancipation Proclamation made him a moral hero to some people and a political and social reject to others. His memory is a tribute to his great courage; he ranks with our founding president, Washington, in the hearts of his countrymen. His famous Gettysburg Address gives us insight into the foundation of his courage and the basis of his hope for a restored nation. His words continue to ring 150 years later:

This nation, under God, shall have a new birth of freedom. . . .[241]

THE COST OF COURAGE

Although courage is the backbone of our personal and national character, courage is not without cost. A price must be paid in acquiring courage. To obtain courage, one must sacrifice self and personal ambition on the altar of service. He or she must dispel fear with faith. And one must pursue truth and justice rather than "political correctness."

There is also a cost in being courageous. Lincoln lost friends— and then his life.

A century later, when Dr. Martin Luther King announced, "I have a dream. . . ," he was not living in a dreamland. He knew that liberty had a price, as captured in the words of Thomas Paine: "That which is bought too cheaply is esteemed too lightly."[242] His courage to confront injustice in the entire social order cost him dearly. He paid with his life. His courage issued from his faith, despite his own frailties.

The fifty-six signers of our Declaration of Independence counted the cost in pledging "our lives, our fortunes, and our sacred honor."

Freedom is the sure possession of only those who have the courage to defend it. No freedom can exist apart from truth and justice. Freedom is not free.

What is freedom worth to you? Do you have the courage to defend it? Will you defend it? If so, at what cost?

Consider expressing actively your courage this week in the following form:

- Courage of conscience, to do what is right;
- Courage to conform, to do what the law requires of you;
- Courage to change your own thinking;
- Courage to communicate, to speak on issues of importance;
- Courage to consider, to rethink preconceived notions;
- Courage to care, to take *personal* responsibility for others and your nation;
- Courage to confront, to stand up to untruth and injustice;
- Courage to challenge, to change the way you've always done it if it has been wrong;
- Courage to correct, to change your own behavior if it is wrong; and
- Courage to confess, to acknowledge your personal wrongs toward others, your lack of courage, and your sin and rebellion against God.

Don't be afraid to go out on a limb if the limb is worthy. That's where the fruit is.

Cultivating Courage

As light becomes known in darkness, so courage manifests itself in the waning light of moral, spiritual, social, and political strife, turmoil, and decay. When darkness and discouragement abound, the light of courage pierces the darkness, radiating to the unseen extremities of the blackness that surrounds us. It carries on its wings a message of hope. It reveals an unseen dimension beyond the pain of the present.

But courage cannot be merely mustered from one's own bootstraps. We wish it were so, but such is not the usual tale of history.

"This is the way to cultivate courage," said J. F. Clarke, "first, by standing firm on some conscientious principle, some law of duty. Next, by being faithful to truth and right on small occasions and common events. Third, by trusting God for help and power."[243]

Cicero reminds us, "A man of courage is also full of faith."[244] We must, as Americans, humble ourselves before God so that we can be in position to receive His faith and the courage that naturally flows from it. "It takes more courage for us to repent than to keep on sinning."[245] If we will repent, turn, and decide once again to cooperate with God's plan and purposes, as did our forefathers, we will once again see the return of courage in our land. And although we stand trembling, "prayer gives strength to the weak, faith to the fainthearted, and courage to the fearful."[246] "Men ought always to pray, and not to faint."[247]

Take Courage

"On many of the great issues of our time, men have lacked wisdom because they have lacked courage," declared William

Benton.[248] We have certainly experienced both lack of wisdom and lack of courage in our national life. It has resulted in a sense of aimlessness—a feeling of lack of direction.

"A decline in courage may be the most striking feature which an outside observer notices . . . in our days," writes Aleksander Solzhenitsyn. "From ancient times decline in courage has been considered the beginning of the end."[249] But we need no longer wander in trepidation and fear. We must take courage.

Courage is taken as we appropriate underlying truth or substance upon which courage can be based. Courage must be based on solid ground, not on the fleeting fancies of men's minds.

I had the opportunity to obtain an original page of a volume of the first printing of the *King James Version* of the Bible, published in 1611. The entire Bible was no longer intact, but I had a choice of several pages, and I chose the title page of the book of Joshua, which I have mounted on my office wall. At such a time as this, I think it most fitting to conclude this chapter with a quotation from God's own directive for success and courage.

This book of the law shall not depart out of thy mouth; but thou shalt meditate therein day and night, that thou mayest observe to do according to all that is written therein; for then thou shalt make thy way prosperous, and then thou shalt have good success.

Be strong and of a good courage; be not afraid, neither be thou dismayed: for the Lord thy God is with thee whithersoever thou goest.[250]

Is God with you? Are you with Him? If so, take courage. If you have a breached relationship with Him, turn right now, determine to follow God's way, and then do it. Courage will once again rise in your heart.

The next generation is depending on you. Based upon your courage quotient, what is America's future? What is the future of your family? Are you willing to stand alone against the tide? Your courageous example is what will make a difference. Take courage.

SOUL-STIRRING QUESTIONS FOR PERSONAL AND GROUP REFLECTION

1. How would you define courage?

2. Patrick Henry cried out, "The battle is not to the strong alone; it is to the vigilant, the active, the brave." On a scale of one to ten, with one being "cowardly" and ten being "brave," how do you rank?

3. Courage arises from a sense of responsibility and duty. Some people are never at home when duty calls. Are you?

4. Courage is the backbone of moral character. Why?

5. What part does conscience play in courage?

6. Courage is not without cost. What personal cost are you willing to pay to stand for what is true or right? Will you risk your time or your treasure? How about your reputation or position? Or is your motto, "Peace at all costs"?

7. From where does courage come?

8. How can a man or a woman "take courage" if he or she doesn't seem to have it?

9. Based upon your courage quotient, what is America's future?

Chapter 12

FAITH AND FREEDOM

IT WAS THE DARKEST HOUR of the American Revolution. By mid-December 1777, only eleven thousand men remained in the ranks of the Continental Army. They had just completed a daring attack on the British at Germantown and had suffered heavy losses.

Desertion was a serious problem. Troops were weary, and their clothing was torn and tattered. Blankets were scarce, and shoes were even scarcer. Only a month earlier, on Thanksgiving Day, Lieutenant Colonel Henry Dearborn had written of the American army, ". . . God knows we have little to keep it with, this being the third day we have been without flour or bread."[251] Food could have been plentiful, but the civilians often hoarded it, and transporting it was difficult.

The Continental Congress then governing the colonies had just adopted the Articles of Confederation, a weak and toothless document that purported to join the colonies but gave little support for marshaling and supporting troops. Patting themselves on the back for their labors, most members of the Continental Congress went home for Christmas, closing their eyes to the plight of the army they claimed to support.

But General Washington could not close his eyes. He was responsible for men who had staked their lives, their fortunes, and their sacred honor on his leadership. Amid criticism, he chose to gather his troops together for the winter rather than risk another attack and certain defeat in their weakened condition. So it was that they set up camp twenty miles from Philadelphia at a place which is embedded with pain in the memory of every American— a place called Valley Forge.

As the troops dragged themselves to Valley Forge, Washington said, ". . . you might have tracked the army from White March to Valley Forge by the blood of their feet."[252] And things there did not improve. Shelter was meager, at best. Amid snow and biting cold, the soldiers bound their feet in rags as they built huts and lugged water on a two-mile round trip for survival. But many of them did not survive. Starvation, exposure, disease, and death claimed the lives of 2,600 troops.[253]

In this test of mettle, General Washington remained the "General" to his men. It was not his title but his tough but tender tenacity of inner strength and character that held his troops, that preserved their resolve and gave them endurance. He seemed to draw strength, direction, and purpose from a wellspring not found in the soil of Valley Forge but in the soil of his own heart. And indeed he did.

In that darkest hour, Washington the General drew upon his faith in God. His was not a foxhole faith but a faith borne of long-standing relationship to his God. He knew the Source of his strength and of his ability to lead. He knew that true leadership stems from humility, humility before one's Maker. He knew that he was a servant and that the "Ruler of Nations" was the Supreme Commander.

And he bowed his knee and his heart in humble service to the King of kings. Washington's private faith has been publicly memorialized for all Americans in the famous painting depicting him kneeling in prayer in the snow at Valley Forge. That prayerful image is further memorialized in stained glass in the chapel just off the rotunda of the United States Capitol.

But the personal faith of Washington was also memorialized in the lives of his troops. Whether they individually accepted his God, and Jesus Christ his Lord, we cannot attest, but one thing is certain—they honored and respected their general for his own steady faith in God and received the blessings of that faith in his leadership. Upon Washington's death in 1799, a former cavalry officer, Henry Lee of Virginia, who had become a member of the House of Representatives, honored the General by declaring him to be ". . . first in war, first in peace, and first in the hearts of his countrymen."[254] Perhaps the words of John Marshall, one of America's greatest Supreme Court Chief Justices, best conveys the spirit of Washington's faith: "Without making ostentatious professions of religion, he was a sincere believer in the Christian faith and a truly devout man."[255] "To Christian institutions, he gave the countenance of his example."[256]

In the fury of life's battlefields, which are many, godly faith will always form the foundation of freedom. The hope of true freedom, without godly faith, is futility.

NOT GLORY BUT GRACE

The filtered eye of history reflects the glory of the American Revolution. Acts of bravery and the spirit of patriotism ride high in our memory. As the bell of freedom rings in our hearts, we rejoice and savor that moment of our history that gave rise to the precious blessings of liberty that we now enjoy.

But the American Revolution was not a "moment" for those whose lives were wrapped in its fury. It was the light of freedom being hammered out in the crucible of faith. Time and again, the colonial troops were faced with overwhelming odds. The crack British Redcoats were a well-oiled, well-financed war machine that ruled the seas and were the preeminent military power of the day. Yet, account after account of colonial victory against great odds and protection against annihilation by superior British forces revealed increasing the truth that it was not by men's glory but by God's grace that America was born as an independent nation.

Freedom was born in the womb of God's grace through men of faith who were faithful. Washington himself, in his First Inaugural Address, publicly recognized this fact.

No People can be bound to acknowledge and adore the invisible hand, which conducts the Affairs of men more than the People of the United States.[257]

Neither time nor space will permit the recounting here of the details of how God, in His divine grace and mercy, repeatedly protected the colonial troops, caused dense fogs to fall and rise at critical moments, caused confusion among the British, rendered enemy leadership directionless or inactive at moments of the freedom fighters' greatest vulnerability.

OUR VALLEY FORGE

America is in desperate need of the intervention of the invisible hand of the Ruler of Nations at this dark hour of our history. Freedom is at stake. Destiny is at risk. We need a resurgence of true faith in this critical hour. We do not need faith in faith; that is mere bootstrapping. We need a mighty awakening in our hearts and souls, an awakening of faith in the God who rules and governs in the affairs of men. We need a personal faith, a faith that can stand against the tide and tyranny of political correctness and the stripping of moral absolutes from our personal and national wardrobe.

We are in our own Valley Forge. As Americans who believe in the cause of true freedom under God, we have become weary and have lost direction. Our feet are bloodied, our moral and spiritual clothes are tattered, and we have been on a spiritual starvation diet. We are weakened. Many of us have died morally and spiritually, even in our churches.

We need faith in America. Again, the faith that we need in this land is neither faith in faith nor a patriotically inspired, bootstrapped, emotionally hyped faith in America. The faith we need is faith in the God who has *preserved us a nation*. We cannot look to a charismatic leader or wait for a euphoric uprising of "good feelings" from another Gulf War. We need faith in God Almighty, and we need it now!

But there is no national faith without personal faith. The question is not whether my neighbor, or the president, my congressman, or even my pastor or priest has faith. The question is whether *I* am a man or a woman of faith. Have I put my personal faith and trust in my Creator? Am I yielded to Him and to His will? Or have I become part of the problem? Am I faithless? Have I turned my faith in God gradually to faith in myself, in man's inventions, in the government, in education, in anything or anyone but the Most High God? We can see the wasteland of that kind of faith all around us. Let's take another look.

FAITH WASTELAND

Charles Colson, former "hatchet man" for the Nixon administration and redeemed by the grace of God from the pit of

Watergate and self-exaltation, has become a statesman to America generally but even more specifically to the professing Christian church in America. In his book *The Body*, he writes with characteristic poignancy to those of us who claim to be called by the name of Christ as Christians. He states that we have developed a "McChurch" mentality, flitting about in search of what makes me feel good rather than for a faith that is rooted and grounded in substance.[258]

We have grown to love the froth rather than the faith. We run hither and yon in search of "what's in it for me?" And we have lost the substance of the faith that we purport to embrace. Self-support has replaced self-denial. Love of self has replaced love of God. And American society careens off into faithlessness.

Men and women search for a tailor-made god, a god made in their own image, custom-shaped to their own personal perception of what *they* want or what *they* need—or at least what *they* think they need. For such people, it is no longer an issue of what they owe to their God but of what their God owes them. In such an environment of "I-ism," we no longer bear responsibility. We no longer need forgiveness of sin because we only make mistakes. We are products of our environment, of a dysfunctional family, of too little, too much, too late. And life careens off into a wasteland, an endless and tumultuous sea, where there are no absolutes suitable for anchor, no compass by which to gain perspective, and no maps with which to chart direction.

We are plunging recklessly and almost frantically ever deeper into the faith wasteland, the wilderness without chart or compass; yet, we are oblivious to where we are headed. All of this at a time when pollsters talk about the continued significant presence of religion in America, liberals cry about the political power of the "Religious Right," and Bible-believing Christians fight to preserve the remaining vestiges of religious freedom under the First Amendment.

How can we make sense of this confusion? How can we gain some perspective to sort out truth from fiction. And what effect does all of this have on our lives and in the life of our nation?

TELLING STATISTICS

"Overall, 64 percent of the adults in America believe that they are religious," said George Barna in his 1991 report on *What Americans Believe,* indicating a decline from 72 percent in 1985. Because nine out of ten senior citizens describe themselves as religious, it is easy to see what has happened to the younger generation—traditional religious commitment has dropped off dramatically.[259] Barna also reports that "two-thirds of all adults either agree strongly (22 percent) or somewhat (44 percent) that America is a Christian nation."[260] A decade later, George Gallup reported that 45 percent of all adults classify themselves as born-again or evangelical Christians.[261] Ninety-five percent of Americans say they believe in God.[262] Yet, "a profound gulf lies between America's vowed ethical standards and the observable realities of American life. What may be even more damming," notes George Gallup Jr. "is the gap between what Americans *think* they do and what they *do.*" Gallup calls it a "national schizophrenia, justifying his newsletter headline, "Religion is gaining ground, but morality is losing ground."[263]

"God is alive and very well," declares Patterson and Kim in *The Day America Told the Truth.* "But right now in America, fewer people are listening to what God has to say than ever before."[264] That is quite a statement coming from two advertising executives! Apparently, God is not the one who has changed; Americans have changed.

A couple of years ago, as our family was graciously hosted at one of Mississippi's finest antebellum plantations, our attention was attracted to a little plaque that we now display in our own home. The words seem appropriate here: "If you don't feel close to God, guess who moved?"

As Americans, we have strayed gradually from our faith in God and from our commitment to His purposes in our individual lives, families, communities, and even churches. One of the primary reasons for this increasing estrangement has been our redefining of the laws or the center of truth.

To our Founding Fathers, that the Bible was the center and source of all ultimate truth was nearly a foregone conclusion. The Bible was the most oft-quoted source in the writings of our Founding Fathers, and it was from that platform of dependable, unwavering truth that they announced to the world the American experiment in representative democracy—a Republic—promising liberty and justice for all. Without absolute confidence—faith—in the truth and authority of the Bible as the faithful expression of the Truth and the will of God himself, the American experiment of a democratic republic was foolhardy at best. It was the difference in foundation, the difference in faith, and the difference in worldview that made possible even the concept of a government of, by, and for the people. And it was the Founders' confidence in the truth of the Christian way, based upon the Bible, that fueled the fires of the American Revolution, giving birth to a nation pursuing liberty and justice for all. As Noah Webster so aptly stated, "The religion which has introduced civil liberty is the religion of Christ and His apostles . . . to this we owe our free constitution of government."[265]

But now, as we stand tall in our national pride, we have dismissed that "Divine Friend" as only remotely relevant and have decided that we can pick and choose the portions of His Truth that patronize our personal feelings and predilections. The source of truth is no longer fixed and dependable but variable with every personal whim and cultural shift. And as culture shifts almost daily with the vagaries of human passion and prejudice, so our new comprehension of truth shifts, continually being redefined to serve the mandate of the moment, from the church house to the White House.

Perhaps no more poignant expression of the sacrifice of principled truth on the altar of pragmatism exists than that revealed by the Rev. Jesse Jackson on the issue of life itself, grounded in the fundamental conviction that men are truly created in the image of God. His shift over just one generation from principle to pragmatism is breathtaking. Consider it with an open heart.

In 1977, Rev. Jackson sent an open letter to Congress opposing use of federal funds for "killing infants." Jackson wrote in a 1977 *National Right to Life News* article, "It takes three to make a baby: a man, a woman, and the Holy Spirit." With great conviction he asked, "What happens to the mind of a person, and the moral fabric of a nation, that accepts the aborting of the life of a baby without a conscience? What kind of person, and what kind of society will we have 20 years hence if life can be taken so casually?" He concluded, "Failure to answer that question affirmatively may leave us with a hell right here on earth." Then Jesse Jackson ran for president, and thereafter totally reversed his convictions to pander to the shifting cultural cry. Thousands of people, both black and white, have followed his example.[266]

What kind of society do we now have some twenty-three years later? We have, in fact, so eroded, corroded, and "outmoded" our foundation that we are left with virtually no foundation. And faith is foundering—yes, yours and mine—believe it or not. We have been cut loose on this sea of relativity together, and we are in desperate need of catching a glimpse of light from God's "lighthouse"—the Truth from a God who does not change with every vacillation of human experience and who can steer us clear of the looming shoals of personal and national destruction.

It is most disheartening that 75 percent of all adult Americans have come to believe there is no such thing as absolute truth, truth that remains constant, relevant, and applicable throughout the changes and shifts in life's experiences and culture. Among even those who claim to be born-again Christians, 66 percent concur that no absolute, dependable truth exists upon which to base one's life, behavior, and decisions.[267] Shockingly, fewer Americans in mainline Protestant churches today believe in absolute truth than the population at large. Clearly, no portion of the American populace escapes the sinister blight of unbelief and faithlessness, whether they are professing Christians or non-Christians. Yet, the very foundation of our nation was the firm conviction that God's truth, as expressed in the Bible, is fully dependable for personal and national life and practice.

Billy Graham wrote in *The Saturday Evening Post* about national abandonment of faith: "When John Wycliff translated the Bible into English, he unwittingly outlined prophetically the course of history. For the Bible became not only the book of the English people of his day: it became the foundation of freedom for a nation's unborn that would be called America."[268]

So profound is the shift off our biblical foundation that despite the fact that we have more Bibles per capita than any other nation on earth, pollster George Gallup declares, "We are a nation of biblical illiterates." He notes, "Americans revere the Bible but do not read it."[269] It should therefore come as no surprise that we now founder in heavy seas at every level of society—both individually and institutionally.

We now run frantically to and fro in search of surrogate truth. Having rejected absolute truth upon which we could build our lives and preserve our nation, we search for and pursue a plethora of therapeutic remedies to make us feel better and help us cope. But it still isn't working. We seek therapy rather than truth. The consequences are enormous—not only for American society but also for you, me, and our children and grandchildren. We are all caught, to one degree or another, in the swirling waters of unbelief and its consequences.

"As we entered the 1990s, it became suddenly and urgently clear that a tumultuous change was occurring in America," advertisers Patterson and Kim declared. "On every front . . . the ground beneath our feet began shifting. Yesterday's verities had vanished. Unpredictability and chaos became the norm."[270] "We can no longer tell right from wrong," they observe, and "It raises fear and doubt which often leads to depression." "Americans . . . have more of both fear and doubt—and of depression, too—than did any previous generation." "Americans wrestle with these questions in what often amounts to a moral vacuum. The religious figures and scriptures that gave us rules for so many centuries, the political system that gave us our laws, all have lost their meaning in our moral imagination."[271]

If it takes secular advertising executives to sound the alarm, so be it. Somebody must tell the truth.

HOW DID IT HAPPEN?

So, then, how did we get to this point? How did we lose our moral backbone and our spiritual moorings? How did we discard truth and become faithless? Neither time nor space permit a thorough analysis of the scope and depth of these questions here because they reach deep into our minds, hearts, and history, but we should at least take a brief look.

The Prosperity Pinch

As a nation, we have enjoyed fifty years of perpetual prosperity since World War II. True, we have had cycles during which we experienced recession. Some areas of the country have experienced greater prosperity than others, and not all families have prospered equally. But for the most part, we as a people have certainly reaped the "blessings of liberty."

Prosperity carries with it a sense of "resting on our laurels." We gradually relinquish the principles and faith to which we cling in climbing out of the pit of adversity and mounting the high road of prosperity. Most of us do not relinquish our faith and our principles with calculated intention; neither do we do so instantly. It is a gradual process. It occurs almost imperceptibly, until we look back and see how far we have strayed.

And we have definitely strayed over the last fifty years—more than a little. In fact, if we relied upon our faith level today to restart our personal, family, community, and national engines, many of us would not even get a response as we turned the key; others of us would get a brief turnover and die; and a few people would start, sputter, and succumb to silence. And that is true even among a large portion of churchgoers and Bible-toters. We have become weak in spirit. We don't want to admit it—some of us might even argue and dispute it—but it is nevertheless true because the spirit is fueled by faith, and we have run out of fuel.

It is a strange paradox that the very prosperity for which we seek and grasp contains within it the seeds of decline and decay. It is not that prosperity is evil or wrong in itself. It is that we humans are not consistent. We become lax. And we become faithless. We place our lives on "cruise control" and forget to look at where the road is taking us until we realize that we do not like the destination we have reached.

That is precisely where we find ourselves at this moment in American history—lost and without a compass. We feel it in the pit of our stomach. It is unnerving. And so our national headlines have cried out, "Why We're So Gloomy,"[272] "The Glooming of America—A Nation Down in the Dumps,"[273] and "How Our American Dream Unraveled."[274] And we grasp desperately for solutions and hope, anything that will make us feel better. But we don't feel better because our problem is not our feelings—it's our faith. Will our current adversity once again turn our hearts to faith? Will we—you and I—again let God into our lives—on His terms rather than ours? The choice is ours.

The Darkness of Enlightenment

A few years ago, I stood before a judge in a Southern California family law court, arguing a child custody case on behalf of a client. Fortunately, there was little doubt as to which parent had shown consistent parental care and concern. There was also little doubt as to which parent demonstrated a faithful, consistent, and moral lifestyle. The court openly acknowledged these observations, so I do not need to "beat my own drum," or even that of my client, here. That is not why my thoughts are drawn to this incident.

One would think that under such circumstances the choice would have been clear and the court's decision easy. But no. Just as I expected to hear the court confirm custody to my client, I was shocked to "reality" as the court ordered a "psychological" evaluation for the parties. "A psychological evaluation," I thought aloud. "This is not a case for a psychological evaluation!" To which the judge responded, "We live in an enlightened society," and then began to reflect on why we must rely upon the true wisdom of our society residing in the minds of psychotherapists.

You see, my client was a Christian minister whose teenage children dearly loved him. They had planned and considered as a family for nearly a year to remove to another state because of their concern over the living environment of their family. The teenage son and daughter had, with heartfelt conviction, conveyed their own minds and hearts to the court, believing their faith and moral environment to be of greater value than pursuing friends, fortune, and fine living.

These teenagers actually had a personal faith, personal convictions, and personal standards. How could this be? How could they cast away the "opportunities" of Southern California so lightly? Surely something was wrong. We must have an enlightened psychologist look into this matter. And so they did.

I ask you to probe the inner recesses of your mind and heart. Are we, indeed, living in an enlightened society? If so, why has almost every aspect of our society declined? Why do we have such perversion? Why have murder, rape, and other crimes escalated to frightening proportions? Why does the drug culture have us in a headlock that defies the best efforts of law enforcement? Why do we lie to one another? Why can't we find leadership on which we can depend? Why are we—me, you, our relatives, and our friends and neighbors—in a frantic pursuit of therapy?

Out of France about the time of our own Revolutionary War came the seeds of the Enlightenment. The theorists of the Enlightenment said that if we really wanted progress and true freedom, we must cast off the shackles of all that would bind us: tradition, faith, and family. France suffered as a result of this philosophy and has never truly recovered. Our Founding Fathers resisted this philosophy although it was the avant-garde philosophy of the day. Our Founders realized that it was itself a religion—a religion of anti-faith. But this secular philosophy has now crept in and infected the minds of our entire society to one degree or another—even the church. And as the American mind turned, so turned the American heart.

As I conversed with a publishing agent regarding the publishing of this book, he began to relate to me a story of a recent trip to Russia. He had been invited to present ways of providing Christian literature and materials for use in Russian schools. Russian leaders were literally crying out for Bibles and materials to help restore and build a spiritual base in a society that had been officially stripped of faith and family and that had finally collapsed for lack of a sure foundation.

One of the Russian leaders asked the publishing agent, "Could you use these materials in your schools in America today?"

Sheepishly and in embarrassment, the publisher responded, "No, not in America today." Suddenly the Russian leader became obviously angry. In Russian, he began talking rapidly, raising his voice, and pointing at the publisher. The publisher was taken aback, wondering how he had offended the man, and inquired of the interpreter. The words of that Russian leader, as translated by the interpreter should pierce the heart of every American. "Why is America doing this to itself? Can't you see that is what happened in Russia? Can't you see it doesn't work?"

Have we become "too big for our britches"? Do we really know better? Or are we on a collision course with a reality that we really do not wish to experience. I think that we are already experiencing the agony of that reality. Its statistics weigh us down with horror and despair. We are not enlightened. Our foolish hearts have been darkened. But it is not too late to turn.

Did the God who made us and set the universe in its course go off on an eternal vacation? Or does He still have something to say to Americans who will humble themselves, turn from their self-exalted ways, and seek His wisdom and His righteousness? Can we afford this blind pursuit of philosophized and psychologized enlightenment that leads us down an ever-darkening path? Will we, like two-year-olds, continue to put our hands over our faces and say, "Look, God, You can't see me"?

The judge in our custody case did finally grant custody to the father who chose to lead his family in faith. He also permitted those teenage children to follow their father in the pursuit of a life and an environment that enabled them to preserve and define a life of moral absolutes issuing out of personal faith. But the court's decision was not based upon the genuine life substance of that family, which had enabled them to ride above the tumultuous tide of the society around them.

Following the presentation of the psychological evaluation, the court invited final argument. I recounted factually and passionately the stability of that family, the respect that the children had for their father, their unifying faith, their moral and spiritual convictions, their mutual desire to seek a living environment that would foster moral purity and family stability and a desire to see all of these characteristics borne out in their continued education. The court responded, "Mr. Crismier, the court is interested in things related to the best interests of these children, and I have not yet heard you address these matters."

A lawyer is seldom without words, but I was speechless, dumbfounded. To my mind, I had just recounted and touched upon the most foundational and substantive issues that could affect the lives of children within the family unit. Already established to the court's satisfaction were employment, housing, extended family availability, and schooling. And so, in frustration, I inquired what other information the court could possibly consider "essential" to the best interests of the children that had not already been presented. The court's response reflects, I believe, the shallowness of enlightenment thinking and its hopelessness in presenting any redeeming social (or other) value to American society. The court proceeded to ask for availability of enrichment activities such as sports, music lessons, and youth activities.

What a commentary on American life and values! And I thought of the parents in hundreds, if not thousands, of families whom I had encountered in my two decades of law practice—families that were disintegrating, that were full of activities but void of active faith, running fast and furiously to provide enrichment to their children's minds and bodies but impoverishing their souls and spirits. I recalled young children longing for time with mom while being rushed from ballet lessons to girl scouts to flute lessons while mom got her nails painted so she would feel good enough about herself to spend her weekly hour with her therapist to try to find some meaning in her treadmill existence.

I thought of fathers who were too tired to take their families to church by 9:30 A.M. on Sunday morning but could be found regularly on the golf course by 7:00 A.M., who worked six or seven days a week to provide a car for their sons on their sixteenth birthdays while having provided those sons with no sense of moral responsibility or understanding of how to provide moral or spiritual leadership to their own families.

And I thought of "Christian" families in which dad's behavior and values on Monday bore no relationship to dad's "profession" on Sunday at church and in which mom's interests and conversation on Tuesday sounded strangely foreign to her hour of glossy show from 11:00 A.M. to noon in the Sunday morning service. I thought of the inner noise of clanging dissonance and hypocrisy of life and practice reverberating in the minds and hearts of America's children, numbing their sensibilities and cauterizing their moral and spiritual perception, leaving them with enlightened minds and darkened spirits, having no sense of their own reason for living, of ultimate value or purpose, or of how to get there. And they call this "enlightenment."

May God help us! And He will if we will let Him. Otherwise, the darkness of enlightenment will engulf us. For if the light that is in us be darkness, how great is that darkness! True enlightenment with which to preserve a nation issues from truth—truth that does not vary with my every whim or desire or with every new idea pumped into the world of thought by armchair philosophers bent on "freeing" us from the truth that will make us free.

Jesus Christ made the matter abundantly clear when He declared, "If ye continue in my word . . . ye shall know the truth, and the truth shall make you free."[275] Whose word will you believe? Our Founders chose to believe the Scriptures, and on that foundation they built us a nation. On what foundation will you *preserve us a nation?*

A Chameleon Church

The primary resource for faith in society is the corporate body of Christian believers. This has been true in America since our forebears first set foot on these shores. Those individual believers might belong or associate together in a variety of local churches, which, if they are Protestant, might either belong to denominations or be independent. Regardless of doctrinal distinctives among various individuals, local churches, or denominations, the central doctrine remains the same; that is, that man is essentially sinful, that he needs a savior, and that Jesus Christ is that Savior. The source of that doctrine is the Bible, and Christians, historically, have been committed to the Bible as ultimate truth for life and practice.

From the landing of the first settlers in Virginia in 1607, the Pilgrims in 1620, and the Puritans in 1630, the Christian church and individual believers have been the guiding light of the nation. Our national vision and purpose was Christian and was, as stated in the Virginia Charter and the Mayflower Compact, to advance the Christian faith on these shores.[276] The mind of those early settlers was unswerving commitment to Christ and His gospel of salvation to everyone who would believe. The heart of those settlers was denial of self in service to Christ and to their fellow citizens as unto Christ. That was America, in both principle and practice, for her first two hundred years. Although not all Americans professed Christ as Savior, virtually all Americans accepted the Bible and its principles as foundational for successful living and government.

These facts were so open and obvious that the Frenchman Alexis de Tocqueville, in his book *Democracy in America*, recites, "Not until I went into the churches of America and heard her pulpits aflame with righteousness did I understand the secret of her genius and power." That book was written in the mid-1800s.[277]

Today, one hundred sixty years later, America's "genius" is in question, and her power is waning. People around the world increasingly "raise their eyebrows" at the nation that once stood for faith, virtue, and honor as they watch America's internal decay and the increasing fomentation of American society at every measurable level.

Not long ago, as I sat in the Cincinnati airport awaiting a connecting flight, I conversed with a man from Zimbabwe. He told of how American missionaries used to come to his country, and when asked why America was so blessed, would respond that America honored God. Then the man's countenance darkened and in a worried tone he said, "In my country we are worried about America. What has happened to America?"

What has happened to America? Could it be that there is a clear connection between America's churches today and the decline of America's genius and power? A few brief observations will have to suffice in response to these questions.

First, America's pulpits no longer flame with righteousness. Instead, they either flame with political rhetoric to patronize the political predilections of the people in the pews or pander to the felt needs of people seeking psychological therapy in religious garb and rhetoric to help them cope with life's struggles, which are largely self-created because they refuse to accept God's standards on God's terms. The messages emanating from America's pulpits preach a gospel of self-help rather than that of salvation. We are creating a custom-made god who is more interested in rights than righteousness.

Second, America's pulpits are no longer pulpits for delivering God's Sacred Word but lecterns for delivering man's quips, quotes, and opinions. This is true for not only the liberal but also the evangelical branches of Christendom. The new authority for life and practice is individual experience, and the Ten Commandments have become the Ten "Suggestions."

Third, America's pulpits have become the place of poise for spiritual chameleons who seek to blend with contemporary culture and experience. As a result, they are leading whole congregations of Christian chameleons to blend, without identity, into the warp and woof of a society that so desperately needs the transforming, purifying, cleansing, preserving, and enlightening power and presence of a Holy God walking in the shoes of those who call themselves by His name.

George Gallup Jr., in *Forecast 2000*, expresses concern that ". . . only 29 percent (of Americans) feel that organized religion is giving adequate answers to moral problems," and "only 35 percent believe that man's spiritual needs are being fulfilled at all by organized religion."[278] "As a people, we lack deep levels of individual spiritual commitment."[279]

How can that be when America still is the most religious nation in the world? It is because our spiritual leaders are not leading.

They are, instead, following popular culture and then cloaking it in religious jargon. And we have followed.

The shepherds of God's flock in America must reconsider quickly the following emphases:

- building men instead of churches;

- working for spiritual growth rather than church growth;

- emphasizing God's truth over human experience;

- communicating the awesome consequences for failure to consider all of the preceding emphases, both to individuals before God and to our society.

If America's churches can't or won't tell the truth, God might even have to speak through secular magazines such as *Time*, April 5, 1993. In the feature article of that issue, "The Church Search," the following warnings ring out to the pastors of America.

A growing choir of critics contends that doing whatever it takes to lure fickle customers, churches are at risk of losing their heritage—and their souls.[280]

[Mainline churches] are suffering because they have failed to transmit a compelling Christian message to their own children or to anybody else.[281]

A pastor has to shake things up. The point isn't to accommodate self-centeredness but to attack it.[282]

. . . it is lethal to reshape churches around the claims of returnees who are ignorant of the heritage, or to capitulate to a random set of cravings nurtured by anti-Christian forces.[283]

[Biblical truth] is being edged out by the small and tawdry interest of the self in itself.[284]

Many of those who have rediscovered churchgoing may be shortchanged, however, if the focus of their faith seems subtly to shift from the glorification of God to the gratification of man.[285]

A living, vibrant, Bible-believing, God-obeying church that stands against the tide of popular culture and the exaltation of self is America's only true hope. In America, let our pulpits once again flame with God's righteousness that we might see truth prevail and the ills of a suffering society dealt with on God's terms. Perhaps then we will also see a glimmer of America's genius and power reappear on the horizon because, as Abraham Lincoln reminded us, "That nation only is blessed whose God is the Lord."[286]

ANTIDOTE FOR DOOM AND GLOOM

In America's past, when we drifted into spiritual complacency and private and public morals waned, God sent men and women into our midst who carried His truth and delivered it potently so we would hear and heed it. He sometimes delivered His truth through unsuspecting sources, once through a baseball player, Billy Sunday, and once even through a lawyer, Charles Finney. Each time, a shaking occurred in America that converted people's minds and turned their hearts, resulting in both restoration of private and public faith and in renewed moral behavior. The soul of the nation was renewed.

An awakening of mind and spirit occurred, bringing renewed life and vigor to the American people. The ultimate consequence was a restoration of national and personal vision and purpose. We—you and I—need such an awakening today. We need to be shaken to our senses so that we can once again hear and heed God's message of hope and healing. The true gospel of Jesus Christ is the "good news" antidote for America's current doom and gloom. It is America's only hope. Because it is our only true and lasting hope, I have devoted greater attention to the matter of our faith than to any other issue of life or character. Genuine faith is the glue that binds it all together in integrity. It is what made America unique among nations and what will revive her once again if we will personally respond and not continue to point our finger at the liberals, the conservatives, the Religious Right, the Religious Left, the government, the preachers, or our parents. "It's *me*, O Lord, standin' in the need of prayer."

THE PRESENT VALUE OF THE ETERNAL

Many of us have developed progressive myopia, a disease that shortens our visual perception and prevents us from seeing "beyond the end of our nose." We have become trapped by the seeming urgency of life's immediate pressing problems and have become spiritually nearsighted. We struggle frantically to remedy and cope with the cracking world around us or become encased in personal peace and affluence so that we lose sight of the interconnectedness of personal faith and events around us. There is present value in today's world—in downtown or suburban or rural America—to a faith that looks also to eternity.

Once again, we look briefly at the findings of secular advertisers Patterson and Kim as they now describe the present, tangible value of committed faith in American life.

People describing themselves as "very religious" definitely make better citizens.[287]

Religious people are more moral than the national average.[288]

Religious people are far less likely to "have a price."[289]

[People of faith are] less prone to do something they know is immoral because other people are doing it.[290]

[People of faith] are also more at peace with themselves.[291]

Religious people are more likely to say they are satisfied with themselves.[292]

Religious people are . . .
  more truthful,
  more committed to family,
  make better workers,
  less prone to carry weapons, and
  less prone to petty crime.[293]

But perhaps more importantly, men and women of strong faith have a sense of direction, of purpose, and of personal worth and value. And it is these intangible needs that Americans are pursuing in every conceivable direction and by every conceivable means—except where they may be found.

WHAT MUST I DO?

A Roman jailer once asked this question. His world had been shaken like many of our lives have been, and he was under pressure for his very life. A tremendous earthquake had shaken the very foundations of not only the jail under his authority but also his life and his future. Locked doors flew open, shackles fell from the prisoners, and the jailer would pay with his life if even one of them escaped. As he was just about to take his own life in despair, a man of faith—none other than the great apostle Paul—

brought a simple message of faith that pierced through the temporal values and pluralistic, everything-goes mind-set that bound the jailer in fetters stronger than those of the prisoners he guarded.

And the jailer cried out in the agony of his own empty spirit, "What must I do to be saved?" to which the apostle responded, "Believe on the Lord Jesus Christ, and thou shalt be saved, and thy house."[294] That is what we must do first if we would hear the bells of freedom continue to ring in America, because freedom rings first in the heart of a man or a woman before it rings in a nation. And true freedom begins with breaking the shackles of sin that imprison each of us and impress us as slaves to do the bidding of him who presides over evil in our world. Then we will know the truth, and the Truth will make us free.

Having set our hearts to pursue the master plan of the God who rules in the affairs of men, let us then:

- reestablish the Bible, God's Word, as the final authority for our individual lives;

- choose to exalt and obey the timeless principles of the Bible over the ever-changing dictates of popular culture;

- teach our children and grandchildren the principles of God's Word diligently, realizing that their future and the future of the nation is at stake;

- be a living, walking example of God's principles of life, truth, and freedom walking in modern shoes;

- seek out a church fellowship that is dedicated in both word and practice to teaching the Bible as the authoritative Word of God—unadulterated by popular culture and the new "therapeutic" gospel; (If you cannot find such a church, consider starting one with others of like mind and heart. If you need help, write to us.)

- serve your neighbor and fellow Americans, especially those in need, as unto God himself.

- do justly, love mercy, and walk humbly with your God.

And America will once again be "one nation, under God." Let freedom ring!

AMERICA'S FINEST HOUR

America's finest hour is not the glory of a magnificent military victory but the outpouring of God's grace upon us as we fall on our faces in repentance for sin and selfishness before our true "Founding Father"—God himself. Then we will see our neighbors differently, our families will be united, crime will diminish, and life will explode with new meaning and purpose as we serve one another under God. This nation will indeed have a new birth of freedom. God will indeed

Shed His Grace on Thee
And crown thy good with brotherhood
From sea to shining sea.[295]

Will you be the first? Today, if you hear God's voice, Christian or non-Christian, "harden not your heart." Today is the day of salvation. There might not be another day for you or for America. Events can turn rapidly the course of history in a split second, as we have so tragically seen, bringing tears to our eyes and agony to our hearts. Why do you linger and heed not His mercy? Come home. Home is where the heart is. Turn your heart to the "Founding Father." Turn your heart to Jesus Christ. Become a man or a woman of true faith.

And may God, through your example of faith, bless America!

Soul-Stirring Questions for Personal and Group Reflection

1. What do you see in common between Washington's Valley Forge experience and our current experiences in America?

2. Do you share the conviction that "the hope of true freedom, without godly faith, is futility"? Why or why not?

3. Why do you suppose George Washington stated in his first inaugural address, "No people can be bound to acknowledge and adore the invisible hand which conducts the affairs of men more than the people of the United States"? What, or who, is that "invisible hand"?

4. Do you believe we need the intervention of that "invisible hand" in our land today? Why or why not?

5. Can the quality of our national faith in God be greater than that of the individuals (you and me) who make up *We the people?*

6. Do you see ways in which we, in our pride and prosperity, have become increasingly faithless while still claiming to be religious?

7. How does prosperity turn our hearts from trusting and obeying God?

8. How must the message from America's pulpits change if the people are to change?

9. Has your own heart been challenged or your soul stirred by this chapter? If so, how?

10. What changes must take place in your own life, attitudes, and ways if you would see America change?

If I would be served, I must serve.

Chapter 13

MY BROTHER'S KEEPER

THE BRITISH TEA ACT WAS enacted by Parliament on May 10, 1773. The Act gave a virtual monopoly for tea distribution to the East India Company, bypassing colonial merchants. Because the American colonies were already chaffing under the tax levied on tea and other goods without representation, the Tea Act was like rubbing salt into open wounds. The colonists cried out in anguish because of the political and economic pain that the tax inflicted.

TEA FOR TWO . . . OR A NATION

On the night of December 16, 1773, the greatest tea party in history unfolded. The cargoes of three tea ships berthed in Boston Harbor were unloaded by self-appointed longshoremen disguised as Mohawk Indians. But their contents, rather than being stored in warehouses, were dumped into the harbor, turning the entire harbor into a giant teacup. And now, two centuries later, the annals of history preserve the flavor of that event for all of us to taste. It remains a symbol of nonviolent colonial efforts to resist British tyranny and oppression. No person or property was destroyed, and the colonists even volunteered to pay for the tea that they had destroyed, but British retaliation was swift. They closed the Port of Boston and imposed the "Intolerable Acts," strengthening and uniting the colonists' resolve. King George declared, "The die is cast. The colonists must either submit or triumph."[296] So a call went out for the Continental Congress to meet in Philadelphia to decide the position of the colonists. Would they submit, or would they triumph?

If anyone's influence had sparked the Boston Tea Party, it was that of Samuel Adams. History records him as being the "Father of the American Revolution." But Sam Adams was not a wild-eyed revolutionary. He was a man of principle, resolve, commitment, and dedicated service. He was indeed a public servant without pay or privilege, and his was one of the first voices heard in the call to freedom from tyranny.

"The rights of the Colonists as Christians," wrote Adams, "may be best understood by reading and carefully studying the institutes of the great Law Giver . . . which are to be found clearly written and promulgated in the New Testament."[297] He found not only the seeds of liberty but also the call to service set forth in the same Scriptures. And his dedicated service was evident to all. Someone said that up to the time of signing the Declaration of Independence, "No one had done more and perhaps no one else had done so much in behalf of American rights and liberties."[298]

As the tea was being dumped into Boston Harbor, Sam Adams and John Hancock looked on approvingly. The British promptly labeled Adams and Hancock as their two most-wanted men.[299] Soon, as Adams and Hancock were ushered to safety under heavy colonial guard, Adams remarked in anticipation of the birth of the new nation, "O! what a glorious morning is this!"[300]

From his early forties, Sam Adams made public business his main concern. Although he continued later service in Congress, as the governor of Massachusetts, and in local offices, his culminating act was his signing of the Declaration of Independence. It was a dream come true after long effort.[301]

Although Adams was educated at Harvard and acted in positions of prominence, he was no self-seeker. "Unlike John Hancock, he cared nothing for personal glory; to him the cause was paramount, and his most important activities were behind the scenes." He was "notoriously indifferent to his private fortunes."[302]

Perhaps no greater honor can be bestowed upon this patriot of unswerving commitment to serving his fellow man issuing from a life dedicated to the God under whose command he served than the observation of one of his fellow-signers of the Declaration of Independence:

> His morals were irreproachable, and even ambition and avarice, the usual vices of politicians, had no place in his breast.[303]

What a heritage to leave to one's children and grandchildren . . . and to the nation!

HERITAGE OF SERVICE

As Americans, we are blessed with tremendous examples of service. Undoubtedly, our first president, George Washington, portrayed the honor of humble service as completely as one could hope to exemplify that trait within the span of seventy years, the years allotted to mortal man. From his early years, he demonstrated leadership in his service. His was not a climb up the social ladder or a self-seeking power grab. Rather, he made himself available to speak, offering his time, his talent, and his treasure to the needs of society around him.

After years of interruption of family life to provide both military and political leadership, Washington was ready to retire to the tranquility of his beloved Mount Vernon. But the needs of a new nation cried once again for his talents. The necessity of the hour prevailed over his longing to withdraw from the arena of public debate to the quiet world of his private retreat overlooking the Potomac River.

Washington wanted to run from obligation. How could it be his responsibility? Hadn't he done enough? But he knew the need. Could he leave the fledgling nation at such a time when his countrymen desperately called for his talents? Had not the God who had miraculously preserved him in battle under the intensity of enemy fire also bestowed upon him abilities tailored peculiarly to the demands of leading the new government?

He could not walk away. He could not turn his back. And so the General was inaugurated as our first president on April 30, 1789. As he took the oath of office[304] with trembling voice, he asked that a Bible be brought, upon which he placed his right hand, committing to serve under the divine authority of Him who came in the form of a servant and taught that whosoever will be chief among you, let him be your servant. And so the servant was honored, even by his contemporaries: First in war, first in peace, first in the hearts of his countrymen.

Washington made a difference among men but not without great personal cost. He did not want to be president, although many people wanted to make him king. In a personal letter that he wrote just thirty days before his inauguration, Washington revealed his feelings in the starkest reality: "My movements to the chair of Government will be accompanied by feelings not unlike those of a culprit who is going to the place of his execution." In the fall of 1788, without complaining, yet revealing his heart about the prospect of being called upon to assume the presidency, he wrote in another private letter, "If I should conceive myself in a manner constrained to accept, I call Heaven to witness, that this very act [acceptance of the presidency] would be the greatest sacrifice of my personal feelings and wishes that ever I have been called upon to make."

Who can envision the consequences of Washington's deciding for his own personal peace and tranquility at Mount Vernon over shouldering the mantle of responsibility? Many people believe that Washington was the key, the essential ingredient to stabilize and steer the new nation. Without him, some people wondered whether the nation could have survived its birth. As Americans, you and I are living testimony to the character of the man who said in his heart when he was torn between self and service, "I am responsible."

SERVANTS OR SLAVES

What will America be tomorrow? Are you responsible? If you and I are not responsible, who is?

It is disconcerting indeed that at this critical hour in the life of our nation, service, responsibility, and commitment have become passé. We now have better things to do—things to improve ourselves, things that will help us get ahead. After all, it's "dog eat dog" in this rough-and-tumble world. And who is going to fight my battles for me?

Service, commitment, and responsibility have become the subject of great concern among both secular and religious writers. That means, folks, that this problem in American society is serious and debilitating. It threatens to eat away the very core of civilized society itself, and it challenges the souls of free men because we will be either servants or slaves.

If we will not choose to serve, neither shall we *be* served, for ultimately each person will serve only himself. When each person serves only himself, our masters shall no longer be our servants but tyrants—and we shall have become slaves.

Responsibility and commitment are rooted in the character of servanthood. If I choose to serve you, I acknowledge my responsibility, and I am committed. If I choose not to serve you, I deny any responsibility to care for you, and I most certainly will avoid any commitment to you.

Most of us love to be served. But can you imagine a diminishing pool of "servers" and a growing body of "servees"? How long will you consider yourself "served" if the pool of "servers" dwindles to only a few? And how long will the remaining few who serve be able to meet the demand?

At its end, we will no longer appreciate service but demand it, seeking to enslave even those few people who remain to serve. Gratefulness will gradually disappear and be replaced by thanklessness, requiring either an enslaving master to satisfy my insatiable craving to have *my* needs met or a violent revolt of the general populace to coerce the meeting of our needs. Either way, we will have become slaves. We will be either enslaved to an outside tyrant or an internal tyrant—selfishness.

THE FREEDOM OF SERVICE

We met Alexis de Tocqueville earlier in this book. He, after having spent several years studying American culture after coming to these shores from France in the mid-1800s, made a shocking observation:

> I can see the whole destiny of America contained in the first Puritan who landed on those shores.

This observation requires some further exploration, because it embodies perhaps the most profound understanding of what the culture and character of America was all about. From it we can also clearly see our cultural drift and the corrosion and redefining of character that has occurred in the ensuing years. John Winthrop was a lawyer of considerable means who devoted his life to the welfare of the Puritan colony. Having come to these shores from England while in his early forties, he sought to establish a unique society in America, a society built around a strong sense of community. The founders envisioned a vibrant, thriving settlement where men and women genuinely cared for one another and sought the good of others as much as their own good. It was not to be a commune but a community. Freedom was to be the driving force—freedom to do what I *ought* and not just what I *want*.

Before setting foot on the soil that would embrace their venture, the Puritans, under Winthrop's leadership, covenanted together under God to establish "A Model of Christian Charity" in New England. In their own words we witness the simple framework that was to lay the foundation for both law and government in the new land.

> Thus stands the cause between God and us: we are entered into covenant with Him for this work.

This love among Christians is a real thing, not imaginary
. . . . We are a company, professing ourselves fellow members
of the body of Christ, [and thus] we ought to account ourselves knit together by this bond of love. . . .[304]

That might sound a bit mushy today, but the fragmentation of
our society and the growing void in our sense of community and
commitment to one another speaks loudly for an injection of the
spirit of John Winthrop and those Puritans. You see, things were
not so wonderful in England when the Puritans sailed for America
in 1630. They saw the corruption and chaos in society and, yes,
even in Christendom. Historian Perry Miller observes, "Winthrop
and his colleagues believed . . . that their errand was not a mere
scouting expedition . . . it was an essential maneuver in the drama
of Christendom. . . . It was an organized task force of Christians,
executing a flank attack on the corruptions of Christendom."

That is the purpose and call of a new group of Christian believers whom the sovereign Lord of nations is stirring at this very
moment. In the great panoply of American history, He is moving
these believers to bring correction, redirection, and new hope and
vision to a society run amuck and a Christian church that has lost
the brilliance of its own light, unable to illumine the way to a
society that is slipping into the abyss. God is calling Christians to
be Christians, that His light and His glory may once again be seen
in the land.

For Winthrop, that was serious business. At the age of twenty-
four, the Cambridge-educated attorney penned the following
words as the goal for his own life:

I will ever walk humbly before my God, and meekly,
mildly, and gently towards all men. . . . I do resolve first to
give myself—my life, my wits, my health, my wealth—to the
service of my God and Saviour who, by giving Himself for

me and to me, deserves whatsoever I am or can be, to be at His commandment and for His glory.

Thus, Winthrop envisioned American destiny in service, not in self. In their book *Habits of the Heart*, sociologists led by Robert N. Bellah at the University of California at Berkeley note that Winthrop "decried what he called 'natural liberty,' which is freedom to do whatever one wants. . . . True freedom—what he called 'moral' freedom, 'in reference to the covenant between God and man'—is a liberty 'to that only which is good, just, and honest.' 'This liberty,' he said, 'you are to stand for with the hazard of your lives.'" After studying American society today and yesterday, these modern-day sociologists from the historic bastions of liberalism had the following comments about Winthrop's view of life, service, and liberty:

His words have remained archetypical for one understanding of what life in America was to be: "We must delight in each other, make other's conditions our own, rejoice together, mourn together, labor and suffer together, always having before our eyes our community as members of the same body."

What is your view? What society do you seek? In what kind of culture do you wish to raise your children? To what philosophy of life do you wish to entrust the future of the America to which your grandchildren will be consigned to live?

INDIVIDUALISM—BLESSING OR CURSE?

We Americans pride ourselves on our individualism. We parade on the silver screen before the world our models of self-expression.

Are we now, as a people, reveling in the sweetness of the fruit of the vineyard that we have planted these last generations? Or has the fruit turned sour?

As early as the 1830s, de Tocqueville observed a different strain of freedom and liberty gaining sway in American society, a turning from the covenant commitment so beautifully expressed by the Pilgrims and Puritans whose influence carried the nation for our first two hundred years. He looked at American mores, referring to them as "habits of the heart." And he coined a word *individualism* to describe a new idea permeating the culture. He said, "Individualism is a calm and considered feeling which disposes each citizen to isolate himself from the mass of his fellows and withdraw into the circle of family and friends; with this little society formed to his taste, he gladly leaves the greater society to look after itself."

In his book *Habits of the Heart*, Bellah notes, "Tocqueville saw the isolation to which Americans are prone as ominous for the future of our freedom." And so it is and has become. As a secular prophet, de Tocqueville described one hundred sixty years ago our current dilemma and the consequences of our shedding the covenant vision of Winthrop and our Pilgrim and Puritan founders. Bellah, in reflecting on de Tocqueville's observations, states, "Such folks [individualists] owe no man anything and hardly expect anything from anybody. They form the habit of thinking of themselves in isolation and imagine that their whole destiny is in their hands. Finally, such people come to 'forget their ancestors,' but also their descendants, as well as isolating themselves from their contemporaries. Each man is forever thrown back on himself alone, and there is danger that he may be shut up in the solitude of his own heart."

My fellow Americans, our worship at the altar of libertarian individualism has not saved us but rather enslaved us. We have perverted God's liberty in favor of man's license. Our greatest blessing has become a curse. "Liberty and justice for *all*" has become "liberty and justice for *me*." The chains of our slavery are being forged on the anvils of our selfish hearts. Like Pontius Pilate of old, we ceremoniously wash our hands within the isolation of our minds and say to our neighbor and our society, "It's not my responsibility."

The Thomas Jefferson whom hyperindividualists and libertarians exalt feared the scourge of such individualism. He was concerned that "our rulers will become corrupt, our people careless." He warned, "If people forgot themselves in the sole faculty of making money, the future of the republic was bleak and tyranny would not be far away." Jefferson's antidote for such individualism in society was to quote the Scriptures and then turn their attention to the nation saying, "Love your neighbor as yourself, and your country more than yourself." So how do we square with that standard?

HOPE FOR A NATION

The problem we face has not changed in six thousand years since the days of Adam and Eve. We merely use different labels today. Adam and Eve had two sons, Cain and Abel. Cain, in the ultimate expression of personal freedom, murdered his brother in cold blood. When confronted by the voice of God, who holds all men accountable, Cain asked a classic question: "Am I my brother's keeper?" And that question continues to ring down through the annals of time. America's answer to that question is a reflection of her character in this generation and a reflection of your character and mine. Yet, the matter goes even deeper because character is rooted in "habits of the heart."

America's life-and-death struggle for survival is not a battle waged in the halls of political debate or in our courts of law. Neither do the multiplied layers of psychological theories, armchair philosophies, and linguistic gymnastics, which seek to re-label, redefine, and camouflage the truth about ourselves, bring any meaningful remedy to the problem. Why not? Because America has heart disease. Our root problems are not political, psychological, or sociological; they go to our very heart.

So what speaks to the heart? Doctors perform open-heart surgery on that mass of muscle that pumps life-giving blood throughout our bodies. Arteries are cleaned, replaced, and rerouted. And those who might otherwise find the sentence of death resting upon them receive new life. But what do we do with our spiritual heart, that which differentiates us as human beings from other living creatures? Can we place political or psychological bandages over the arterial occlusion of our spiritual life supply and genuinely expect to avoid a massive myocardial infarction in the heart and soul of our nation? Is there hope in the land to prevent the encroaching gangrene that is deadening America's cities because of the lack of life supply? Is rigor mortis inevitable, as many people are beginning to believe? Or is there hope for the American heart and the American character? I say resoundingly, "There is hope!" But we must attend to the heart of the matter. The heart of the matter is the heart.

Dr. Tony Evans, a black pastor in Dallas, Texas, formed a response to the blight of America's cities called "The Urban Alternative." In his book *America's Only Hope*, he calls to the Christian church in America to stand up, clean up, and take responsibility as "America's Only Hope." It is interesting that the Frenchman, de Tocqueville, as a sociologist, also saw the Christian religion as our only hope one hundred sixty years ago. He was not a clergyman, but he was an astute observer.

Today, sociologists Bellah, et al., from the University of California at Berkeley, make a radical turnabout for their profession. For generations, sociologists and psychologists have been looking in every nook and cranny of thought for solutions and explanations for our problems while ridiculing matters of faith. Bellah and his associates, after five years of study and dialogue, conclude in their much-acclaimed book *Habits of the Heart* that although our society has been deeply influenced by the traditions of modern individualism, "We have taken the position that our most important task today is the recovery of the insights of the older biblical and republican traditions."

To some people, this statement might seem entirely too theoretical for their blood at this point. But we are not through with our discussion of our responsibility as citizens amid a culture war that is raging violently between the forces of self-centered individualism and those who wish to reestablish a covenant commitment to each other in America. The ideas of men are responsible for the havoc that we now witness in this dear land. Viewpoint is determining destiny. And if we refuse at least a cursory exposure to those ideas, we will remain clueless as to our current dilemma— both as to how we arrived at this mess and as to our only hope for a future that we care to experience.

In an earlier chapter, we quoted President Woodrow Wilson as telling us that a nation that does not know what it was does not know what it is or where it is going. Bellah et al. traversed in *Habits of the Heart* the scope of our history as a nation and found a resting place in the insightful observations of an independent, outside observer—de Tocqueville. Both the secret to our amazingly blessed past and our hope for the future rest in de Tocqueville's comments in *Democracy in America*.

"Tocqueville suggested that the economic and political flux and volatility of American society was counterbalanced by the fact that 'everything in the moral field is certain and fixed' because 'Christianity reigns without obstacles, by universal consent.' . . . while recognizing that religion 'never intervenes directly in the government of American society,' he nevertheless considered it 'the first of her political institutions.'" Christianity had "the role of placing limits on . . . individualism, hedging in self-interest with proper concern for others. The 'main business of religion,' Tocqueville said, 'is to purify, control, and restrain that excessive and exclusive taste for well being' so common among Americans."

Well, there is little room for today's concept of religious pluralism in the observations of de Tocqueville. Although everyone is and should be free to practice the religion of choice, we as a people and as a nation must make some hard choices as to the foundational principles upon which we wish to build or rebuild a society in which it is worth living. We can practice selfish individualism and experience the temporary freedom of every man for himself only so long—and then we pay the awesome price. We are now finding that price too high to pay, and we must return to our roots of righteousness and relationships founded in the Christian faith.

For professing Christians, the task of bringing direction to a society that has enveloped Christendom itself in its headlong pursuit of selfish individualism is indeed challenging. Yet, as Dr. Tony Evans has said, the Christian church is "America's only hope." Yet, for so long, he says, "Instead of setting the agenda for society, the church has been crippled by society." "The church is no longer the church in the world; rather, the world is in the church." "Unless the church applies the Bible's truths to every aspect of life, there is little hope for society."

A lawyer came to Jesus Christ to cross-examine Him on which of the many commandments in Scripture was the greatest. His reply was simple and sets the direction for America today: "Thou shalt love the Lord thy God with all thy heart" is the first and greatest commandment, He said, and the second is like it, "Thou shalt love thy neighbor as thyself."

Another lawyer heard those words fifteen centuries later. His name was John Winthrop. And it was John Winthrop whose simple yet profound acceptance of the truth of those words formed the basis for the American "Covenant," an absolute covenant relationship with God out of which we entered a covenant relationship with our fellow citizens. When the two come together again, we will restore the cross of Christ in America. We must love God, and we must be our "brother's keeper." That is America's only hope! Will you join me?

As we reach out to serve rather than be served and to touch the festering wounds of the sons and daughters of America in the name of Christ, the hand of the great Lord of Nations will again begin to move in blessing. The Son of Righteousness will arise in our hearts with healing and forgiveness. And the propitious smiles of heaven will once again grace our land from sea to shining sea.

What can we do to make a difference? What can you and I do tangibly to touch hurting neighbors, fragmented families, greedy government, and a nation that is rapidly spinning out of control? We will explore some ideas in the next chapter.

Soul-Stirring Questions for Personal and Group Reflection

1. Was your soul stirred by the brief vignette of the life of Sam Adams, the "Father of the American Revolution"? How did his life of selfless service strike you in contrast to the spirit of our age?

2. Why was it a great sacrifice for George Washington even to consider becoming our first president?

3. How are responsibility and commitment rooted in the character of servanthood?

4. What was it about attorney John Winthrop's view of life, service, and liberty in 1630 that has caused modern historians and sociologists to write, "His words have remained archetypical for one understanding of what life in America was to be"?

5. Do you share John Winthrop's view? Why or why not?

6. Would America be a better place if we collectively and individually embraced and lived out Winthrop's vision?

7. What about individualism did de Tocqueville see as threatening to America's future?

8. In what ways (other than physical) does America have "heart disease"?

9. Have you been caught up in the spirit of individualism? In what ways has it affected your life and thinking?

10. How might your life change to show more effectively your love of God in your tangible love to your fellow citizens, neighbors, or . . . ?

Chapter 14

COMPASSION THAT COUNTS

EVERY WEEK, NEW HEADLINES EMBLAZON the pain of a broken society across the front pages of America's newspapers and magazines. Many people long to flee from the torrent of destruction to a tranquil place of personal peace, an island of isolation apart from the maddened crowd. Some people have, indeed, fled to the hinterlands of forested glades or the acreage of farmlands that are removed from the incessant contact of people rubbing against each other in aggravation amid urban life teeming with the pathos of human need.

I have noted the increasing frustration of people who are fed up with political platitudes when society is screaming for practical solutions. I, with most of my countrymen, wince at the crushing burden of a national debt that is fueled by the "passing of the buck" of social responsibility from ourselves, our families, and churches to the federal government. The cry of the poor and downtrodden causes us to turn our faces as we pass their makeshift posters that read, "Will work for food." A twinge of guilt, or compassion, passes across the membranes of our minds, feeling a sense of helplessness yet fearing that if we offer help, someone might take advantage of us.

I thought that the racial issue was under control—until the conflagration of the Los Angeles riots revealed that the coals of racial turmoil had merely smoldered only to erupt in flames that spread more broadly. And now the leaders of America's cities tremble at the tinderbox of social upheaval threatening to explode in violence on Main Street, U.S.A.

Feeling comfortable in my own personal peace and affluence, driving to and from my law office, it was easy to feel relatively insulated from the pain of society, responding only to the needs that passed through my office. It was not that I was living an isolated lifestyle. On the contrary, my law practice placed me in the center of the pushing and shoving of American life in the 1990s. I made my living in America's favorite combat arena—the courts. Yet somehow, as I drove back and forth to church on Sunday mornings as a volunteer pastor, and as I spoke in churches and civic clubs throughout Southern California, I somehow had difficulty bridging the realm of conservative and spiritual principles and the overwhelming needs of society.

In the midst of this cacophony of moral, spiritual, social, and political distress, I attended the National Religious Broadcasters Convention in February 1993 in preparation to launch a daily radio broadcast confronting the issues of America's heart and home. As I worked my way through the numerous exhibits, I turned a corner at the far end of an aisle and stopped short at the massive bronze sculpture in front of me.

Just a year earlier, I had been called by a local church to speak on the subject "The Christian and the Political Issues of the '90s." And I wondered, *What shall I say to people who increasingly despise and distrust politics? Why would God ask me to speak on such a subject when I have not been involved in politics for more than fifteen years?* And I asked God to give me a fresh look, a new heart to respond to the perplexing issues of our time. The process had begun. Save America Ministries was born.

VOICE OF A SCULPTURE

Now, as I stood transfixed by the sculpture before me, I saw modeled in bronze the image of God's living answer to pierce the isolation, brokenness, and hopelessness of a society bereft of meaning, purpose, and direction. It was the image of a "Divine Servant" crafted certainly by divine inspiration in the hands of a Texan, Max Greiner.

I knew then that the future of America would be defined by a spiritual revival within the heart of America and especially among the professing Christians of this great land. It would be a revival that would be translated into humble and sacrificial service to a hurting society in the name of Christ. It would take Jesus himself—well, at least you and me in His name—taking on the form of a servant under His authority. Then, and only then, willing even to "wash one another's feet" as depicted by that sculpture, will the American vision be reborn. Then, and only then, will we experience true reconciliation and restore community. Then, and only then, will peace have more than an empty ring and hope be more than a four-letter word. Then, and only then, will America's soul be renewed.

Will you be the first? If not, who will? Let's start on our knees. Then let's get up and get to work.

WHERE DO I BEGIN?

Now we have begun a new millennium, "testing whether this nation or any nation so conceived and so dedicated can long endure." How can I—how can you—make a difference? What can I do that will count? How can you affect the decaying social, moral, political, and spiritual environment in which you live? What can we do to prevent the tentacles of crime, economic despair, selfishness, moral relativity, racism, illiteracy, malaise, government intrusion, and purposelessness from strangling the remaining life from our families and from a nation that has brought hope to the world, light in the midst of darkness, healing from the anguish of pain, and freedom, direction, and purpose to past generations?

The most common response to America's dilemma in the last two generations has been an increasing resort to either political power or governmental programs. Both options have significant side effects that are seldom considered in the euphoric pursuit of "quick fixes" that often sidestep individual commitment and personal responsibility. Taken alone, resort to political power or governmental programs leads us ever closer to the precipice of social, moral, and cultural collapse. These responses tend increasingly to isolate us from each other. They often create a spirit of antagonism, and they certainly undermine any sense of personal commitment to our neighbor. "Let the government do it," we say. And if we do not say it, we think it because in our hearts we also think, *How can I, alone, make a difference?*

You *can* make a difference! Yes, you, even you can make a mark to change the direction of American life. You can help stop the moral slide of our culture. You can stave off governmental intrusion into our freedoms. You can preserve justice. You can bring hope where there is despair. You can bring direction and light in a society that is groping in darkness. Say it: "I can make a difference—and with the help of God, I will begin now."

So where do I begin? What are the needs I see around me? Each one of us will undoubtedly have many concerns. But what grabs your heart? What quickens your conscience? Act on it! Be moved by biblical correctness, not political correctness. Do not be paralyzed by fear! "God has not given us the spirit of fear; but of power, and of love, and of a sound mind."[305] Begin with the little things. But begin!

"DARE TO CARE"

The late psychiatrist Paul Tournier, having endured the horrors of a concentration camp, said, "Happiness is a door opening outward." Unfortunately, we have increasingly closed our minds and hearts to the needs of those around us. Happiness is no longer pursuing us as a nation. Neither are we pursuing true happiness despite our Declaration of Independence, which provides for the "unalienable rights" of "life, liberty, and the pursuit of happiness." Increasingly, we seek to isolate ourselves from the needs around us. We determine to protect and insulate our families from the encroaching darkness. And we are becoming so very unhappy. There is an antidote for gloom in the midst of social upheaval and cultural crisis. We must dare to care.

Consider blooming where you are planted. To begin the thought process, consider the following possible needs and your options for action.

- Is your neighbor injured or out of work? Take a meal. Talk to your neighbors about assisting. Mow his lawn. Paint her fence.

- Is your mother or father infirm? Take time to talk and care. Coordinate care and concern among the children.

- Assist the teacher in your child's or grandchild's classroom.

- Become involved in the P.T.A. (Parent-Teachers Association).

- When a "politically correct" attitude or thought that is morally wrong is presented in private conversation or in a group—speak up with conviction but kindness.

- Take the lead in setting the "agenda" for thought and action in your school, church, and civic club based on sound and enduring biblical and moral values.

- Take time to teach and model enduring life values for your children and grandchildren. Make it your life "investment." Do not delegate this responsibility to the "professionals."

- Organize, or serve, in a food bank through your church.

- Dare to organize, or serve, in an AIDS hospice.

- Write sincere and thoughtful letters to your elected representatives—before some massive group effort is amassed.

- Care enough to try diligently to keep current on what is happening around you—in your church, neighborhood, city, state, and nation.

- Discipline yourself. Care enough to pray regularly and with specificity for those in need, for leadership, for national healing, for personal repentance—your own, that is.

- Start, or serve, in a program to encourage literacy.

- Serve the youth in your church, as unto God.

- Open your heart, and your home, in hospitality. It is your heart, not the value of your house, that speaks.

- When you see injustice, speak up, but with respect.

- Visit someone in jail or prison. "Adopt" that person by your thoughtful care.

- Really love your husband or your wife with deeds of kindness. And then tell him or her regularly with real words.

- Commit yourself to a local church body. Don't run in from 11:00 A.M. to noon on Sunday morning and leave incognito. Be responsible. Don't be a spectator!

- Openly talk among your coworkers, friends, relatives, and neighbors concerning moral and spiritual values. Your silence can be deemed to be consent. Be kind and considerate. Do not be argumentative or strident!

- Actively listen. You will be amazed at how it will energize and motivate you to positive response.

- Be proactive, not reactive.

- Give liberally of your resources when you see a need. Do not defer to the government or think that the "other guy" will do it. That's our problem. If you shouldn't help, why should anyone else?

- Eliminate "they" from your vocabulary. "They" do not usually do anything. Personally identify with the problem, and the solution likely will follow.

- Be a better example of moral and ethical behavior than you expect of the "other guy." There is a word for the call to virtue without corresponding practice—hypocrisy!

- Love God intensely, and let it be reflected in your attitude, care, concern, and commitment to your neighbor. Who is your neighbor? The people, your fellow Americans, and others whom God brings across your path, not mine. All of us have "neighbors" right where we are planted.

Well, that's a start. Bloom where you are planted. God will do the rest.

THE SURROGATE CITIZEN

What happens if I do not "bloom where I am planted"? What can we expect if we reject service to others and sacrifice? What if we decline to shoulder moral responsibility?

A surrogate is something or someone that replaces the real thing. If a parent refuses to parent, the court will appoint a relative or even a stranger to substitute for the parent. What happens when you or I abdicate our care and responsibilities as citizens? What are the consequences when I demand my rights and shirk my duties? The surrogate citizen steps in to assume responsibility in the form of government. In America, we have euphemistically come to refer to the surrogate citizen as "Uncle Sam."

A surrogate never quite replaces the real thing. Something is lost, usually in spirit if not in substance. We despise and kick up our heels at government intrusion on our liberties, yet more often than not, we bring it upon ourselves. "The death of democracy is not likely to be an assassination from ambush," de Tocqueville observed. "It will be a slow extinction from apathy, indifference, and undernourishment.[306] The health of a democratic society may be measured by the quality of the functions performed by private citizens."[307]

Consider again for a brief moment the following facts.

- Governmental involvement in Social Security came as the result of children, families, and churches increasingly failing to care for their own.

- Governmental insistence upon national health care came as the result of children, families, and churches increasingly failing to care for their own—fueled by growing greed in the entire health-care field that priced care out of reach, bringing on governmental intervention.

- Companies failed to govern the quality and safety standards of products, and that resulted in government regulation.

- Companies failed to respond reasonably to environmental concerns, thereby bringing on the heavy hand of government to overregulate.

- Parents increasingly abused or failed to supervise their children, and that failure resulted in the courts and government responding to excess, interfering with even legitimate parenting under the guise of serving the child's best interests.

Once the surrogate citizen intervenes, it is nearly axiomatic that the citizens forever forfeit the particular area of intervention. The wattage of "freedom's holy light" is reduced—until it is no longer even a flicker. But loving service and compassionate caring keep the flame of freedom burning.

What causes your spirit to come alive—another government program to meet needs, or the sacrificial caring of your neighbor?

The signpost of another government takeover was recently planted. Service and financial provision by individuals, families, churches, and other organizations have so waned that President Clinton proposed *national* service for our youth as a means to pay or compensate for educational "loans."[308] On the surface, it might seem noble, but next it will be national service for adults for various and sundry reasons. In an editorial on the subject, *Newsweek* stated, "The nation is coming apart at the seams and people don't connect with one another anymore." If we will not serve one another, we will serve the surrogate citizen.

COMPASSION THAT COUNTS

Compassion is not a feeling but an act. In reading the New Testament scriptures, one finds numerous instances where Jesus

Christ "took compassion." In each instance, he did something tangible to respond to need. It was an essential ingredient to "fleshing out" the gospel of salvation. It was good news both for the spirit and the body.

Believe it or not, that was also an essential ingredient of the American vision that John Winthrop, the lawyer of whom we spoke in earlier chapters, sought to introduce on these shores in the 1600s. It was part of the American covenant, a covenant to love God that was expressed tangibly in a covenant to touch our neighbor with God's love through human hands. Winthrop spent his own small fortune to instill the reality of that covenant in the fabric of our society in the Puritan colony. And for that reason he could confidently say, ". . . we shall be as a City upon a Hill."[309] Our American "city" is sliding off that "hill" because our spiritual foundations are undermined and decayed, but some of our fellow citizens are working to make a difference.

Crisis Pregnancy Center

A young Christian lawyer in Pasadena, California, was grieved over the massive blight that abortion brought on the nation. He thought that merely to voice objections to abortion was insufficient. Real help was needed. So he helped develop and launch a crisis pregnancy center to counsel and assist troubled young mothers-to-be, affording them alternatives to spare the lives of their unborn babies.[310]

Racial Reconciliation

A white executive of perhaps the largest Christian mission organization in the world intentionally moved his family to riot-torn south-central Los Angeles to be a "human bridge" of reconciliation between white and black Americans.[311]

Uplifting AIDS Sufferers

An evangelical Christian minister became burdened for one of the great tragedies of American society—people who suffer from AIDS. He began giving his time in AIDS hospices to bring encouragement and companionship. His heart expanded to create "Project Compassion," coordinating the efforts of many churches not only to comfort those who suffer from AIDS but to provide housing for the homeless, assistance in crisis pregnancy, job placement, and clothing and food for those in need.[312]

Community Development

A black Mississippi minister, unmercifully beaten by white Americans, forgave those who persecuted him. Having been freed from the bondage of bitterness and hatred, he intentionally moved his family into one of the most dangerous, drug-infested communities in Southern California to provide hope, education, and new vision for kids. He now shares his concepts for reconciliation and redevelopment of America's inner cities around the nation.[313]

Literacy/Public Policy

A young, black Christian lawyer, concerned about the devastating consequences of illiteracy among youth near her Pennsylvania home, developed a literacy program involving four hundred children. That same female lawyer was grieved over the affect of governmental policies that undermine the family, so she established a public-interest law firm to address policy issues affecting the basic building block of our society.[314]

Prison Ministry

A powerful lawyer in the White House, having himself been convicted and imprisoned, was dramatically converted to faith in Jesus

Christ. He translated his new love for God into practical "touching" of the lives of other prisoners, giving them new hope through reconciliation with God. Prison Fellowship has now spread through prisons across America and throughout the world.[315]

Love, Inc.

An ordinary American saw the need to match the love and resources of people in churches across the nation with a wide range of human needs. Now, church people who are concerned about the needy, the hungry, and the homeless are networked with the needy in their neighborhoods. The chronically dependent are being helped to become independent, delivering them from the bondage of welfare.[316]

YOU AND A NEEDY NATION

Are you ready to take compassion? It need not be grand and glorious, but it will be Godly. Can you see the need around you? Are you ready to "speak" with your time, talent, and treasure to the hopelessness and pain of those around you whose cry causes heaven to weep? Is your heart broken by the things that break the heart of God? Where do you fit? Let's break the "culture of complaint," our "victim" mentality, and our dependence on the "surrogate citizen" by reaching out with compassion that counts. Make a difference—today!

Christian, act with compassion in the name of Christ. Add one hundred pounds of integrity to your message. As Bart Pierce well expresses in *Seeking Our Brothers*, it is time to "restore compassionate Christianity to the church."[317] American, if you do not act in the name of Christ, under whose authority do you act? Only two ultimate spiritual authorities exist. Lincoln declared in his Gettysburg Address, "This nation, under God, shall have a new birth of freedom, that government of the people, by the people, for the people shall not perish from the earth." Let's serve under God's authority. Let's reveal the renewal of our soul in the resurgence of our service.

SOUL-STIRRING QUESTIONS FOR PERSONAL AND GROUP REFLECTION

1. How does our demand for government programs reveal a gradual abandonment of individual commitment and personal responsibility?

2. How does walking away or refusing to embrace personal responsibility to care for others result in increasing government intervention in our lives?

3. Which is more likely to encourage your heart? Another government program to meet your needs or the sacrificial caring of your neighbor?

4. Government is a surrogate, or substitute, citizen. Why is it that "if we will not serve one another, we will serve the surrogate citizen"?

5. Compassion is not a feeling but an act. In what ways have you shown compassion to others recently?

6. As you read this chapter, did any need or opportunity for compassionate service come to your mind? Are you willing to be part of the answer to that need?

Chapter 15

A CIVIL
BODY POLITIC

ON NOVEMBER 21, 1620, FORTY-THREE Pilgrims were about to set foot on American soil for the first time. They were concerned that the nature and purpose of their endeavor, which had been taken at great risk and had already cost many Pilgrims their lives, be expressed clearly to preserve the future of their intentions. So they penned a short document to memorialize their intentions. That document, known as the *Mayflower Compact*, together with the Virginia Charters of 1606 and 1607, were the first documents setting forth the meaning of America and setting the tone for the nation that would grow and prosper under that vision. The Mayflower Compact stated in part,

> Having undertaken for the Glory of God, and Advancement of the Christian Faith, and the Honor of our King and Country, a voyage to plant the first colony in the northern Parts of Virginia; do by these Presents, solemnly and mutually in the Presence of God and one another, covenant and combine ourselves together into a civil Body Politick, for

our better Ordering and Preservation, and Furtherance of the Ends aforesaid. . . .[318]

All that would fulfill their goal of "Advancement of the Christian Faith" "for the glory of God" in establishing the new nation was to be accomplished by "a civil Body Politick," which would be created as they would "combine ourselves together" "for our better Ordering and Preservation." Thus was instituted for the first time in history a government of *We the people.*

If our government is *We the people,* logic and reason dictate that without *We the people,* we have no government. Therefore, government in America requires you and me. We are all part of the "Civil Body Politick." We cannot escape that fact. That is what is meant by self-government.

American government is not a "they"; it is a "we." In a sense, government for us is a nondelegable duty, except that we do elect representatives. When we elect representatives, we elect people like ourselves whom we collectively believe represent who we are, what we believe, and our goals and aspirations. For that reason, someone has said, "we get the government we deserve."

If I am an American, I am involved in politics because I am part of the "Civil Body Politick" in a self-governing nation. If I am not involved in politics, I am not part of the "Civil Body Politick" and must question whether I am an American. Politics is, therefore, the means whereby we work out our relationships with one another in covenant commitment. It does not mean that I must run for office. It does mean, however, that in some way we are all necessarily politicians because we all must work out our relationships with one another under the umbrella of our covenant "for better Ordering and Preservation and Furtherance of the Ends" for which the nation was established.

Viva La Difference!

What difference does it make? Why must we grind into our consciousness the fact that we are self-governed? We must do so because it is that which set America apart as unique from all previous governments in the history of civilization. It is what makes us what we are. It is the foundation of all that made America great. And it is the basis on which we became "one nation under God." For *We the people* voluntarily chose, in establishing the nation, to submit to God's authority. We established the nation "for the Glory of God, and Advancement of the Christian Faith."[319] That theme, from the Pilgrims, was repeated by the Puritans. And Puritanism, believe it or not, "laid the egg of democracy."[320]

The concept of freedom and liberty enjoyed by Americans was born out of religious freedom. The Pilgrims and the Puritans were convinced that true freedom and liberty for all would continue only to the extent that the colonists submitted to the authority of God and His will as expressed in the Bible. The people had to repeatedly choose to submit to God's authority. They found a critical link between their prosperity as a "Civil Body Politick" and their intentional choice to submit to God's authority in their individual and corporate lives.[321]

That theme continued for a century and a half to the time of the American Revolution. Even Benjamin Franklin, who was not particularly known for his faith, publicly addressed chairman George Washington in the Constitutional Convention, "I have lived, Sir, a long time, and the longer I live, the more convincing proofs I see of this truth—that God governs in the affairs of men." Franklin went on to say, "We have been assured, Sir, in the Sacred Writings, that except the Lord build the house, they labor in vain that build it."[322]

Who is building the American "house" today? Who is maintaining it? *We the people* have a choice. The "house" of our "Civil Body Politick" must be maintained continually. If it is maintained, it is maintained by *We the people.* If we do not maintain it, the house begins to deteriorate and crumble. Look around you. Does the fracturing of our society indicate anything about the condition of the "house" of our "Civil Body Politick"? Have our mortal minds and consciences become so seared that we cannot assimilate the meaning of the statistics that we ourselves publish? These statistics are not about them; they are about us.

Self-government means that we must govern ourselves. If we fail to govern ourselves, we are not self-governed. Our ability to govern ourselves has historically proven to be in direct proportion to our willingness, both individually and corporately, to submit to the governance and authority of God.

This is not religious talk. This is real-life stuff! How long can we, who pride ourselves as the most scientifically advanced nation in the world, continue to ignore the cause-and-effect relationship between our national sickness and our national sin? Can we afford to continue pretending in our individual lives and families and as a nation?

America's number one crisis is not the economy; it's not abortion, crime, health care, violence, AIDS, divorce, or any of the other numerous problems that threaten to overwhelm us. America's number one crisis is an "authority" crisis! And *We the people,* as self-governors, must make a choice. Will we return to being "one nation under God"? Or will we arrogate ourselves to the throne of our lives and declare ourselves "god"?

If our Declaration of Independence is to have further value to us, we must, both individually and nationally, declare our *dependence* upon the "Power that hath made and preserved us a nation."[323] Power politics and political platitudes are utterly ineffectual in the face of our national crisis. Have we not yet realized that fact? Or are we still building our hopes on the sand of eternal optimism that things will just get better? As we wait, our nation is crumbling. We do not need a new paint job; we need reconstruction from the inside out.

We must humble ourselves, pray, seek the face of God himself and His forgiveness, and repent.[324] That is true for all of us, including all brands of the Christian church in America, because the very Scriptures that we purport to believe declare, ". . .judgment must begin at the house of God."[325]

A CHOICE FOR THE PEOPLE

We have a choice! It is a life-or-death choice. Time is too late for us to mince words. Our first president warned us in his Farewell Address, "Reason and experience both forbid us to expect that National morality can prevail in exclusion of religious principle."[326] John Adams, our second president, warned us again, "Our Constitution was made only for a moral and religious people. It is wholly inadequate to the government of any other." "We have no government armed with power capable of contending with human passions unbridled by morality and religion."[327]

Moses similarly warned the nation of Israel after delivering God's laws and authority to them, saying, "I have set before you life and death, blessing and cursing:" Then he gave them a "subtle" hint for their self-governing choice—"Choose life," he said, "that both thou and thy seed may live . . . and that thou mayest dwell in the land. . . ."[328] Israel's history is a cyclical history of blessing when they chose to honor God's authority and of cursing when they chose to come out from under that authority.

Abraham Lincoln, our sixteenth president, pointedly declared the source of America's blessing: "It is the duty of nations, as well as of men, to own their dependence upon the overruling power of God and to recognize the sublime truth announced in the Holy Scriptures and proven by all history, that those nations only are blessed whose God is the Lord."[329]

America stands at the crossroads of history. So do you and your family. As Joshua of old cried out to ancient Israel, so I cry out to you, my fellow American, ". . . Choose you this day whom you will serve . . . but as for me and my house, we will serve the Lord."[330]

BE INVOLVED

Having made our fundamental choices, we must be involved in the fray. If we will be self-governed, we must govern ourselves. That means that we must be informed and be involved. It is our civic duty arising out of our covenant to one another as a "Civil Body Politick." But the goal is to serve, not to coerce or to "lord it over" our fellow citizens. Public service means public *service*. Our attitude is as important as our position.

LABELS ARE LIBELS

Have we lost our ability to speak with clear and convincing speech? Political correctness has gained a stranglehold on our ability to communicate in good faith with one another. That is a violation of our covenant. We cannot "mutually covenant and combine ourselves" "for our better Ordering and Preservation" when we create artificial barriers in the common language that prevent any sense or hope of mutuality.

Our labels become libels when they preempt discussion. As a "Civil Body Politick," let us strive openly and in good faith in the "public square" in open forums. Resist the temptation to conform to political correctness. It is an adult form of peer pressure. It is insincere. And it is calculated to squeeze you into the labeler's mold. It is designed to remove critical subjects from both public and private discourse. Avoid it like the plague!

A BLOW TO THE LEFT— A BLOW TO THE RIGHT

To the Left

To my fellow Americans on the "left," or "liberal" end of the political spectrum—do you really, in the name of compassion, want to continue the expansion of government control and involvement in our private lives that squeezes out the lifeblood of the very freedom and liberty you purport to champion?

On the other hand, in the name of liberty, do you really want the tyranny of social anarchy in exchange for the formal and systematic removal of "the God Who gave us liberty" from the schools for our young and the halls of public debate? For if my history is correct, virtually every significant social reform in American history that you now tout so highly was spearheaded or encouraged by strong, Bible-believing Christians in the name of Christ.

And was it not your standard-bearer, Jefferson, who declared, "Indeed I tremble for my country when I reflect that God is just, that His justice cannot sleep forever"?[331] And was it not that same Jefferson who penned the words in the great Declaration of Independence declaring it to be a "self-evident truth" that all of the rights of liberty that you purport to espouse were "endowed by their Creator"? Does that document of liberty not conclude with "a firm reliance on the protection of Divine Providence" and commence with an acknowledgment that "the laws of nature and of nature's God" entitle men to a station of authority to be independent?[332]

Perhaps there should be some intellectual integrity in acknowledging Mr. Jefferson's letter to the Danbury Baptists in 1803, which called for a "wall of separation" keeping the government out of the church rather than keeping the church out of the government. Perhaps ground would also be gained in restoring the nation by acknowledging that interpretation as being the clear understanding of the courts of the land for one hundred fifty years until an increasingly liberal Supreme Court decided to ignore legal precedent, set aside the rules of judicial interpretation under *stare decisis*, and, excise the words *wall of separation* from the context of Jefferson's letter, thus redefining an otherwise clearly understood doctrine to suit a liberal notion.[333] Have you not undermined the very Divine Authority that made and preserved us a nation, as declared in our National Anthem?

Such mental, legal, and historical gymnastics present insurmountable hurdles for "conservatives" and appear to be nothing short of intellectual dishonesty under the cloak of law. Are not the very foundations of the Republic at risk when individual rights are radically promoted without corresponding responsibility while at the same time God's authority to speak in our individual and corporate life is mocked, repudiated, and locked out of the halls of public debate?

To the Right

To my fellow Americans on the "right," or "conservative," end of the political spectrum—where, I must admit, this author generally falls—could we not more effectively articulate what we are "for" as compared to what we are "against"? Have we not unnecessarily alienated some by giving the perception that people are secondary to economics?

And specifically to the so-called "Christian Right," from the confessions of one of our standard bearers, have we not failed to formulate an "overarching, universal theme which could be articulated about where [we] wanted to take America"? "Because of this lack of unifying message, the movement created misunderstanding, resentment, and even fear among potential allies."[334]

Did we not lack visible compassion? And by that lack, did we not "forfeit the trust of the populous and abdicate the right to lead the nation"? In our "self-proclaimed quest for national righteousness . . . [didn't] the Christian Right overlook God's equally important imperatives for justice and mercy for the oppressed, the poor, the less fortunate, and for our neighbors?"[335]

Is it not true that "Because our message was not perceived as being firmly rooted in a foundation of love and compassion, we lacked the moral authority to command loyalty and we lacked the vision to attract zeal, energy, and sacrifice"?[336] Was not "the failure of the Christian Right to follow Christ in serving our community the major obstacle to accomplishing its national objective"?[337] Perhaps it truly is time for "compassionate conservatism," where truth and mercy can be espoused credibly from the mouth of one whose mind and heart have been spiritually renewed, thus renewing the soul of a skeptical nation.

Racism, Rhetoric, and Reconciliation

Racism is a reality! It has no place in our "Civil Body Politick" and is repugnant to our covenant with God and our fellow man. *We the people* must, with God's help, eradicate this blight from our hearts and society.

But fundamentally, racism is not a problem that can be remedied by legislation or litigation. It can only be accomplished by heart surgery. And there is only one qualified for such surgery and that is the Great Physician. Liberal demands, confrontation, and stridency serve no ultimate purpose and only provide a national excuse to drive the roots of racism deeper. On the other hand, conservative games of "let's pretend that racism is neither real nor rampant" only exacerbate the frenzy of strident activists.

So where does that leave us? Black America, so long our preeminent minority, has a unique place in our history. A spirit overshadows the nation with roots deeply entwined in the fabric of our society and culture. Racism has become a two-way street if not a multi-hubbed intersection. It defies solution by coercion or ingenuity. It is a matter of the heart. And habits of the heart must be dealt with in the realm of our faith under the authority of God himself. There is that authority problem again.

The first two great spiritual awakenings in our nation resulted in massive social consequences and the cleansing of many social evils. In each awakening, revivalists confronted slavery. George Whitfield was a champion against slavery before the Revolutionary War. Charles Finney cried out in opposition to slavery before the Civil War. And we are long overdue for another spiritual revival in our "Civil Body Politick" in America.

I—along with many other observers—am convinced that America faces her greatest crisis ever in this precipitous moment of her history. A mournful cry issues from saint and sinner alike amid the agony of the tearing of the flesh and fabric of our society. Prayer goes up from churches across the land as Christians plead for revival as America's only hope. Yet, the "hand of the Lord is not short that it cannot save, neither is His ear heavy that it cannot hear."[338] I am convinced that the God who gave us liberty will no longer tolerate a church that in both black and white congregations not only tolerates but also perpetuates America's national sin of racism, often to preserve power, perks, and position. Our iniquity has separated us from not only each other but also "our iniquities have separated between us and our God that He will not hear."[339]

The time has come for judgment to begin at the house of God in our "Civil Body Politick." We are praying for revival with unclean hands. God has winked at our failure to cleanse this stain of racism from His church in America in two previous awakenings. I am convinced that the intentionalized reconciliation of both black and white professing believers in American Christendom is a coextensive condition—if not a precondition—to the great move of God's hand and spirit so desperately sought and so drastically needed across the face of the United States. Neither may we ignore nor forget the Native Americans whom both blacks and whites have oppressed and whose covenants we have spurned.

The Supreme Ruler of Nations desires to strip out the Mason-Dixon Line from His church in America. He will not tolerate a church with spot or wrinkle . . . or any such thing.[340] And here's further food for thought: I recall reading in the Sacred Writings that God did not send His Spirit in power until His people were "in one accord."[341]

Harriet Beecher Stowe left us a message in 1852 that echoes through the words of her famous novel *Uncle Tom's Cabin*, which we would do well to take to heart for our mutual healing:

> A day of grace is yet held out to us. Both North and South [black and white] have been guilty before God; and the Christian church has a heavy account to answer. Not by combining together to protect injustice and cruelty and making common capital of sin, is this Union to be saved, but by repentance, justice and mercy.[342]

CHOICES

It is twilight on the American horizon. Unless Divine Intervention occurs, history will record the rise and fall of another empire. But the choice is ours. Will we—you and I—submit to God's authority? Or will we continue the cry of our age, "I'll do it my way"? The jury is still deliberating, and their verdict is not yet in. There is still time to settle this issue. But what we do, we must do quickly. And this is a decision that we must make both individually and corporately.

Alexis de Tocqueville noted a century ago, "Not until I went into the churches of America and heard her pulpits aflame with righteousness did I understand the secret of her genius and power."[343] Let our pulpits again flame not with rhetoric but with righteousness. And may that flame kindle in each of our hearts so that the blaze of a Holy God's light and glory may sweep across our land and renew the soul of America.

SOUL-STIRRING QUESTIONS FOR PERSONAL AND GROUP REFLECTION

1. What is meant by the term *self-government?*

2. How is it that "we get the government we deserve"?

3. Why has ability to govern ourselves historically proven to be "in direct proportion to our willingness, both individually and corporately, to submit to the governance and authority of God"?

4. Why is America's number one crisis an "authority" crisis?

5. How does political correctness pervert or prevent us, as a people, from legitimate and good-faith communication?

6. What do you see as the greatest issues or problems dividing so-called political liberals and political conservatives? How do our labels frustrate legitimate and honest communication on issues?

7. Why is racism repugnant to our covenant with both God and our fellow citizens?

8. What habits of the heart perpetuate racism in your home? In your community? In your church congregation?

9. Do you think that God, who made man in His image, will continue to bless any person, family, community, or church (regardless of race or color) that not only tolerates but also perpetuates racial division to pursue power, perks, or position?

10. What does being "in one accord" with God and man have to do with receiving God's power and blessing?

Chapter 16

THE INTEGRITY GAP

ON JUNE 14, 1777, THE Second Continental Congress
adopted the following resolution:

> Resolved, that the flag of the United States be thirteen
> stars, white in a blue field, representing a new constellation.[344]

History may never fully verify or resolve the question of
whether the creator of that first flag was really Betsy Ross, but it
does confirm the blessing that those Stars and Stripes have
brought to Americans and even to the world.

I can never remember a time, even as a young boy, when my
heart did not skip a beat when I spotted Old Glory waving in the
breeze. Perhaps that has something to do with the fact that my
birthday happens to be Flag Day. After all, not everyone is privi-
leged to have an entire nation put out its flags on one's birthday.
But I know that other Americans have shared and felt the same
bond, unity, and sense of pride and purpose that our flag represents in our hearts.

AN ALLEGIANCE GAP

But a flag is a symbol, not the substance, of something. And when the substance that it represents changes, dissolves, or is distorted, the symbol also begins to lose its meaning. When the nation loses its integrity, the flag loses its bond of allegiance, and when the flag no longer holds respect among the people, clear evidence exists of severe internal decay. Such is our current plight in this great land that we hold so dear. We are developing an allegiance gap because we have an integrity gap.

In 1892, Francis Bellamy wrote our "Pledge of Allegiance," and it was published in the magazine *Youth's Companion*.[345] Millions of Americans since that time have stood proudly in public gatherings and saluted the Stars and Stripes. As we respectfully placed our hands over our hearts, declaring those familiar words—"I pledge allegiance to the flag of the United States of America. . . ."—we shared an understanding. It was a mutual conviction that America was good, that America stood for justice, truth, virtue, and honor, that led us to continue our pledge: ". . . and to the Republic for which it stands." And now we are beginning to ask ourselves, "What do we stand for?" And I ask you, "What does America stand for today?" What do *you* stand for? If we don't stand for something, we'll fall for anything.

Our children once saluted the flag daily in schoolrooms across America. Today—well, some do, some don't. It's "ho-hum, take it or leave it." Virginia's legislature recently had to pass a law to mandate the flag salute that teachers and children formerly recited from their hearts. Today, we have little sense of national purpose, direction, or virtue. Quietly, we wonder why. And then most of us just shrug our shoulders and go off to business as usual. We bellyache about the waning American dream. But what has happened to the American spirit? Will tragedy alone revive our symbol and our spirits; and, if so, for how long? Is there a link between our soul and our flagging symbol? How have we lost our allegiance?

We need not look far to answer the question. It is not a mystery because the allegiance gap is, at its root, an integrity gap. We began questioning our leadership during the Vietnam War. Then came Watergate and, later, Iran-gate. These scandals were followed by "Rubbergate," the check-bouncing scandal in which members of Congress intentionally overdrew their accounts in the House Bank.[346] That scandal brought us to the 1992 presidential election and "Character-gate," when America decided that personal integrity was a value well worth sacrificing for the promise of temporary economic relief, causing *Newsweek* to note, ". . . everything's an issue of integrity." [347]

Now, after passing through Travelgate, Chinagate, and Monica-gate—in which fidelity to spouse, loyalty to country, and commitment to truth became national casualties—we are trudging our way through "moral-gate" into a world in which moral principles that have guided and protected us for centuries are given short shrift and are cast away as unwanted refuse in the face of a cry for individual rights and selfish, politically correct pursuits. So profound and unabashed is our collective abandonment of moral truth and principle that our forty-second president, in 1997, made what may well be the most arrogant public statement ever made by a sitting president, reflecting in public what was already practiced in private: "We are redefining in practical terms the immutable ideals that have guided us from the beginning."[348]

No wonder we don't like what we see in our national mirror! How can I, you, or we pledge allegiance to a nation that is losing its integrity? Can tragedy alone inspire us? Will Rogers, an inveterate optimist who said he never met a man he didn't like, made an interesting observation in his autobiography back in 1949. He said, "If we ever pass out as a great nation, we ought to put on our tombstone, 'America died of the delusion she had moral leadership.'"[349] In other words, moral leadership is the key to the greatness and even the survival of our nation. In 1953, President Eisenhower, in his first inaugural address, reflected, "Whatever America hopes to bring to pass in the world must first come to pass in the heart of America."[350]

What is in the heart of America today? What is in *your* heart? America is not a feeling or a political whim or a patriotic euphoria. America is *We the people.* And for America to change, *We the people* must change. We cannot expect the president or Congress to change unless we are willing to change. An editorial in *Time* magazine states, "As voters we profess shock that our candidates should behave as we do. The paradox is striking. Voters are demanding in their leaders the personal virtues that they decreasingly demand of themselves. There is a word for the profession of virtue accompanied by practice of vice—hypocrisy."[351] And so *We the people* widen the allegiance gap, unwilling to clean up the image we see in the national mirror. As goes our integrity, so goes our allegiance.

THE INTEGRITY GAP

The U.S. Supreme Court was asked some years ago to define pornography. The oft-quoted response of one of the justices was, "I'll know it when I see it." Similarly, most of us have some ill-defined conception of what integrity should look like. We believe that we will know it when we see it, meaning that integrity is something that we believe we can observe. Yet, integrity is not an object. It is not something we can reach out and touch. But we know, in our hearts, that it is very real when it is present—and a very real need when it is absent.

The trouble that we have in America today, however, is that with the erosion of moral absolutes, the lines of integrity have become blurred. If everyone is allowed the "freedom" to define his own morals, does not everyone have the right to define his or her own integrity? Without a moral consensus among *We the people,* we forfeit the right to a common expectation of standard integrity.

Thus, a thief who is consistent in his thieving, who steals from the "right" people for the "right" purpose is an "honorable" thief under the then-prevailing "moral" expectations or "politically correct" motivations of the general society. It should not take a theologian or a rocket scientist to comprehend where the denial of moral absolutes is leading us. We are making it increasingly difficult to identify integrity "when we see it." We have an "integrity gap."

George Barna, in his assessment on the results of polling Americans on our beliefs, values, and direction, titled his book-length report *Absolute Confusion.*[352] And he is only one of a rising chorus of voices to make this assessment. But there is yet hope if we will, as individuals, seriously explore our personal and individual roles and responsibilities, both in how we contributed to our current confusion and in how we will respond to restore life-giving, hope-inspiring integrity to a decaying culture. Clearly, if we sincerely wish to bridge the "integrity gap," we must get a better grip on the meaning of integrity.

WHAT IS INTEGRITY ANYWAY?

Although we believe in our hearts that we will know integrity when we see it, most of us find it easier to identify integrity—or its absence—in "the other guy" rather than in ourselves. If any real bridging of the integrity gap in America is to occur, it must begin with you and me. Are you a man or woman of integrity? What does your wife or husband think? What would be the private report of your business associates, your coworkers, or your neighbors? Has your life been a living definition of integrity for your children or your grandchildren? Has your behavior, your individual daily acts, reflected your professed values? It is time to "get real" about these things! This is the "stuff" of integrity.

The word *integrity* is related to the word *integer*, which basically means "whole." Does your life "come together" in a visible, identifiable whole? Do my individual acts, words, attitudes, and thoughts line up consistently with some standard that I value? If so, what is that standard? Can you define your life standard for your children? Is your life the living testimony to those around you of that standard?

Don't try to get off the hook by saying, "Well, nobody is perfect!" We all know that. The time for excuses is long past. The question is, "Does my behavior and my life demonstrate a consistent, observable course in the direction of my professed values?" Or perhaps we could ask, "Do I meet the standard for integrity that I hold for others— my boss, my spouse, my congressman, my pastor or priest?"

Let us briefly explore the recesses of our lives together. Following are some questions that can begin the process. I am sure that we all can add a few other questions of our own. Are you ready? I wince as I begin, for I know a few of my own imperfections. But let's get on with it. Let us each ponder "the shoe that fits" and begin to do something about it.

A PROBE FOR INTEGRITY

Raise your right hand. Do you now solemnly swear that the testimony you are about to give shall be the truth, the whole truth, and nothing but the truth? Please state and spell your name for the record. Now, please answer the following questions:

- The last time you received too much change by the cashier, did you return the excess?

- The last time you were undercharged by the waiter, cashier, or salesperson, did you voluntarily offer to pay the additional amount due?

- Did you do anything recently that would grieve you or make you angry if you knew that your spouse had done the same thing?

- Did you this last year call in sick to your employer and then go off and do personal pleasure or business?

- Have you permanently "borrowed" your employer's supplies (i.e., pencils, pens, etc.)?

- Have you delayed in paying a bill when you could have made the payment timely by adjusting your personal desires?

NOTE: This is the "stuff" that tears up America's integrity quotient. Shall we go on?

- Have you told your secretary to say that you are not in or your child to say that you are not home when you really were?

- Did you report all of your "cash" income last year on your tax return?

- Did you write an "illness" note to your child's teacher when you really took the child for some family fun activity?

- Do you complain about the violence and sex excesses of television or the movies and then watch them anyway, or rent a video so you can watch it in your home so no one will see you, or in the hotel room when you are away?

- Did you take care of personal affairs on your boss's time and report it as work time?

- Do you make personal long-distance calls from work so you don't have to pay for them on your tab at home?

Time out: The list could be endless. I think it necessary, however, to touch my Christian brothers and sisters a little in some important areas.

- Do you say that you believe the Bible is God's divinely inspired, authoritative Word? If so,

- Have you used the Lord's name loosely? Ponder this awhile. Some people have developed a habit.

- Do you give at least a full tithe to the church?

- Do you read your Bible daily?

- Do you give to the poor or seek out the needy?

- Did you divorce your spouse if he or she had not committed adultery?

- Have you cheated on your spouse?

- If your children were a jury, would they convict you of being a godly example?

Time for a breather! The list might not be exhaustive, but it sure is exhausting, isn't it? It's time now for the leaders of Christian ministries. Are you ready?

- Do you raise money under false pretenses?

- Do you pay all of your ministry bills? On time?

- Do you attempt to manipulate people for ministry purposes?

Publishers:

- Will you publish almost anything if you think it will make a big profit?

- Will you make deals with celebrities to have books published under their name to increase the profit margin when they didn't write the book?

- Will you delete aspects of books or refuse to publish them if you feel the truths contained in them will not "sell" or "market" to maximize profits?

Pastors:

- Are you so hungry to lure people to your church that you would modify, compromise, or just not talk about the straight truth of God's Word as it would impinge upon the rough-and-tumble areas of people's lives?

- Do you preach "the whole counsel of God" even if it is uncomfortable, or you feel you may risk your position, or it might not be politically correct, or it might cost you in diminished giving to fund ministry projects?

Have we gone beyond such trivia? It is such "trivia" that has burned a hole in the soul of America. Is this chapter for any of us—or just the other guy?

Some readers might say, "That's just legalism." This falsely premised mind-set reveals a perverted heart and has, perhaps more than any other single factor, revealed our profound authority crisis from pulpit to pew, leading to compromised integrity in our churches. Remember, it was Christ himself who four times in John 14 declared in differing ways, "If you love Me, keep My commandments."[353]

THE DEATH OF ETHICS

Ethics is closely related to and a significant component of integrity. While American professionals run from one ethics course to another, true ethics lies gasping on its deathbed in the "land of virtue." "The number one cause of our business decline is low ethics by executives. Who says so? Workers and the executives themselves."[354]

Syndicated columnist Cal Thomas, in his book *The Death of Ethics in America*, notes, "The lack of any personal accountability to a moral code has made immorality respectable in our nation."[355] He calls it "An American Tragedy."[356]

Richard C. Halverson, former chaplain of the U. S. Senate, made the following observation:

Abandoning an absolute ethical/moral standard leads irresistibly to the absence of ethics and morality. Each person determines his own ethical/moral code. That's anarchy. Evil becomes good—good becomes evil. Upside down morality! Good is ridiculed! Evil is dignified![357]

A news reporter interviewed a candidate for political office on television. When asked about ethics and character issues in his personal life, he angrily retorted, "That's none of your business! What I do on my own time doesn't make a bit of difference as far as my candidacy for political office is concerned."[358]

Is this true? Do you believe that? Such was not always the case in the United States.

A discussion of ethics and integrity would be seriously deficient without a reminder from the life of our sixteenth president, Abraham Lincoln. His life was replete with examples of honor, ethics, and integrity—yes, even as a lawyer. Justice Sidney Breese of the Supreme Court remarked that Lincoln was "the fairest lawyer I ever knew."[359]

But two examples stand out to test the mettle of our own ethical standards. Lincoln, having discovered on one occasion that he had taken six-and-one-quarter cents too much from a customer, walked three miles that evening after the store closed to return the money.[360] On another occasion, he weighed out a half pound of tea, or so he supposed. It was the last thing he had done before closing up that night. On returning the next morning, however, he discovered a four-ounce weight on the scales. He immediately closed the shop and hurried to deliver the rest of the tea. His care in his personal ethics earned him the nickname "Honest Abe."[361] And it was that integrity that enabled him to lead the nation through its darkest and most difficult hour to that time.

What will enable you and me to lead our nation in this dark hour at the beginning of both a new century and a new millennium? Are we qualified? We can and must act promptly in our individual lives. Lincoln practiced what he preached. America is waiting for a repeat performance from you and me.

SPEAKING OF PREACHING

If we would practice what we preach, what we preach suddenly becomes very important. So what do we preach? Our lives are an open book. Our children, grandchildren, neighbors, and coworkers cannot hear the good things we say for seeing the contradictory things we do—consistently. Our behavior preaches loudly, regardless of whether we like it. And while character is made by many acts, it may be lost by a single act. And the collapse of character often begins on compromise corner.

While our behavior preaches loudly, what we say is nevertheless critical. So then, what have we been saying about integrity? We can answer that question only by looking behind the desired integrity to the components that, together, comprise the label of integrity. Those are qualities of character and moral behavior. So what have we been saying about moral behavior? Precious little!

From the Secular Side

An insightful article in *Forbes*, a premier business magazine, gives a "Message to society: What you applaud, you encourage. And: Watch out what you celebrate."[362] What do we celebrate, applaud, and encourage generally as a society? We need only look at the entertainment we pipe into our homes and pump through the delicate membranes of our minds and hearts.

Michael Medved, co-host of the weekly PBS television program "Sneak Previews," in an address to hundreds of college students, declared, "The Hollywood dream factory has become a poison factory." As a film critic who is recognized in the industry, he states, "The crisis of popular culture is at its very core a crisis of values." He then observes, "No movie is morally neutral, no movie fails to send a message, no movie doesn't change you to some extent when you see it. Movies have a cumulative, potent, and lasting effect."[363] The title of his book, *Hollywood vs. America*,[364] gets the point across quite succinctly.

On the formal education side of the ledger, the policy exclusion of the Bible as a standard of moral truth for America's youth in the case of *Abington vs. Schempp* (1963) rendered the field of moral and character development an ephemeral issue to blow hither and yon with the sands of time at the whim of every student, as he or she should choose, for any reason, at any time, depending upon however one might "feel" at a given moment. The result: "There is absolutely no moral consensus at all. . . . Everyone is making up their own personal moral codes."[365]

Allan Bloom, in his critique of higher education in our nation, *The Closing of the American Mind,* decries the death blow dealt to our national soul and character. The introductory page facing the title page says it all: "How Higher Education Has Failed Democracy and Impoverished the Souls of Today's Students."[366]

In our supposed "value neutral" education these past thirty years, we have, in fact, "preached" a new set of values and have subverted the values espoused generally by American society for the previous three hundred years. The result: an integrity crisis. And the crisis of integrity has invaded the very citadels of truth and the guardians of moral righteousness—our churches.

A CALL TO CHRISTENDOM

The assault of moral neutrality has laid siege against "America's Only Hope," the Christian church. But for the Scripture's declaring that "the gates of hell shall not prevail"[367] against God's church, one might be even more concerned for the breach of the pillars of truth in Christendom, both Protestant and Roman Catholic.

Situational morality has threatened the moral and spiritual integrity of the Catholic Church, resulting in major confrontations among both priests and parishioners on the authority of the Scriptures and their governance in the affairs and personal lives of citizens. This critical and growing confrontation led Pope John Paul II to issue his encyclical titled "The Splendor of Truth" throughout the Catholic Church. With fervor, he proclaims that good is clearly distinct from evil, that morality is not situational, and that right is right and wrong is really wrong. Only absolute morality, argues the Pope, provides the basis for the democratic equality of all citizens. Only when people hold to the same standards of good and evil can they be free and equal.[368]

Protestant Americans are likewise confronted with the assault of an increasingly valueless popular culture. *Time* magazine, April 5, 1993, presents a cross on its front cover with illustrations revealing the "cross"-roads of American society, calling us "The Generation That Forgot God." The lead article, "The Church Search," discusses the efforts of the "baby boomer" generation to seek after religion—but on their own terms, "shopping for a custom-made God."[369]

The *Time* article observes, "A growing choir of critics contends that in doing whatever it takes to lure those fickle customers, churches are at risk of losing their heritage—and their souls."[370] Folks, that means that our churches are jeopardizing their integrity! Analysts say that mainline Protestant churches have "failed to transmit a compelling Christian message to their own children or to anybody else."[371] The result is that the highest incidence of moral uncertainty is among mainline Protestants, where seventy-five percent of the respondents do not believe in an absolute truth upon which to guide human behavior.[372] When two-thirds of born-again Christians, who claim to be carriers of the truth, contend that there is no absolute moral truth, how can the church even pretend to bridge the integrity gap?

But evangelical Protestants are also caught in the vice-like grip of the integrity crisis. Resorting to technology and marketing techniques, concern is mounting that rather than the churches "using some marketing techniques . . . marketing techniques are beginning to use the church."[373] Evangelicals have followed the suit of their liberal predecessors to placate popular culture. Even among conservatives, warns David Wells in *No Place For Truth*, biblical truth "is being edged out by the small and tawdry interest of the self in itself."[374] The Christian gospel, he says, is becoming "indistinguishable from a host of alternative self-help doctrines."[375] "And in this wilderness, voices crying about a loss of spiritual integrity are not easily heard."[376]

The *Time* article concludes, "Many of those who have rediscovered churchgoing may ultimately be shortchanged, however, if the focus of their faith seems subtly to shift from the glorification of God to the gratification of man."[377] Os Guinness declares that we are "Dining With the Devil" in playing the game of enticement with popular culture.[378] I ask: If the church won't tell the truth, who will?

Warren Wiersbe, evangelical author and pastor, has lovingly but firmly warned the evangelical community of believers in his book *The Integrity Crisis.* He states, "Our values are confused. And we're so comfortable in this snare of our own making that we don't really want to get out! The vested interests in the evangelical world are enormous, and revival might cost us financially."[379] He concludes with a message of hope: "You and I can help to make the difference."[380] But then he warns, "Our greatest danger is that we may waste our opportunity."[381] Wiersbe concludes, "The wrong kind of preachers have created the wrong kind of Christians by declaring the wrong kind of message, compelled by the wrong motives."[382] That, my friends, is an integrity crisis.

America's only hope, declares Dr. Tony Evans, is the Christian church. But "instead of setting the agenda for society, the church has been crippled by society." The church is no longer the church in the world; rather, the world is in the church."[383] In unmistakable clarity, Evans points the way to the restoration of integrity in both the nation and the church. "As God's people go, so goes the culture. Until we decide to be His church rather than a group of religious-looking people, our society is hopeless." That means we must "infiltrate the culture with God's righteousness."[384]

To the church, we either is, or we ain't. Let's clean up our act. As de Tocqueville stated a century and a half ago, let our pulpits once again "flame with righteousness," and let our lives demonstrate the same. To all appearances, we have enough dirty laundry to keep the laundromat of God's forgiveness busy for a century. But it is time for us to repent, confess our sins to God and our faults to one another that we may be healed.

The Lord, the Supreme Ruler of Nations, set His own conditions for revival, renewal, and restoration. He said,

If my people which are called by my name,
shall humble themselves,
and pray,
and seek my face,
and turn from their wicked ways;
then [and only then] *will I hear from heaven,*
and will forgive their sin,
and will heal their land.[385]

That is the condition for real change, folks. America needs a church worthy of the name of the Lord, a church of integrity, without spot, or wrinkle, or any such thing. As David of old cried out, "Let integrity and uprightness preserve me."[386]

A NOTE TO MOMS AND DADS

Parents are the most important leaders in the nation. What you do in modeling integrity for your children will determine not only the future of America, but will determine if there will be a "land of the free and a home of the brave." May I leave you with a few helpful suggestions to help you work through the minefields of moral training as you seek to develop allegiance on the foundation of integrity?

DEVELOPING ALLEGIANCE IN YOUR KIDS

Allegiance is a form of loyalty. If Mom and Dad are loyal to God and loyal to the principles they profess, the children will likely follow. Like father, like son; like mother, like daughter.

Integrity is the true basis for allegiance. Integrity is behavior consistent with what I say that I value. If moms and dads model that integrity consistently within the home, the kids will likely develop allegiance to those values.

Allegiance is a matter of relationship. Our children will develop allegiance to God if they develop a relationship with Him. They will be more prone to develop that relationship if they see it genuinely modeled by Mom and Dad. Similarly, they are more likely to develop an attitude of respect and allegiance to their country if those attitudes are alive and well in their parents.

Rules without relationship breed rebellion; rules with relationship breed allegiance.

Relationship depends on integrity for survival. Neither you nor your children will commit to a spouse, a church, or a nation where no allegiance exists. No allegiance exists where there is no relationship, and there can be no relationship where no integrity exists. Integrity is the bottom line, folks. So teach your children well.

THE ENEMY WITHIN

In a May 2, 1992, address in Washington, D.C., Chuck Colson spoke of a "fundamental change in the values of American life" resulting from "a breakdown of character. . . ." He noted that the previous year, ten percent of the members of the U. S. Senate were under investigation, a HUD official was under indictment for skimming, the Department of Justice successfully prosecuted 11,050 office holders, and the president of a major university resigned for multimillion-dollar fraud. These facts, he said, are the reflections of a "loss of character."

And then Colson notes, "A democracy isn't held together by law. A democracy is held together by shared values—a certain understanding of right and wrong." "Without a moral consensus, there can be no law." And "America will collapse if everyone does what is right in his own eyes."[387]

The enemy is within! No power could do to us what we have done to ourselves. We must restore a moral consensus in our society. The only workable consensus is one based upon the Bible. It is the source from which our forefathers drew their wisdom and from which issued their integrity of life action. Lincoln advised, ". . . but for the Book we could not know right from wrong."[388] And it was he who said, "This Nation, under God, shall have a new birth of freedom . . ."[389] That is still true today.

We can talk about a "pluralistic" society all we want, but we must look at the fruit of a valueless culture that is utterly lacking in integrity. The social consequences to date have been horrendous. But we have seen nothing yet compared to what lies ahead if we do not individually, as families, and as a nation immediately begin an abrupt change of course. We are engaged in a moral and spiritual experiment that will have increasingly grotesque consequences.

To repeat, our founding president, George Washington, in his Farewell Address, warned, "Let us with caution indulge the supposition that morality can be maintained without religion. . . . Reason and experience both forbid us to expect that National morality can prevail in exclusion of religious principle."[390] If we would be restored *outside*, in our society, we must first be renewed *inside*, in our soul.

Washington, as Commander-in-Chief of the Continental Army, made the following statement during an address before the Battle of Long Island. The words seem strangely appropriate here, although our enemy is within.

> The time is now near at hand which must probably determine whether Americans are to be freemen or slaves; the fate of unborn millions will now depend, under God, on the courage and conduct of this army. Our cruel and unrelenting enemy leaves us only the choice of brave resistance, or the most abject submission. We have, therefore, to resolve to conquer or to die.[391]

The colonial soldiers took the challenge against the enemy without, and God honored their commitment. We have reaped the blessings of their faithful courage to this day. Will our children and grandchildren be able to say the same of our triumphal victory over the advancing enemy within? It is up to you and me.

INTEGRITY BEGINS AT HOME

Integrity begins at home—in the little things. It begins with not calling in sick to my employer when I want to go shopping. It begins with reporting my untraceable cash income on my tax return. It begins with paying for goods and services that I purchase in a timely manner. It begins with the way we run our churches and present God's truth. It begins with truth, the whole truth, and nothing but the truth. It begins with you and me.

At its root, the allegiance gap is not a problem of the American spirit but of the soul and spirit of Americans. In 1954, the words *under God* were added to our Pledge of Allegiance by an act of Congress. This act was not meant to signal a change in our nation's spiritual direction. Instead, these words were added to reflect the essential role that God and His Holy Scriptures had played in our national life since the first settlers landed on these shores. But now, in our pride, we seem to have determined that we no longer need this "Divine Friend."

In 1962, we officially removed prayer from our schools. The next year, we removed the Bible, and our Supreme Court has told us that we can't have the Ten Commandments in our schools because the students might read them; and if they read them, they might obey them. And many of us, including professing Christians, no longer consider the Bible to be authoritative. The Ten Commandments have become the Ten Suggestions. We have turned from being "One nation, under God" to being "One nation, under Greed." As the September 1992 issue of *Forbes* magazine warned, "It is a terrible thing when people lose God."[392] And are we not experiencing terrible things? Do we not see the cause-and-effect relationships in every social indication in our beloved nation?

If we would once again pledge our allegiance with conviction of heart, we must once again become men and women of integrity. And—bottom line—our integrity crisis is a spiritual crisis, a crisis of the soul. If I, as a father and a husband, am not "under God" and submitted to His authority, the nation has no hope because the nation is only a mirror of *We the people*. Things will look up when we do.

America has entered its time of reckoning. This is "an hour of truth that will not be delayed."[393] As we have seen, our real crisis is a "crisis of cultural authority."[394] We must once again choose, as did our Founding Fathers. It is a crisis that "goes to the heart of America's character and strength. It is both a sobering time and a time of great opportunity to rebuild. We must resolve our current identity crisis." Who are we? As Os Guinness has so aptly said, "At stake is the vision of America that will become America's vision."[395]

May our motto, "In God is our trust," become an undistorted reflection of our national mind and heart. And may God, through your integrity, begin the process of renewing the soul of America.

SOUL-STIRRING QUESTIONS FOR PERSONAL AND GROUP REFLECTION

1. What is integrity? What is allegiance?

2. Why do American schoolchildren and their teachers no longer want to salute the flag?

3. What does America stand for as a nation today?

4. Do you think that things have changed in our nation during the past two generations that have affected significantly what we do or do not stand for? What are some of those changes?

5. If every person were allowed to define his own morals, should everyone also be allowed to define his own integrity?

How would this situation affect the very measuring of the word integrity?

6. Most of us find it easier to identify integrity—or its absence— in the "other guy" rather than in ourselves. Do you meet the standard for integrity that you hold for others? Where are you most likely to fall short?

7. What aspects of the integrity of your life will light the way in your spheres of influence for our nation in this dark moral and spiritual hour?

8. The collapse of character begins on compromise corner. Have you in some way compromised, thereby tarnishing your character?

9. How can the church (professing Christians) in our land recover integrity to lead and light the nation?

10. In what ways would your life, behavior, attitudes, position, and thinking have to change for America to be truly "under God"?

Chapter 17

HERITAGE AND HOPE

HERITAGE IS WOVEN THROUGHOUT THIS book. Its thread comprises the fabric of our lives both as individuals and as a nation. It forms our viewpoints, frames our values, and focuses our voices in response to the issues of our time.

America's heritage is a composite of the viewpoints, values, and voices of our past that have defined our path throughout roughly four hundred years of history. Yet, it also has declared our promise and purpose for the future. Therefore, remembering that heritage is important. Heritage thus becomes an ever-accruing monument to the past to be remembered for the future. If we fail to remember, we risk falling into the historical trap that "the only thing we learn from history is that we don't learn from history."[396] Clearly, our hope for the future hinges significantly to our heritage. Let's take a closer look.

WHY PRESERVE US A NATION?

Why should America be preserved? This question is not only valid but also necessary, demanding more than a simplistic patriotic answer. Is purpose and principle behind our patriotism? If our founding purpose and principle are buried in the dust of history, forgotten or even denied by subsequent generations, do we have a continuing reason to exist? Do we have *raison d'être*, a reason for being?

Patrick Henry, the stirring voice of the American Revolution, declared in a speech in the Virginia Convention on March 23, 1775, "I know of no way of judging the future but by the past."[397] The past not only judges the future but also gives purpose to the future. The real challenge, then, is whether we can glean from our past that which is worthy of both forming and informing our future. Can we find hope in our heritage?

What is America? From what seed was she conceived? What events caused the seed to become fertilized? What womb of purpose prospered her gestation? When was she born? The answer to these questions depends largely upon viewpoint. Viewpoint has and will continue to determine the nation's destiny.

For historic purposes, America is twofold. Just as we all have one head but two eyes, so America has two primary windows through which her history and heritage can most accurately be viewed. Those two windows are political and spiritual (or religious). Did the political existence of America proceed from the spiritual? Or did the spiritual issue out of the political? These questions must be answered, and answered with great integrity, to identify where our hope, if any, lies in our heritage.

Throughout world history, religion and politics have always found themselves entangled, and not always by intent. It is the very nature of our life together as humans (our polity) that renders it impossible to sever matters of faith from those of government. It should not be surprising, therefore, that religion and governmental polity are continuous and running patterns throughout our national life, extending back four hundred years. But which area—

religion or politics—if either, prevailed as the driving force in the foundation of the nation? Did a longing for political freedom foster religious faith? Or did a longing for free worship in faith foster a pursuit of political freedom?

When was the nation conceived? And when was she born? That which is born will necessarily resemble the DNA of the seed. Because conception always precedes birth, establishing these facts by the weight of historical evidence should help us immensely over modern hurdles of political correctness and historical revisionism, which often become artificial barriers to identifying our heritage. If the seed of the nation is primarily political, our primary reason for preservation becomes the perpetuation of political freedom. If, on the other hand, the seed of the nation was primarily spiritual, our primary reason to preserve us as a nation must lie in fulfilling some spiritual calling or purpose.

Precisely because of the momentous significance of the answers to these questions, and the public perception of them, historical revisionists have worked overtime for a generation to sanitize America's history textbooks of almost all of our religious roots. What few religious roots they have allowed to remain have been so revised, distorted, or secularized as to render them virtually unrecognizable. This sanitization process is the root struggle of the so-called "culture wars" that have raged this past generation. The culture-war battles are mere symptomatic skirmishes on a much bigger, winner-take-all battlefield for a spiritual-versus-secular heritage for America. Hope lies in the balance.

REMOVING THE ANCIENT LANDMARKS

Pulitzer Prize winning author Pearl S. Buck, in a letter to the *New York Times*, November 15, 1941, offered an observation that is worthy of every American's attention. She wrote, "When hope is taken away from a people, moral degeneration follows swiftly after."[398]

If hope is linked to heritage, either the gradual loss of remembrance of that heritage or the intentional revision of that heritage will have, over time, a calamitous effect upon the hope of the people. When hope wanes, confusion ensues, followed closely by chaos. Therefore, we should not be surprised that the word *Chaos* is plastered boldly over a background of the United States Constitution on the front covers of the December 2000 issues of both *U.S. News and World Report* and *Newsweek*. Heritage hangs in the balance and has all but disappeared in the memory and moral imagination of *We the people*.

Humankind needs help to remember. We are all highly susceptible to cultural, moral, and spiritual drift if we are not tightly moored to fixed points in our memories. For this reason, when the patriarchs of ancient Israel needed to protect personal or corporate memory of a momentous event that showed God's mighty hand at work among the people, they often set a stone or a pile of stones as a memorial. Mountaineers build cairns of available rocks on mountaintops to memorialize for themselves and others the memory of their achievements.

Historically, when men wanted to memorialize the boundaries of their land, they erected landmarks to preserve memory and to put the uninformed on notice of their claims. Americans have done this as well, not only to protect their land but also to preserve the memory of the initial and sustaining source of their liberties, laws, and life itself. Consider again the memorials upon which our national memories and message are literally engraved in stone.

IN THE CAPITOL BUILDING

Preserve me, O God: for in thee do I put my trust (Psalm 16:1).

IN THE SUPREME COURT

The Ten Commandments are inscribed over the head of the Chief Justice.

IN THE LIBRARY OF CONGRESS

What doth the Lord require of thee, but to do justly, and to love mercy, and to walk humbly with thy God? (Micah 6:8).

IN THE LINCOLN MEMORIAL

As was said 3,000 years ago, so it must still be said, "The judgments of the Lord are true and righteous altogether."

IN THE JEFFERSON MEMORIAL

Can the liberties of a nation be secure when we have removed the conviction that these liberties are the gift of God?

IN THE CONGRESSIONAL BUILDING

In God we Trust.

The God who gave us liberty declared, *Remove not the ancient landmark, which thy fathers have set.*[399] Removing landmarks erases memory and memorials that declare fixed points in our moral imagination. For two generations, the "ancient landmarks" have been selectively removed from before our eyes and consequently from our minds and hearts.

A minority of loud and angry men and women, rebelling against the God who "hath made and preserved us a nation,"[400] have co-opted our courts and usurped the ministry of legitimate government to defy the very "laws of Nature and of Nature's God"[401] to strip away all remembrance of God's rule, reign, or authority among *We the people.* The consequences have been nothing short of devastating. Rebellion is the ultimate affront to the God who, in His wisdom, determined that "all men are created equal; that they are endowed by their Creator with certain unalienable rights; that among these are Life, Liberty and the pursuit of Happiness."[402] Rebellion against God's authority by removing these ancient landmarks has led to rot in America's homes and riot in her streets.

Because the ancient landmarks are a summary expression of our heritage as American people, removal of the landmarks, both actually and figuratively, erases our true heritage. As went our heritage, so went our hope. So we must ask ourselves, *If the landmarks are removed, can they be restored? If so, how? And what part will I play in their restoration?* Before we can answer those questions, however, we must be firmly convinced of how far this process has gone in changing the "unchangeable" and what efforts have been made to restore historical memory.

REDEFINING IMMUTABLE IDEALS

The final decade of the twentieth century concluded by revealing a nation that is profoundly divided. An Associated Press article following Presidential Election 2000 was headlined, "Nation, it seems, is split in half."[403]

Perhaps at no time since the Civil War has division so threatened our existence as a nation. The fleeting euphoria of patriotic feelings has not changed the underlying division. A familiar and oft-quoted truth is that "if a house be divided against itself, that house cannot stand."[404] Someone also said that "Every kingdom divided against itself is brought to desolation."[405] These statements should give every sincere American citizen cause for pause.

Jeffrey Goldfarb, a sociologist who studies cynicism, has expressed worry over the public's flagging morale and lack of unity.[406] "Americans, it seems, are of two distinct minds," he wrote.[407]

How did this division happen, and can it be corrected? What enemy has successfully penetrated our ranks to bring such confusion? During America's Revolutionary War, the enemy was obvious: clearly, we battled the "Redcoats." During the Civil War, some people battled the "Blue Coats" and other people battled the "Gray Coats." But today we battle uncertainly. We know not what coats the enemy wears, for as someone so poignantly said, "We have met the enemy, and it is us."[408]

We have allowed the ancient landmarks that formerly guided us to higher ground to be stripped, thread-by-thread, from our national wardrobe. As these eternal boundaries have been removed from the frontal lobe of our personal and collective memories, some people have considered it a badge of twisted honor to demolish yet one more moral or spiritual landmark. Political correctness has redefined both constitutional correctness and biblical correctness, rendering each malleable on the anvil of progress to conform to the fleeting whims of a new god made in man's image.[409]

No public statement better reflects the brazenness now employed in the destruction of these ancient landmarks than that of the last president of the twentieth century. He made the statement on November 8, 1997, at a fundraiser for the nation's largest gay and lesbian rights group. Although he carried a Bible to church on Sunday, he swung a wrecking ball at the moral and spiritual landmarks on Monday through Saturday. He set the tone by stating, "We have to broaden the imagination of America."

Then he uttered words that strike like a death warrant the historical moral and spiritual sensibilities of the American people. Absorb his words slowly. Consider their dramatic implication for every level of civil society.

We are redefining in practical terms the immutable ideals that have guided us from the beginning.[410]

Do these words defile our heritage? If so, they also destroy our hope!

RESTORING THE ANCIENT LANDMARKS

At the time of our nation's bicentennial in 1976, a natural resurgence of interest in our roots as Americans, both spiritual and secular, occurred. Much was made of our forefathers' struggle for freedom. Others focused on the search for a place in which to practice the purity of faith. Perhaps no one better linked these pursuits in the imagination of the American heart than Peter Marshall and David Manuel in their deeply moving book *The Light and the Glory* (1977).[411] Peter Marshall, the son of a celebrated former chaplain of the U.S. Senate, repainted a picture of America's past that was nearly lost. He began restoring the ancient landmarks in the moral imagination of *We the people.*

Educators had begun rebuilding the foundations of America's spiritual heritage in the early 1960s. Perhaps the leading voice was Verna Hall with her *Christian History of the Constitution* (1960),[412] *Self-Government with Union* (1962),[413] and culminating in 1975 with *The Christian History of the American Revolution*—which traced the hand of God in American history and was published by the Foundation for American Christian Education.[414] Marshall Foster expanded the resurrecting vision with *The American Covenant—The Untold Story* (1981).[415] Memory of a godly heritage was beginning to reemerge.

In 1989, the Providence Foundation, under the leadership of Mark Beliles and Stephen McDowell, published a wonderfully readable account, *America's Providential History*.[416] But it remained for David Barton, a former high school teacher, to make a connection between our lost Christian heritage and the dramatic downturn of the nation's social structure. Barton's *America: To Pray or Not to Pray* (1988)[417] was a simple statistical analysis distilled from U.S. governmental records revealing the profound decline in every area of America's social life following the official removal of prayer from our public schools in 1962 and the removal of the Bible in 1963. Barton has toured the nation, addressing governors, legislators, pastors and citizens, speaking often more than four hundred times a year. He speaks with a sense of holy mandate in a defining moment in the nation's history, proclaiming, as his classic video states, *America's Godly Heritage* (1990).[418]

Others have taken up the torch. Pat Robertson gave us *America's Date with Destiny* (1986).[419] William J. Bennett, Secretary of Education under the Reagan administration, attempted to translate the trend of a renewed spiritual vision to fill the moral vacuum in the land with his *Book of Virtues* (1993)[420], followed by *The Moral Compass* (1995).[421] *The Theme Is Freedom* (1994)[422] was an effort by M. Stanton Evans to connect, for elite thinkers, religion, politics, and the American tradition.

Perhaps no one in the closing decade of the twentieth century did more to fuel the rising tide of a revived memory of Christian heritage, however, than William J. Federer in his book *America's God and Country* (1994).[423] This massive encyclopedia of quotations from leaders of the past has made available to every man, from pulpit to pew, and from church to Congress, the collective heritage of a Christian worldview, well expressed by our founding president in his 1789 inaugural address:

> The propitious smiles of Heaven can never be expected on a nation that disregards the eternal rules of order and right which Heaven itself has ordained.[424]

THE INTERMARRIAGE OF CHRISTIANITY AND CONSERVATISM

The "handwriting was on the wall."[425] By the time of our bicentennial, American society was unraveling. From the viewpoint of many Bible-believing Christians, as well as political conservatives, the nation had been "weighed in the balances, and was found wanting."[426] Heritage was nearly lost. Fear fanned the flames of faith. A spark ignited hope when the Nixon "hatchet man" of Watergate fame, Chuck Colson, became "born again." His book by that name served, inadvertently, to naturalize into the American culture Christ's two-thousand-year-old admonition to a Jewish lawyer named Nicodemus,[427] turning a Christian convert into a new American brand-name—"Born Again."

Congressman John Conlan of Arizona began touring the country, passionately exhorting evangelical Christians to enter the political fray. I, among many others, responded, running twice for California's legislature in 1976 and 1978. Columnist and commentator Rus Walton wedded our Christian heritage to the call to political action in his classic *One Nation Under God* (1975).[428] He selected as the biblical text to undergird the movement Proverbs 29:2:

> *When the righteous are in authority, the people rejoice; but when the wicked beareth rule, the people mourn.*[429]

Evangelical Christians were presumptively "the righteous," in our own eyes, and therefore needed to "be in authority" to enable the nation to again rejoice. The battle was joined. Pursuit of political power became the means to achieve spiritual power in the land. To that end, Third Century Publishers issued a citizen's guide to politics, *In the Spirit of '76* (1995).[430] On the front cover, Billy Graham noted,

> If America is to survive, we must elect more God-centered men and women to public office; individuals who will seek Divine Guidance in the affairs of state.

Bible-believing Americans who had abandoned the world of politics as "dirty business" were awakened to a new tool in the evangelistic arsenal. The "Sword of the Spirit" became used interchangeably with the sword of secular electioneering power. Successes at the ballot box brought a new power base to American politics, and its secular opponents labeled it the "Religious Right."

President Ronald Reagan became the poster boy of the new movement. He gave evangelical Christians the political favor for which they yearned. It became a holy alliance of secular and spiritual power. Evangelicals reveled in their new seat at the table. Parachurch ministries were born in an effort to stave off further moral decay, speaking from an evangelical platform into national politics. Jerry Falwell's "Moral Majority," D. James Kennedy's Coral Ridge Ministries, Dr. James Dobson's "Focus on the Family," and Pat Robertson's "Christian Coalition" were all prominent in promoting "cultural salvation" by restoring a moral base. Restoring the moral base became linked to preserving the heritage.

All of these efforts were undergirded by evangelistic promotion of an annual National Day of Prayer, which had been long on the books but little practiced. Evangelical Christians were deeply divided over the presidential candidacy of Pat Robertson in 1988, however, and his defeat by the senior George Bush for the Republican nomination severely dampened the fever-pitched evangelical euphoria.

Meanwhile, the vital signs of the nation were not good. Every moral and spiritual indicator revealed a country reeling, staggering like a drunken man into a moral and spiritual abyss. The culture wars raged between the secularists and the spiritualists. Yet, on another plane, many people wanted to reclaim the moral base without embracing the spiritual foundations. What to do? How to preserve the culture? These questions became the pressing concerns for evangelical leaders and politically conservative leaders.

The answer seemed simple. The "Religious Right" and the conservative movement must unite in a marriage of convenience. Marriages for political purpose and promise have been common throughout world history. But marriage invariably involves compromise; hence, the biblical injunction, "Be ye not unequally yoked together with unbelievers."[431] This marriage has not only produced the inevitable confusion of unholy compromise but also was born out of the confusion of compromise in a state of desperation.

What has been the fruit of this alliance? Has our heritage been preserved? On the secular side, William J. Bennett reports "facts and figures on the State of American Society" in his *Index of Leading Cultural Indicators*. Conservative talk show host Rush Limbaugh laments on its front cover that these are "Some of the most chilling statistics I have ever read. . . . His numbers are like a kick to the solar plexus."[432]

From the spiritual viewpoint, America's favorite pollster, George Gallup Jr., reports that although America's religious heritage seems to persist in outward appearance, "The religious or spiritual condition of America today can best be described in terms of gaps." He speaks of an "ethics gap," a "knowledge gap," and a "faith gap." "While religion is highly popular in this country," he says, "evidence suggests that it does not change people's lives to the degree one would expect from the level of professed faith."[433]

In light of the past generation of American history, what is the status of America's hope? To answer that question, we must reexamine whether heritage has become our servant or our master. Has our Godly heritage guided us back to God, or has it become our god?

GODLY HERITAGE, OR UNGODLY IDOLATRY?

Truly, as the psalmist of old reflected, we have a "goodly heritage."[434] Despite all of our national downsittings and uprisings, the blight of slavery, graft in government, and a variety of other glaring ungodly deeds by everyone from president to pastor to parishioner, we have a godly heritage from the perspective of history. Most of this book confirms this wonderful treasure.

But let me ask you a personal question. If we revel and rejoice in our goodly and Godly heritage, yet refuse to obey and submit our lives personally and corporately to the God of that heritage, have we not elevated our Godly heritage to a position of worship, politely dismissing God himself, except when we desire His aid?

I fear that, in this precipitous moment of our history, having had the glorious memory of a Godly heritage restored to us during the previous generation by so many dedicated people among us, we now glory in that memory rather than in the God who made and preserved us a nation. And that, my American friend, is a prescription for personal and national disaster. For it is written as the first of all commandments, "Thou shalt have no other gods before me."[435] Please do not dismiss this lightly. Remember, in God's eyes, "the nations are as a drop in the bucket." Despite our Godly heritage or the fact that our nation might be called "America," "All nations before Him are as nothing. . . ."[436] Heritage is not something to worship in pride but to honor in humility.

As Abraham Lincoln suggested in his call to the nation for a day of humiliation, fasting, and prayer, "It behooves us to humble ourselves before the offended power."[437] As syndicated columnist Cal Thomas and his colaborer in the "Moral Majority" Ed Dobson now lament, even those of us who sought sincerely to preserve, protect, and resurrect our Godly heritage have ultimately become *Blinded by Might*.[438] We have subtly, and sometimes not so subtly, shifted our trust from God to government, from the Cross of Christ to the Congress, from the Prince of Peace to the president. In grasping for heritage without leading the nation, or even the church within the nation, to submit to the God of that heritage on His terms, we have unwittingly put hope at grave risk.

Ultimately, heritage is a matter of the heart. Christian Coalition directors Don Hodel and Randy Tate declared in preparation for their "Road to Victory '98" conference that it needed to be "A time of spiritual renewal, a time of revival." "Even if every leader in this country, from the White House to the school house, shared our political goals," they commented, "this nation still would not change. America cannot change until the hearts of the people change."[439]

The heritage of the past provides hope for the future only when it is lived out from our hearts in the present. How secure is America's hope based upon living out our heritage through your heart today? Living out that heritage as a legacy of hope is the subject of the next chapter.

SOUL-STIRRING QUESTIONS FOR PERSONAL AND GROUP REFLECTION

1. Why should America be preserved? Do we have a reason for our being a nation?

2. Did the political existence of America proceed from the spiritual, or did the spiritual issue from the political? On what do you base your answer to that question? Why does it matter?

3. When was the nation truly conceived? What was the initial seed that resulted in the nation's ultimate birth?

4. What is heritage?

5. Pearl Buck said, "When hope is taken away from a people, moral degeneration follows swiftly after." In what way is our hope linked to our heritage as a nation?

6. Of what significance to our heritage is the engraving of Bible passages on most of our national buildings and monuments?

7. When the last president in the twentieth century declared, "We are redefining in practical terms the immutable ideals that have guided us from the beginning," what were the implications of his view on the role of nearly four hundred years of heritage and history in our nation's future?

8. Do you think it is important to "restore the ancient landmarks" of our past to bring focus and healing for our future? Why, or why not?

9. How can a Godly heritage become an idol?

10. If America's future depends upon your example of living out our heritage today, what is America's hope?

Heritage in the past without purpose in the present destroys hope for the future.

Chapter 18

A HOPE AND
A PURPOSE

WHEN AND HOW CAN HOPE well up in our hearts from the wellspring of our heritage? It is not enough that we be informed of our goodly and Godly heritage. We must be transformed by it. Information without transformation leads to frustration, stagnation, and ultimately termination. This is true for individuals, families, and, yes, even nations. Often the missing link is proper application. Without proper application of the abundant information regarding our heritage, we are void of vision and will soon perish for lack of purpose.[440]

The connecting link between heritage and hope is purpose. Heritage in the past without purpose in the present destroys hope for the future. It is at the point of purpose that our hearts make connection with our heritage. When purpose is either forgotten or abandoned, we lose heart. And a people who have lost heart have lost hope.

Do we now, or did we ever, have a national purpose? If we can identify that purpose, we might define our destiny—or, regrettably, determine our destruction. How far back must we go to pinpoint our purpose? We must go to the very first settlers because their defining purpose becomes our defining purpose, unless we abandon our heritage. Hope lies in the balance. Our search here must be brief, yet bold.

THE GREATEST OF ALL CAUSES

The story we are about to recite is one of the most amazing stories in the tablets of human history, and it is still being written. It includes a cast of millions over a span of two millennia. Some of the cast members stand prominently in our heritage; yet, this unfolding story continues to fuel the fires of faith and freedom for America's hope. Let's begin a short tour through the pages of this story.

America as a nation owes her birth to the "Great Commission." You might ask, *What is the "Great Commission"?* Please follow this brief distillation of our history and watch the great panoply of America's purpose unfold.

Jesus Christ, after His crucifixion and resurrection, ascended into heaven to God the Father. Just before His ascension, He gave to His church the following simple instructions, known as the "Great Commission":

> *Go ye . . . and teach all nations, baptizing them in the name of the Father, and of the Son, and of the Holy Ghost: Teaching them to observe all things whatsoever I have commanded you* (Matthew 28:19–20).[441]

These words have inspired and motivated followers of Christ for the past two thousand years to take the gospel, or good news, of Christ around the world and to all nations. Many people have toiled and suffered great hardship, even loss of life itself, to accomplish this holy purpose.

Although this holy enterprise often became entangled with the pursuit of unholy prizes, with holy ends being used to justify unholy means, the divine purpose has persisted through twenty centuries to the brink of the seventh millennium. Hope has indeed sprung eternal, with many people believing that this seemingly impossible commission might finally be accomplished in our generation. For this reason, the end-time words of Christ to His disciples are engraved above the entrance to the headquarters of the Christian Broadcasting Network:

> This gospel of the kingdom shall be preached in all the world for a witness unto all nations; and then shall the end come.[442]

Regardless of what we might think of Christopher Columbus in our generation, his was a "Great Commission" vision that paved the way to the New World in preparation for the first settlers to arrive on our eastern shores. Although he pursued gold, he also was convinced that God had given him a holy mandate to carry the gospel to heathen lands. Christopher, the "Christ-bearer," wrote in his journal, quoting the Book of Isaiah:

> *Listen to me, O coastlands, and hearken, you peoples from afar.*
> *The Lord called me from my mother's womb . . . I will give you as*
> *a light to the nations, that my salvation may reach to the end of*
> *the earth.*[443]

THE CROSS AND THE COLONIES

It took a century for Columbus's vision to yield the first meaningful signs of implementation. When Queen Elizabeth I rose to the throne of England after her miraculous deliverance from the reign of "Bloody Mary," she asked her adviser how she could give thanks to God for what He had done. He answered that she should fund from her personal resources a scholarship for poor boys. One of those "Queens Scholars" was Richard Hakluyt.

Young Hakluyt, following an education at Westminster and Oxford, felt called to be a pastor. God soon gave him a vision for the colonization of America. His crusade for colonization did not become reality for a generation. In 1584, he wrote his defense for American colonization in *Discourse on Western Planting*. The reasons he offered for English settlement of the "Western Land" were clearly stated:

> The blessed Apostle Paul the converter of the Gentiles, Romans 10, writeth in this manner: Whosoever shall call on the name of the Lord shall be saved: But howe shall they call on him in whom they have not hearde? And howe shall they heare withoute a preacher? And howe shall they preache except they be sente?
>
> Then it is necessary for the salvation of those poore people which have settled so longe in darkness and in the shadowe of deathe, that preachers should be sent unto them: But by whome shoulde these preachers be sente? By them no doubte which have taken upon them the protection of the Christian faithe: as The Kinges and Queenes of England have the name of Defenders of the Faithe: By which title I thinke they are so to inlarge and advance [the faithe of Christ] accordinge to the commandmente of our Saviour Christe.[444]

Hakluyt's life call and vision were fulfilled when James, King of England and Defender of the Faith, on April 10, 1606, named him to be one of nine patentees of the First Virginia Charter to establish a plantation "in that parte of America commonly called Virginia." Hakluyt became rightly known as the "Father of Colonization." Consider the stated purpose for colonization in that First Virginia Charter.

> Wee, greatly commending and graciously accepting of theire desires to the furtherance of soe noble a worke which may, by the providence of Almightie God, hereafter tende to the glorie of His Divine Majestie in propogating of the Christian religion to suche people as yet live in darkenesse and miserable ignorance of the true knowledge and worshippe of God may in tyme bring the infidels and savages living in those parts to humane civilitie and to a settled and quiet governmente, doe by theise our lettres patents graciously accepte of and agree to theire humble and well intended desires. . . .[445]

Based upon this First Virginia Charter, the "cross of the covenant" was first planted on American soil. Virginius Dabney, in his renowned *Richmond, The Story of a City*, records in the opening words of the first chapter that after the English explorers planted a cross at the cape on the Chesapeake Bay, they sailed to Jamestown from which, after ten days, they sailed up the James River.

> Over the seething rapids of the James River and into the silent forest echoed "a great shout," followed by a prayer "for our King and our own prosperous success in this his action." One-armed Captain Christopher Newport had led a small band of intrepid English explorers upriver from Jamestown . . . and had planted a wooden cross at The Falls, near the heart of today's downtown Richmond. It was May 24, 1607.[446]

THE COLONIES AND THE GREAT COMMISSION

The psalmist of Scripture wrote, "Ask of me, and I shall give thee the heathen for thine inheritance, and the uttermost parts of the earth for thy possession."[447] According to the renowned historian Will Durant, by the fourth century, even the mighty Roman Empire had bowed her knee to Christ as Lord. Writes Durant,

> There is no greater drama in human record then the sight of a few Christians, scorned or oppressed by a succession of emperors, bearing all trials with fierce tenacity, multiplying quietly, building order while their enemies generated chaos, fighting sword with the word, brutality with hope, and at last defeating the strongest state that history has known. Caesar and Christ had met in the arena, and Christ had won.[448]

Thirteen centuries later, the church was marching across the Atlantic to the New World. Ready to endure hardship, "as good soldiers of Jesus Christ,"[449] the church embarked in the shoes of Puritans and Pilgrims on an "errand into the wilderness" along the American shores. They carried their gospel treasure of God's good news of salvation imperfectly in earthen vessels,"[450] just as we are, but carry it they did.

The 1606 Virginia Charter provided full authority for their spiritual enterprise to be underwritten by their business endeavors. Because Virginia as then known comprised nearly 80 percent of what is now the continental United States, as reflected on their own world maps, a commission to transmit God's truth to Virginia was, in effect, a commission that embraced the entire nation-to-be. We should not be surprised, therefore, to learn that the Mayflower Compact, penned by the Pilgrims on November 11, 1620, should contain the identical purpose that was set forth in the Virginia Charter fourteen years earlier.

The Pilgrims had been blown off course by storms. Their landing at Cape Cod in Massachusetts placed them outside the official lines of Virginia and therefore outside the scope of the jurisdiction of the Virginia Company under whose charter they had embarked. Yet, their purpose remained firm. Authority among their band must be preserved to secure their purpose. So they drafted a compact, which became a cornerstone of America's experiment in a democratic form of government.

The Mayflower Compact was an extraordinary document in American and world history because it set forth the principles of representative government by the people to effectuate the greater life purpose of the people. The civil government facilitated or undergirded, through civil liberty, the proclamation of spiritual liberty in Christ. It is important for us to revisit its words:

In the name of God, amen. We whose names are underwritten . . . Having undertaken, *for the glory of God and advancement of the Christian faith* and honor of our King and country, a voyage to plant the first colony in the northern parts of Virginia, do by these presents solemnly and mutually in the presence of God and one of another, covenant and combine ourselves together into a civil body politic, *for* our better ordering and preservation and *furtherance of the ends aforesaid*[451] (emphasis added).

It is indeed fascinating to note that all but one of the original thirteen colonies found as its purpose the Great Commission. They did not seek religious liberty alone. Rather, the civil government's insurance of religious liberty in the temporal realm was to provide a secure and favorable environment from which to display and deliver an eternal message of salvation from the bondage of sin through the Savior, Jesus Christ.

"Whether it was the Anglicans of Virginia, the Puritans of New England, the Catholics of Maryland, the Presbyterian of the Carolinas, the Separatists of Rhode Island or the Quakers of Pennsylvania—reliance upon Christ's commission to the church united them all. This fact is significant historically and eschatologically (evaluating end-time events), because it provides indisputable documentary evidence that the real purpose for the colonizing of America was a missionary one, to extend the Christian faith to a people who did not know God."[452]

"Undoubtedly many who came to America were not motivated by this noble purpose. And . . . those who came with that purpose oftentimes failed to carry it out. Notwithstanding the failures of men . . . God has honored the dedication of America's early founders by sending revival to America generation after generation and by establishing her as the greatest missionary nation that the world has ever known. The recitation of the Great Commission is important also politically and legally, for it has provided the only foundation upon which the United States of America may claim its legitimacy as a nation."[453]

THE COMMISSION AND BROKEN COVENANT

A few years ago, while waiting for my connecting flight in the Cincinnati airport, I became engaged in conversation with a gentleman sitting near me. As we briefly discussed our basic travel purposes, he indicated that he was from Zimbabwe in Africa, and then he quietly queried me with words that continue to haunt my heart, ringing a warning in my ears. Here are his simple words.

When I was younger, missionaries came to my country from America. We would ask them how it was that America was so great and prosperous. And they would always say, "America is blessed because she and her people love and obey God." Sir, would you tell me what has happened to America? We in Zimbabwe are very concerned about America.

Talk about a blow to American pride! But in truth, it is more an observation of fundamental failure of American purpose. Failure to fulfill our great commission, in whole or in part, lies at the root of our current cultural anguish. The languishing of the American dream is rooted in loss of the true American vision. The American vision is deeply connected to an understanding of covenant.

"The legacy of Puritan New England to this nation, which can still be found (if we look closely) at the core of our American way of life, may be summed up in one word: *covenant*."[454] Covenant implies absolute commitment. Although men may break their contracts, they are bound to keep their covenants. The concept of covenant was at the very core of our earliest founder's theology. Liberty itself was intimately laced to our covenant both with God and with each other. This fact prompted John Winthrop, attorney and first governor of the Massachusetts Bay colony, to warn, "This liberty you are to stand for with the hazard of your lives."[455]

"Covenant speaks of total commitment to Christ and to one another which is deeper and more demanding than most of us today are willing to make. And as a consequence, most of us modern American Christians are of little use to God in the building of His Kingdom. For the building of that Kingdom, as the Puritans demonstrated, requires total commitment."[456]

Fulfillment of the Great Commission was an essential element of our earliest founders' covenant with God. They saw themselves as covenantally commissioned. Every covenant has a benefit and a burden. Repeatedly throughout the Scriptures God declares, "If you . . . then I. . . ." For this reason, John Winthrop, in his "A Model of Christian Charity," which was written before disembarking on American shores, to guide the lives and intentions of four boat-loads of Puritans, warned,

> Thus stands the case between God and us. We are entered into covenant with Him for this work. We have taken out a commission.
>
> But if we neglect to observe these articles . . . and—dis-sembling with our God—shall embrace this present world and prosecute our carnal intentions, seeking great things for ourselves and our posterity, *the Lord will surely break out in wrath against us and be revenged on such a perjured people, and He will make us pay the price of the breach of such covenant*[457] (emphasis added).

Today, we define the "State of the Union" by the state of our economy. If the economy is strong, we declare the Union strong. But for Winthrop or any of our other early American fathers, the condition of the Union was defined by commitment to the covenant. If we fail in the commission, we fail in the covenant. Such failure is not without consequence.

THE CONSEQUENCE OF BROKEN COVENANT

Just as a breach of contract results in civil damages, so a breach of covenant incurs consequences. A covenant is a cousin to a vow, and both temporal and eternal consequences flow from its breach.[458] For generations, we Americans have gradually lost our sense of commitment, having abandoned God's concept of covenant. We do well to take heed to the prophetic words of the Godly governor who for the first thirty years guided the Massachusetts Bay colony.

If we deal falsely with our God in this work we have undertaken and so cause him to withdraw His present help from us:

- We shall be made a story and a byword throughout the world.

- We shall open the mouths of enemies to speak evil of the ways of God and all believers in God.

- We shall shame the faces of many of God's worthy servants and cause their prayers to be turned into curses upon us, till we are forced out of the new land.[459]

Winthrop's words require a moment of solemn reflection, don't they? Could his words of warning be operative in our culture nearly four hundred years after he spoke them? Pause with me for a moment of soul-searching.

- We are, as a nation, becoming increasingly "a story and a byword" throughout the world. We are despised for our pride, derided for our morals, and denigrated for our materialism.

- We have, as a nation, "opened the mouths of enemies to speak evil of the ways of God." While professing to be a nation "under God," we have the highest rates of social breakdown among the industrialized nations, including:

1. the highest divorce rate,
2. the highest murder rate,
3. the highest violent crime rate,
4. the highest illegitimacy rate, and
5. the highest sexually-transmitted disease rate.[460]

- We are "shaming the faces of many of God's worthy servants." Pulpits that once flamed with a call to righteousness now flow with a call to political correctness. The pursuit of happiness has replaced the pursuit of holiness, and the fear of man has preempted the fear of God. Because "the fear of the Lord is the beginning of wisdom,"[461] having lost holy fear, "we are confounded," and "shame hath covered our faces."[462]

Having failed increasingly in our purpose, we are also failing in our promise. Destiny now awaits our decision. Will *We the people* re-embrace our founding purpose, or will we pursue personal pleasure and its illusive perks? Destiny is written in our decision.

We the people begins with you and with me. We cannot look to "the other guy." Each of us must decide. America's hope—or horror—is resident in each of our hearts. For the God who "made and preserved us a nation" declared,

> *Every branch in me that beareth not fruit he taketh away.*[463]

It has oft been said, "To whom much is given, much is required."[464] That principle is as true of nations as it is of individuals. In God's eyes, all nations are as "a drop in the bucket" and are "counted to him as less than nothing."[465] That principle is true as well of the land of the Stars and Stripes, the world's only remaining superpower. Our promise and our hope is predicated upon fulfilling our God-given purpose. Will we do it? Will you? Do you personally know this God who "hath made and preserved us a nation"?[466]

THE COMMISSION OR THE CURSE

This matter of national purpose becomes increasingly, if not intensely, personal. I can deny the commission or embrace it. I can believe *in* God, but refuse to believe Him. Could it be that belief in God is killing America?

If I claim to believe in God, but demonstrate my disagreement with Him by refusing to do what He requires of me in the Scriptures, has not my claim of belief actually been deceptive? Could it be that *We the people* have, for at least two generations, so drifted from our spiritual understanding that, while claiming to believe "IN" God, we profoundly disagree with Him as evidenced by our personal and corporate attitudes and behavior? What might be the consequences of such a disconnect between alleged purpose and actual practice? Could it result in both a personal and a collective curse?

Indeed, a direct connection does exist between the curse that we are experiencing as a nation and our failure to fulfill our Great Commission. Pollster George Gallup Jr. alludes to the cause of this "curse" when he notes that although "Americans today appear to be just as attached to religion as they were a half-century ago (96 percent)," "only 13 percent of Americans have what might be called a truly transforming faith, manifested in measurable attitudinal and behavioral ways." He acknowledges that we are a "churched" nation, having "a belief in God, but a lack of trust in God."[467]

On the surface, such a condition seems impossible. Americans have more Bibles per capita than the people of any other nation on the face of the earth. *We the people* worship in at least 350,000 professing Christian congregations. Our senses are bombarded with messages from more than two thousand Christian radio stations and perhaps a similar number of Christian television outlets. And the three-billion-dollar-per-year "Christian" publishing industry is so lucrative that it is being bought out piece-by-piece by secular media. We are obese with biblical information but lack spiritual transformation.

"Something is terribly wrong," observes Dr. Michael Brown in his book *The End of the American Gospel Enterprise*.[468] Indeed something is terribly wrong, and it connects with our reformatting the Great Commission into what professing Christians have deemed to be a marketable version of truth for our time.

"The test of the vitality of a religion can be seen in its impact on culture," wrote Elton Trueblood.[469] Now, "the measure of the decadence of American culture can be seen in its impact on Christian character."[470] How does this curse connect with the Great Commission? This Great Commission of which we speak, set forth succinctly by Christ following his crucifixion in Matthew 28:18–20, is twofold in nature:

1. *Go ye therefore and make disciples.*
2. *Teach them to obey everything I have commanded.*

The American "Gospel Enterprise"—whether liberal, evangelical, or fundamental—has, for at least two generations, embraced the first half of this commission while neglecting the heart of the call. We have, in essence, engaged in making converts but have fundamentally failed in making disciples. We have evangelized, but we have not done the harder and more basic work of teaching converts to obey Christ's commands. Why? Because obedience doesn't market well in modern America. Yet, Christ himself made clear the most essential qualification for discipleship—obedience: "If you love Me, keep My commandments."[471]

This fact might seem entirely too "religious" for some people because we have drifted so far from the memory of our founding purpose. But recollection of our purpose must be restored if we are to have real hope. Weighing in on this issue, America's most prolific syndicated columnist, Cal Thomas, observes,

> In what has come to be known as "The Great Commission,"
> Jesus put discipleship at the head of his list of priorities. . . .

We have too often had other priorities. That is why the Church of Jesus Christ lacks . . . the power to transform lives.

But we must start with ourselves before we can transform others. Why is there so much apathy? The answer is that there are too few disciples. We prefer a "low-fat" Jesus who doesn't require us to make disciples.[472]

How has this failure to disciple affected our country? By any measure of numerical majority, with 96 percent of the American people professing to be Christian, America has been fully evangelized and could be called a Christian nation. But, as James Russell points out in his *Awakening the Giant*, "by any measure of obedience to the commandments of Jesus Christ as the Christian standard, the United States could be called a heathen nation."[473] What we have failed to realize is that what we are in reality in the church house is what we read about daily in our newspapers, what is taking place in the White House and in the school house. We are, in fact, unwittingly exporting this heathen or pagan version of the gospel to the entire world.

So profound is this undiscipled condition in our land that pollster George Barna laments, "You might say we are among the spiritually undeveloped nations of the planet."[474] "The most persistent, perplexing, demanding question of all is this: With all this widespread belief in Jesus, how can we as a nation be in the advanced stages of moral decline?"[475]

The ancient prophet Daniel gives us hope in the midst of such horror. His own nation had lost purpose and hope. He lamented,

O Lord, to us belongeth confusion of face, to our kings, to our princes, and to our fathers, because we have sinned against thee. . . . Neither have we obeyed the voice of the Lord our God, to walk in his

laws. . . . Yea, all Israel have transgressed thy law . . . therefore the curse is poured upon us . . ."[476] (Daniel 9:8–11).

FROM CURSE TO BLESSING

"What a nation needs more than anything else," writes the former president of Zambia, "is not a Christian ruler in the palace but a Christian prophet within earshot."[477] Strange voices are now stepping into the church's silence to "disciple" the staggering nation. *Time* warns that "many are traveling from church to church or faith to faith, sampling creeds, shopping for a custom-made God,"[478] one made in our own image. Even *New Age* warns, "We expect to be entertained, and spiritual discipline isn't often entertaining." "Picking and choosing from an array of religions [or from a smorgasbord of Christian promises without obedience] may be tempting, but it can also cheat you out of the chance for real transformation."[479]

America's promise rests in re-embracing our purpose. Hope lies in fulfilling our purpose. Parents, let us dare to disciple our sons and daughters in true and clear obedience to the Word of our God, who "hath made and preserved us a nation." Pastors, preaching to and teaching your parishioners the whole truth might not be popular, but it has promise. Only a discipled nation at home can disciple the nations abroad. Destiny knocks at your door.

Let George Gallup Jr., America's best-known pollster, address pastor, people, and president alike, declaring our hope:

> Whatever strategies are developed to revitalize religious faith in our churches and in society as a whole, they should be considered with urgency. The observation that the church is "only one generation from extinction" applies today as perhaps never before.[480]

For Such a Time As This

What is your response? Do you feel even the slightest tug on your heart? Could your purpose on earth at this critical juncture in national and world history somehow link with God's greater purposes? Maybe you do not or cannot now see the future or how you fit into God's purpose. But it is God who, by His Spirit, opens the eyes of the "blind." Blessing lies on the other side of spiritual blindness.

"Our best response is to fall on our knees and cry out, 'Forgive us, oh God! Heal our land, and give us another chance to fulfill our mission!'" "When enough of us fall on our faces before a holy and sovereign God, in brokenness . . . the church will be revived . . . the saints will live in righteousness . . . the world will be drawn to Christ . . . and will be blessed."

Dr. Bill Bright, founder and president of perhaps the largest independent ministry in the world, declared in the twilight of his life, "God will give us a second chance if we renew our covenant with Him and become, as our forefathers expressed, 'stepping stones' for the gospel to the 'remotest parts of the world.'"

"The question is," according to Dr. Bright, "Are we, like our forebears, willing to be used to that end? If we will truly return to God, we stand a second chance of seeing an era of renewal in this nation. We can yet see our homeland revived and receive the blessing God reserves for those who are faithful to Him."[481]

Will you put your heart and hands to the plow, not to restore America to her former glory but to future promise? You and I have been placed here for such a time as this.

SOUL-STIRRING QUESTIONS FOR PERSONAL AND GROUP REFLECTION

1. Do we now, or did we ever, have a national purpose?

2. What does our national heritage say about our national purpose?

3. Richard Hakluyt was known as the "Father of Colonization." What was his basis for defending the American colonization as early as 1584?

4. The First Virginia Charter was granted in 1606. What did it provide as the basis for settling the colony of Virginia, which, according to maps, comprised about 80 percent of what is now the continental United States?

5. What is the Great Commission?

6. What did the Mayflower Compact say about the Great Commission and the reason for the Pilgrim's settlement?

7. Constitutional attorney Herbert Titus stated that the Great Commission is important politically and legally, "for it has provided the only foundation upon which the United States of America may claim its legitimacy as a nation." How could he make such a bold statement? Based on what you've read in this book, does sufficient documentary evidence exist to back up that claim?

8. What did attorney John Winthrop, first governor of the Massachusetts Bay Colony, say would happen if we broke covenant with God and failed to accomplish His commission?

9. Are we experiencing the very things of which Winthrop warned?

10. If America's promise depends upon your part in fulfilling her purpose, what is America's future?

Chapter 19

DECISION
AND DESTINY

TEARS STAINED THE PAGES AS this chapter was being written. Our heritage, hopes, and hearts connect here with the heart of God because America will be restored, not on our terms but on God's terms. If, as Francis Scott Key declared, God is the "power that hath made" us a nation, then He is the only power that can "preserve us a nation."

"America is in danger!" declared the late Leonard Ravenhill, yet *America Is Too Young to Die.*[482] He states that "this is the most critical time in American history."[483] Will the "Land of the Free" meet her demise or fulfill her destiny?

ONE LAWYER'S LEGACY

"When he opened his mouth he was aiming a gun. When he spoke, bombardment began. The effects of his speaking were almost unparalleled in modern history. Over half a million people were converted through his ministry. . . . In an age when there were no amplifiers of mass communications, he spearheaded a revival which literally altered the course of history." Such was the description of the impact of lawyer-turned-preacher, Charles Finney.[484] According to Harvard professor Perry Miller, "Charles Grandison Finney led America out of the eighteenth century."[485]

Some people might look upon it as divine humor for God to retain a lawyer to resuscitate a nation spiritually, yet that is precisely the record of history. So astounding to saint and sinner alike were the results of Finney's pleading God's ultimate cause among a nationwide jury of American citizens that it bears a closer look for its implications in our time.

How does such a thing happen? How could city after city be turned right-side up, radically changing both powerful business moguls and busy housewives—and all that seemingly by the mere words of a lawyer who forsook his practice to plead the case of a lifetime? Let's take a moment to look over the shoulder of history at the man and his times.

The American Revolution began, for all practical purposes, with "the shot heard 'round the world" on the green at Lexington and Concord in 1775. The Revolutionary War pushed the colonists' backs against the wall. Faced with the world-dominant British Army, the rag-tag colonial regulars were no match. Time and again their disheveled troops faced imminent destruction. But for divine intervention, their doom would have been sealed. So great was the common recognition of God's hand in making and preserving the nation that General Washington, in his first inaugural address on April 30, 1789, proclaimed:

> No people can be bound to acknowledge and adore the Invisible Hand which conducts the affairs of men more than the people of the United States. Every step by which they have advanced to the character of an independent nation

seems to have been distinguished by some token of providential agency.[486]

For approximately thirteen years, the fledgling nation had felt the heat of King George's Redcoats. The colonists and their commander-in-chief had cried out to God for power, purity, and preservation. By the time of the Constitutional Convention, political pursuits quickly took preeminence over matters of faith. In 1787, when Benjamin Franklin, not generally known for his spirituality, stood before the Constitutional Convention after its delegates had for six weeks wrangled fruitlessly, it must have truly embarrassed many of the delegates when he reminded them,

> In the beginning of our contest with Great Britain, when we were sensible of danger, we had daily prayer in this room for the Divine protection. Our prayers, Sir, were heard, and they were graciously answered. . . . And have we forgotten this powerful Friend? Or do we imagine we no longer need his assistance?[487]

In his January 1, 1795, Thanksgiving Proclamation, President Washington warned the people of their national proclivity to wander in pride under the blessings of prosperity. He called upon the "kind Author of these blessings graciously to prolong them to us; to preserve us from the arrogance of prosperity, and from . . . delusive pursuits. . . ."[488]

Celebrating the bicentennial of the landing of the Pilgrims, Daniel Webster, one of the greatest of America's orators, warned on December 22, 1820, "If we abide by the principles taught in the Bible, our country will go on prospering . . . , but if we and our posterity neglect its instructions and authority, no man can tell how sudden a catastrophe may overwhelm us and bury all our glory in profound obscurity."[489]

Unfortunately, as with ancient Israel, our nation and her people drifted. The Industrial Revolution began to swing into full gear. Early nineteenth-century America was on the move to a degree undreamed of by previous generations. But the people forgot the God "who hath made and preserved us a nation." There was a wilderness to conquer, money to make, empires to build. The nation was losing her men to mammon.

How did God get America's attention? He retained Charles Grandison Finney for the task.

"Charles Finney was unquestionably the most impressive religious revolutionary that America ever produced."[490] America would never again be the same. Finney, whose father had been a soldier in Washington's Continental Army, had almost no religious training as a child. At age sixteen, he became a rural schoolmaster, but in 1818 he was persuaded to enter the legal profession. A leading New York attorney, Judge Benjamin Wright, opened his office to the twenty-six-year-old law student. Although an admitted heathen, Finney's heart yearned for truth and that the God of which he read privately in the Bible would become real.

The evening of October 7, 1821, changed history. Said Finney, "I made up my mind that I would settle the question of my soul's salvation at once . . . and make peace with God."[491] In his law office late one night, he "wept like a child," repenting of sin in his life.

God stirred another fire within Finney almost immediately. His memoirs record, "I received a mighty baptism of the Holy Ghost. Without ever having any thought that there was such a thing . . . the Holy Spirit descended upon me . . . like a wave of electricity . . . in waves of liquid love. . . . It seemed like the very breath of God."[492]

City after city shortly felt that electricity as the love of God was poured out in power, like a flame from his mouth. The Second

Great Awakening, the most powerful spiritual revival in America's history, spanning twenty-five years, was launched with Finney's ordination in 1824. Rochester, New York, would never again be the same.

THE ROCHESTER REVOLUTION: "UNPARALLELED IN CHURCH HISTORY"

America was exploding. New towns sprang up almost overnight. One of those towns was Rochester, New York, which in 1812 was unbroken wilderness, but by 1830, it had become a booming marketing and manufacturing center.[493] In Finney's words, Rochester "was a young city, full of growth and ambition, and full of sin. The inhabitants were intelligent and enterprising in the highest degree."[494]

Finney had, at that time, planned to go to Utica, where he was expected to start meetings. He had declined going to Rochester because of its perceived spiritual resistance. But God changed his mind during the night.

"I felt ashamed to shrink from undertaking the difficulties,"[495] he told his wife. Meetings were begun at Third Presbyterian Church, where they had extended an invitation but were without a minister and "religion was in a low state."

Mrs. M——, the wife of a prominent lawyer in that city, was one of the first converts. Said Finney, "She was a women of high standing, a lady of culture and influence. The lady who introduced her was a Christian woman who had found that she was very troubled and persuaded her to come. . . ." "Mrs. M—— had been a worldly woman, very fond of society . . . a very proud woman." She afterward told Finney that when she first came to Rochester, "she greatly regretted it and feared there would be a revival, which would greatly interfere with her pleasures and amusements."[496] But the pride of her heart broke, and "with tears streaming down," she turned her face toward heaven.

The conversion of Mrs. M—— caused much excitement in Rochester. Finney's meetings were thronged with lawyers, physicians, and merchants. Lawyers, especially, became anxious about their souls. It was like a spiritual explosion. For weeks, as Finney preached, people from all walks of life flooded in to have their hearts reborn and revived. Letters went far and near. The work spread like waves in every direction to surrounding states.

"The great majority of the leading men and women of the city were converted."[497] "As the revival swept through the town, converting most of the influential people, the change in the city's order, sobriety, and morality was wonderful."[498]

Finney spent six months in Rochester, but the transforming power of that spiritual revival endures, by the testimony of its citizens, to this day. Rochester, in two unusual studies done half a century apart, was designated "The Kindest City in America." In a feature article, *Reader's Digest* proclaimed Rochester "the most caring city in America." According to this heart-stirring, nation-inspiring study, "Charles Grandison Finney's coming to town was the pivotal experience that changed Rochester. . . ." He scorched their consciences," "angrily denounced the evils of selfishness and deliberately aimed his message at the wealthy and powerful."[499]

It was Rochester's moral and spiritual rebirth. Now Rochester is a city of more than a quarter million people and home to some of America's greatest corporations, and "Finney's powerful message is still felt." "Generation after generation stayed in the city and preserved the Finney legacy." "Rochester became a city where love for one's fellow man was more than an empty phrase."[500]

CAN HISTORY REPEAT ITSELF?

What about your city? Has your heart been stirred? Is Los Angeles, Portland, Houston, or Boston beyond the reach of the God who revived Rochester? If God can revive Rochester, can He revive America? Is there any other hope to prevent our moral and spiritual demise?

Revival always produces reaction. Finney minced no words. He was direct and forceful. Clergy and laity alike criticized him for his confrontational approach to preaching. Said a banker, a leading citizen of Utica, New York, when he first heard Finney, "That man is mad, and I should not be surprised if he set the town on fire." He refused to attend the meetings but later affirmed to the director of the bank, "Say what you will, there is something very remarkable in the state of things at Rome. Certainly no human power or eloquence has produced what we see there. . . . There is no accounting for that . . . unless there is something divine in it." Shortly afterward, he was converted.[501]

What would it take for God truly to touch you? What would He have to do to reach you in the deepest recesses of your heart? Are you and I different than the spiritually numbed but busy and entrepreneurial citizens of Rochester—the lawyers, doctors, bankers, pastors, and printers? Our hope and healing has always been revealed in revival, and it will dramatically change our lives. As the late Leonard Ravenhill declared, "Revival shatters the status quo. We can no more have a Spirit-born revival without a moral and spiritual upheaval than we can have an earthquake without destruction." The preservation of the nation demands nothing less than a great spiritual awakening. "America," says Ravenhill, "is too young to die."[502]

EFFECTS OF THE SECOND GREAT AWAKENING

Charles Finney was the galvanizing force of the Second Great Awakening. His revival meetings covered cities, small and great, in most of the industrializing states in pre-Civil War America. "No more impressive revival has occurred in American history. . . ."[503]

What happened in Rochester was the fullest expression of what took place elsewhere, righting that which was wrong among *We the people*. As was said of Rochester, so could be said in a modified manner of the nation:

> The atmosphere . . . seemed to be affected. You could not go upon the streets, and hear any conversations, except on religion. The entire character of the city was modified because so many of the converts were leaders of the community, who "would remake society and politics. . . ." The man who became district attorney soon after the revival [spoke] concerning the drop in the crime rate not only in 1821 but for years afterward.[504]

Whereas Finney was the most enduring focus of the Second Great Awakening, Lyman Beecher of Boston inherited the mantle as the evangelical leader of the awakening. He had many a dispute with Finney over methods and message, but ultimately he concluded that the Rochester revival was the greatest work of God, and the greatest revival of religion, that the world has ever seen in such a short time. "One hundred thousand," he said, "were connected with churches as a result of that great revival. This is unparalleled in the history of the church. . . ."[505]

The denominations—Baptist, Methodist, Presbyterian, and Congregational—exploded. The Baptists multiplied eight hundred fold in fifty years. Bible societies were founded. Ministries to the nation's social concerns were raised.

"The Second Great Awakening brought massive and permanent changes to this country and the world," including fueling the abolitionist movement. Finney did not hesitate to denounce slavery as sin. "The considerable excitement that Finney's preaching stirred up resulted indirectly in Harriet Beecher Stowe's *Uncle Tom's Cabin* and a ground swell of anti-slavery sentiment that rapidly led to Abraham Lincoln's *Emancipation Proclamation* and the end of slavery."[506] "*Uncle Tom's Cabin* sold more books following its publication in 1852 than almost any other book up to that time in the history of American publishing."[507]

Harriet Beecher Stowe concluded *Uncle Tom's Cabin* with words that could well fuel a new and desperately needed awakening in our own time if we have ears to hear and hearts to heed.

> A day of grace is yet held out to us. Both North and South [all of us] have been guilty before God; and the Christian church has a heavy account to answer. Not by combining together, to protect injustice and cruelty, and making a common capital of sin, is this Union to be saved, but by repentance, justice and mercy.[508]

AMERICA'S GATHERING STORM

The Second Great Awakening prepared the rapidly expanding nation for a brewing war, the most destructive war in American history. We refer to it as the Civil War, but it was far from civil. The blood of at least six hundred thousand of America's choicest men soaked American soil to wash away the stain of slavery. States' rights and personal rights were both at stake. Had it not been for the grace of God in spiritually preparing the hearts and souls of the people for more than twenty-five years leading up to that tumultuous storm, it is highly questionable whether the country would have survived. But a silver lining was behind the dark cloud of war that threatened to tear the nation apart.

Marching back in time just under a century, another dark cloud could be seen rising over the American horizon. The colonists were increasingly antagonized by the actions and attitudes of King George and the British Parliament. Tensions were mounting and had become explosive. But another development within and among the colonists themselves also threatened their survival.

Trouble brewed in the cities. The thirteen colonies now claimed a population of 1,500,000 settlers, many of whom came for purposes other than those of the founding Pilgrims and Puritans. The rising god was gold.

Slaves were being transported to America in droves. One of every six inhabitants was a slave. Prostitution proliferated. Drinking, gambling, and brawling were common pastimes. Colonial churches and their pastors were losing power to affect an increasingly worldly society. Pastors and people alike lost their memory of God's work among their forefathers. Church membership was in decline, and the impact of the Christian faith on society was decreasing radically.[509]

It had been 134 years since the men of the Virginia Company landed at Cape Henry, Jamestown, and Richmond, when Jonathan Edwards stepped, as a visiting preacher, into the pulpit at Enfield, Connecticut, on July 8, 1741. The colonies would never again be quite the same.

Reading in a monotone voice from his scripted sermon, the thirty-six-year-old preacher told the parishioners, "The wrath of God is like great waters that are dammed for the present. They increase more and more, and rise higher and higher, till an outlet is given, and the longer the stream is stopped, the more rapid and mighty its course, when once it is let loose."

One eyewitness observed, "Before the sermon was done, there was a great groaning and crying out through ye whole House."

Edwards concluded that day, "Let everyone that is out of Christ now awake and fly from the wrath to come."[510] And awake they did!

That sermon, "Sinners in the Hands of an Angry God," became the most noted sermon in American history. A single revival sermon caused a tidal wave throughout the colonies known as the First Great Awakening. Tens of thousands of people fell on their faces in repentance. Christians were revived. Pagans were converted. John Wesley, the father of "Methodism," preached powerfully throughout the colonies, followed by the impassioned George Whitfield, who "upped the ante" as thousands upon thousands of people cried out in deep contrition for God's mercy. The hearts of the people were being prepared for the conflict just ahead that would determine the nation's destiny—the Revolutionary War.

Only two major wars have been fought on American soil: the Revolutionary War and the Civil War. It has been one hundred and thirty-five years since the last war was fought to "preserve us a nation." Is another storm gathering? Will it be civil war, foreign attack, or both? Or is the greatest battle already within our gates, destroying the moral and spiritual fiber of our people like an insidious and aggressive cancer? Only time will tell, but time may be short. A rising chorus of voices is lifting again from the fruited plain, calling for massive spiritual revival. Increasingly, the message is clear: "Revival, or perish."

RED SKY IN THE MORNING

It is amazing how ancient sailors, without technological tools, were able to determine weather patterns and sailing schedules, deciding their course and destiny by reading the skies. Their sage wisdom is best expressed in the familiar proverb:

A red sky at night is the sailors delight.
A red sky in the morning is the sailor's warning.

As he taught the people, Jesus Christ, referring to this ancient meteorological wisdom, rebuked the religious leaders of his day, saying, "Ye can discern the face of the sky; but can ye not discern the signs of the times?"[511]

That question echoes provocatively to our times. If anyone should discern the nature and relative position of their time, in light of both history and eternity, it should be our leaders, especially our religious or Christian leaders. Yet, the Scriptures of old reveal that in times of profound moral and spiritual decay, it becomes "like people, like priest."[512]

In such a time, God raised up a prophetic voice to pierce the darkening night. A.W. Tozer notes in his foreword to *Why Revival Tarries,*

God has always had His specialists whose chief concern has been the moral breakdown, the decline in the spiritual health of the nation or the church. These appeared at critical moments in history to reprove, rebuke, and exhort in the name of God and righteousness.

"Such a man," said Tozer, "was likely to be drastic, radical, possibly at times violent, and the curious crowd that gathered to watch him work soon branded him as extreme, fanatical, negative.

He was simpleminded, severe, fearless, and these were the qualities the circumstances demanded. He shocked some, frightened others and alienated not a few, but he knew who had called him and what he was sent to do. His ministry was geared to the emergency, and that fact marked him out as different, a man apart."[513]

For this reason, in his *America Is Too Young to Die*, the late Leonard Ravenhill states, "In a day of faceless politicians and voiceless preachers, there is not a more urgent national need than that we cry to God for a prophet!"[514]

Are we in such a day? If so, what sign in our national "sky" would demand such an urgent call?

The founder and president of perhaps the largest independent ministry in America and the world declared in 1998, "A red sky is rising in our nation, warning all who read the signs that we are indeed on the verge of moral and spiritual collapse." "America," says Dr. Bill Bright, "has only two choices: continue in its ungodly path to destruction, or respond to God's call for repentance." "Today," he warns, "we stand on the brink of decision."[515]

That decision for destiny will be made first by those manning America's lighthouse. Yet, in the remote recesses of our hearts, we must all reach the conviction that a nation can, indeed, shipwreck. Without that profound witness in the heart and mind of *We the people*, history and human nature testify that we will change neither our personal ways nor the course of this great ship of state.

What will it take to touch our hearts and minds? What more evidence is required to bring us, both individually and collectively, to see the red sky rising high on the national horizon? What can you do? What must we do? What does it mean to repent? Could the message of the Titanic open our understanding, dismissing the illusion that a technologized salvation might deliver us from the iceberg of moral and spiritual decadence?

Soul-Stirring Questions for Personal and Group Reflection

1. Why might Leonard Ravenhill write *America Is Too Young to Die?* Do you agree with him that "this is the most critical time in American history"? Why, or why not?

2. Harvard professor Perry Miller, said, "Charles Grandison Finney led America out of the eighteenth century." Why would God retain a lawyer to spiritually resuscitate the soul of a nation? Why did He inspire attorney Francis Scott Key to give us our national motto, "In God we trust"? Why did He embolden attorney Abraham Lincoln to emancipate slaves and declare, "This nation, under God, shall have a new birth of freedom"? Why did He empower attorney John Winthrop to write, "A Model of Christian Charity" and to set the vision for a "City Upon a Hill"?

3. How did God use Charles Finney to renew America's soul?

4. Would you like to see your city experience the "Rochester Revolution"?

5. What will it take for God to reach you and renew your soul? Does your soul need renewing?

6. What might you expect to happen if the soul of *We the people* was truly renewed?

7. A rising chorus of voices is echoing across the fruited plain: "Spiritual revival, or perish." Do you agree?

8. Dr. Bill Bright writes, "A red sky is rising in our nation, warning we are on the brink of moral and spiritual collapse." He continues, "We stand on the brink of decision." What decisions must you make for your own destiny and that of our nation?

If America is to correct her course,
I must correct my course.

Chapter 20

CHANGING COURSE: CAN A NATION SHIPWRECK?

FEW CATASTROPHES CAPTURE THE IMAGINA-TION like a catastrophe at sea. The memory of the sinking of the *Titanic* in freezing Atlantic waters now spans three generations. It is a vivid reminder that despite man's best efforts, his dream of creating the unsinkable ship remains an illusion. A sinking feeling grips the pit of the stomach as the mind reflects on men and women scrambling frantically for lifeboats that don't exist. The agonized cries of mothers pierce the darkness as they search for children lost in the mad scramble for self-preservation. The dream has become a nightmare.

TITANIC MEMORIES

"When Edith Brown Haisman last saw her daddy nearly 90 years ago, he was standing on deck, smoking a cigar and smiling at his wife and daughter. 'I'll see you in New York,' he said confidently, as his family was bundled into Lifeboat No. 14." As *Newsweek* reported, "There had been no sense of urgency when the Titanic first struck an iceberg. . . ." "Everyone kept saying, *She's unsinkable*," recalled Haisman, then over 100. She wondered why they were abandoning the most magnificent moveable thing ever built. . . . Not until she was lowered into the 28-degree ocean did she see how much of the 882-foot liner was underwater."[516]

Indeed, viewpoint does determine destiny. Changed perspective can prescribe changed response.

Huddled together against the cold, in profound silence, Haisman and her mother watched as the band played the hymn "Nearer My God To Thee." "The lights flicked out and in a thunderous roar, everything on the supership seemed to break loose." "The black hull tilted perpendicularly; its three great propellers reared against the heavens. And then it was gone, along with Mr. Brown. . . ."[517]

Such wrenching memories were renewed in the recasting of *Titanic* on celluloid during the closing moments of the twentieth century. Pleasure and pride were together swallowed by the great deep as 1522 souls were lost. It seemed impossible! But in the darkness of the night, the ship began taking on water despite the best opinions and inspections of experts.

Slowly at first. Then with accelerating speed the ship took on water. The bilge pumps were no match. The pounding force of the unrelenting sea caused the unsinkable ship to pitch violently, then to list. Men and women trampled over one another to reach the deck. Some screamed in agony as bodies were crushed and broken; others whimpered in fear. Few escaped. Children and parents disappeared into the darkness forever. Business tycoons, political power brokers, and common citizens perished together. And the mind gropes to provide solace for a heart that struggles to fathom the agony of such disaster. The unthinkable happened to the unsinkable.

It was called "A Night to Remember." Indeed, seventeen movies, eighteen documentaries, and at least one hundred thirty books detailed the disaster. Historian Steven Biel notes the horror of the *Titanic* to be one of "the three most written-about subjects of all time," trailing "Jesus and the Civil War." "It's a moment in time that encapsulates what life is about." "It took nearly three hours to sink," "during which people—rich and poor, young and old—had to make choices. . . ."[518]

And so America, the land of opportunity, similarly struggles on the edge of a new millennium to keep her ship of state righted amidst the raging seas of individualistic morality and pluralistic thinking. Her hold of truth has taken on the water of "everything goes" faster than her citizens can bail. Her people surge toward the upper decks in vain search for the welcome glimmer of the lighthouse that would warn of impending disaster on the shoals of moral and spiritual relativism and guide them to safety. We all—both rich and poor, young and old—face choices.

Fear grips the American heart. Mothers weep for children trampled in the mad pursuit of parents seeking self-expression. A growing number of our citizens plunder and brutalize, like pirates, taking advantage of the chaos and weakness. For many people, the faint glimmer of hope of rescue has long-since faded. It's every man for himself. Many other people whimper privately, resigned to their fate. Still others further demoralize the rest with vain promises of political saviors who will allegedly deliver us from the consequences of our collective resistance to and rebellion against the true Savior, who promised to save us if we would only submit to His rule.

PERSPECTIVE PRESCRIBES CHOICES AND COURSES

The story is told of the captain of a great battleship that was making its way through the murky fog as night deepened. His radar beam picked up a distant object in the water. As a good captain should, he crisply warned, "Change course twenty degrees."

The response from the blip on the radar screen was polite, but firm. "Thank you for advising of your position, but *you* must correct course twenty degrees."

The captain, a bit indignant, again barked his order on his radio, "Correct your course twenty degrees. We are rapidly approaching!" But the sharpness of his tone seemed to have no effect.

"I'm sorry, sir, but you must change *your* course."

The captain was outraged by this affront to his stature and authority. He reared up with pride in his position and confidence in his craft. "Correct your course twenty degrees," he insisted. "This is a battleship!"

"No, sir, correct your course," crackled the radio. "This is a lighthouse!"

We the people stand tall in our national pride as we lumber like a great battleship through the fog of enlightenment thinking that enshrouds us. Convinced that we can rely upon our historical power and political prowess, we are plowing through heavy seas that pound our decks and already have swept many people overboard.

"This is America," we assure ourselves, and we dismiss those who crackle warnings to us as mere lightweights, extremists, or fanatics who have no legitimate standing to comment on matters of national life and direction. Meanwhile, this great ship of state plows forward in self-delusion, blithely unaware that the very life of the nation and her people lies in the balance as we barrel forward on a collision course for shipwreck on the rocks of faithlessness.

Truth lies trampled in the streets of a nation whose first president "could not tell a lie." As writer David Wells declared in the title of his recent book, there is "No Place for Truth." So life careens into an endless and tumultuous sea that has no absolutes suitable for anchor, and we have no compass with which to gain a clear perspective and no maps with which to chart our direction. We are plunging recklessly and almost frantically into uncharted waters, oblivious to where we are headed.

Together, we have been cut loose on the sea of relativity, and we are in desperate need of a beacon from God's lighthouse—the truth from a God who does not change with every vacillation of human experience, a truth that can steer us clear of the looming shoals of personal and national destruction.

WHERE IS THE LIGHTHOUSE?

Recently, I stood on Tybee Island near that romantic city of the Old South, Savannah, Georgia. Jutting above the rocky shoreline stood one of America's oldest lighthouses. Completed in 1736, it was one of the first public structures in the original thirteen colonies. Its beam is visible for seventeen miles.

As I gazed at its simple yet regal bearing high above the landscape, I thought of God's lighthouse that graced our eastern shoreline a century before: the Christian church. My heart was broken and torn as I considered the condition of that lighthouse today. The foundations of truth have been questioned and compromised even by the pastors, priests, and people who purport to man the light-house. America's pulpits have become the place of poise for spiritual chameleons seeking to blend with contemporary culture, leading whole congregations of Christian chameleons to blend, without identity, into the warp and woof of a society that desperately needs the transforming, purifying, cleansing, preserving, and enlightening power and presence of a Holy God walking in the shoes of those who call themselves by His name.

It is time for our spiritual leaders once again to lead instead of following popular culture while cloaking it in religious jargon. But it is not just pastors, priests, and potentates who are caught in the vortex of the storm. We are all caught, to one degree or another, in the swirling waters of unbelief and its consequences. We now run frantically to and fro in search of surrogate truth. Having rejected the absolute truth upon which we could build our lives and preserve a nation, we search for a plethora of therapeutic remedies to make us feel better and help us cope. But it isn't working. We seek therapy rather than truth. The consequences are enormous—we are threatened with shipwreck.

Yet there is hope! Although severely tossed and buffeted by howling winds on the sea of relativity, we have not yet capsized. Although the line to the anchor of truth has grown threadbare, it has not yet broken completely, and we have not yet run aground. A faint though flickering glimmer from the lighthouse can still be seen through the fog. And, in the words of one of America's favorite gospel songs, "If it weren't for the lighthouse, where would this ship be?"

Where will this ship called *America* be if the light in the church house of America does not again blaze brightly and broadly—and quickly? Even as the nation is *We the people,* so the church is merely people—those of us who profess to be the sons and daughters of

God the Father through faith in Christ. We have been called "the light of the world,"[519] but, in the words of Christ, "If the light that is in thee be darkness, how great is that darkness."[520] What will turn us? The captain of the *Titanic* faced a gut-wrenching issue. Unfortunately, he placed his trust in technology before he faced the truth. *We're unsinkable,* he thought. *That's what everyone says.* And so he plunged confidently full speed ahead in troubled waters, oblivious to the dangers of which he had been warned. Then came the chilling words "Iceberg ahead!" It was immediate impending disaster . . . a confrontation of technology with truth. Blithe confidence quickly waned.

The spine-tingling interchange between the captain and the crew as portrayed in the sound track of an earlier film depicting the terror aboard the *Titanic* at the moment of truth will echo into eternity.

Captain: Come on! Come on! Turn. What's taking her so long? Turn! Turn!

Crew (in chaos): Hey, what's happening?

(NOTE: Why is it that the truth of what was happening did not register immediately? They knew that they were surging full speed through waters that were dangerously strewn with major icebergs.)

Crew Member: I'm closing the water-tight doors.

First Mate to Captain: We struck something, Sir. I'm afraid she's hit it.

Captain's Response: *In silent shock, he whispers.* Dearest God. Impossible! This cannot have happened!

A living, vibrant, Bible-believing, God-obeying church that stands against the tide of popular culture, disbelief, technological idolatry, and self-exaltation is America's only true hope. Only such a people who themselves turn can begin the timely turning of a nation that is plunging blindly full speed ahead to her destruction. May the light in the lighthouse be turned on once again, blazing the light of God's truth from sea to shining sea. And may it begin with you and me.

SOUL-STIRRING QUESTIONS FOR PERSONAL AND GROUP REFLECTION

1. Do you believe that a nation can shipwreck?

2. What similarities do you see between the Titanic and America?

3. Can the unthinkable really happen to the unsinkable?

4. Are you among those who think, *This is America! Destruction could never happen to us?*

5. Do you agree that the Christian church was historically the moral and spiritual lighthouse of our nation? If so, what made her that lighthouse?

6. According to the *Los Angeles Times*, 78 percent of Americans believe that America is in severe moral crisis. Do you agree? Do you believe that this statistic also reflects an underlying severe spiritual crisis?

7. How have changes in the Christian church, the lives of those of us who profess to be Christians, contributed to muting the warning, clarifying, and purifying light that our nation needs?

8. What would be necessary for the light in the lighthouse to be turned on once again for a new spiritual awakening that would renew the soul of America?

9. Are you willing to change your own course? Or are you among the 89 percent of all Americans who continue to believe that their life and ways have nothing to do with the profound moral and spiritual problems in our land?

10. If America collapses, will you join the captain of the *Titanic*, saying in silent shock, "Dearest God. Impossible!"?

If I would see the light, I must be a light.

Chapter 21

THE LIGHTHOUSE

". . . as one small candle may light a thousand, may the light kindled here shine unto many, yea in some sort to our whole nation."

—William Bradford (1647)
Of Plymouth Plantation

THE MESSAGE OF THIS BOOK began with a lighthouse and concludes with a lighthouse. The Statue of Liberty that "spoke" to us in chapter 1 is undoubtedly the world's most recognizable and famous lighthouse. As its light blazes from under the seven-spiked crown in New York Harbor, the promise of political liberty and freedom is shed across the seven seas and the seven continents. But there is another lighthouse without whose light liberty becomes license and license turns to lawlessness. That lighthouse is the subject of this chapter. You might or might not have ever entered this lighthouse. But all who desire true and lasting liberty must enter it.

A fundamental rule of politics is to go to strength. So what is— or was—the strength of America? If this basic rule of politics were applied to the life of the nation as a whole, where would you expect to find it? If we can reasonably identify that strength, we can also likely identify the troubles that might be expected in the nation if that source of strength deteriorates. And having identified areas of real or potential deterioration and decay, we ought also to be able to pinpoint with some degree of precision where restoration of our former strength is required and to respond accordingly. Among a vast and nearly unending host of witnesses, two secular sources can help us identify the fundamental historical strength of our country.

THE SOURCE OF OUR STRENGTH

Five sociologists from the University of California at Berkeley set about to identify the principle threads that bound the nation together and how they affected public and private life. In researching our modern habits of the heart from coast to coast and in the context of our history and heritage, those sociologists were profoundly impressed by the observations of the French social philosopher Alexis de Tocqueville.

To refresh our thinking, perhaps a little review would be helpful. Alexis de Tocqueville came to America from France in the 1830s to study what about the nation made her great, the thing that distinguished her from France, which had politically befriended her. He compiled his several years of careful observations into his book *Democracy in America*.

In the opinion of the five Berkeley sociologists, expressed in their bestseller *Habits of the Heart*, de Tocqueville offered "the most comprehensive and penetrating analysis of the relationship between character and society in America that has ever been written."[521]

Alexis de Tocqueville came to America near the midpoint of our country's four-hundred-year history. Almost exactly two hundred years after the English attorney John Winthrop landed four boat-loads of Puritans on our eastern shores, penning his "A Model of Christian Charity," de Tocqueville stated, "I think I see the whole destiny of America contained in the first Puritans who landed on these shores."[522]

One hundred seventy years have passed since de Tocqueville came to these shores. His perspective can assist us, as we enter the third millennium of history, to regain our perspective. Carefully consider his words.

> I sought for the greatness and genius of America in her commodious harbors and her ample rivers, and it was not there; in her fertile fields and boundless prairies, and it was not there; in her rich mines and her vast world commerce, and it was not there. *Not until I went into the churches of America and heard her pulpits aflame with righteousness did I understand the secret of her genius and power.* America is great because America is good, and if America ever ceases to be good, America will cease to be great[523] (emphasis added).

The Christian church is and has always been the lighthouse of this nation. Although we enjoy freedom of religion and respect men of other faiths, it was the Christian church that sowed the seeds of America's birth vision. It was the church that nurtured those seeds during the nearly two centuries before the nation's political birth. And it is only the church that can again breathe new life into a nation that is gasping through every fiber of its being for the oxygen of faith and a flow of moral truth that will restore her character and revive her heart.

It gives great pain, however, to confess that the light in America's lighthouse, the Christian church, no longer blazes its illuminating, purifying light into our national soul. Its flickering flame reveals a cold and waning faith insufficient to fan the spiritual fire necessary to revive a foundering nation. It is not the nation, but the church, that must cry to her Lord for revival. We dare not continue to bless ourselves with blithe mantras of "God bless America" until the message of the gospel again becomes good news to the American mind and transforms the American heart.

What has happened? How has the light in the lighthouse grown so dim? Is it actually true? What incontrovertible evidence could support such an admission? If it is indeed true, what must be done to restore the light of the Christian church in America? Who bears responsibility for her waning influence, and who carries hope for her revival? These are tough but essential questions because America's survival depends on the church's revival.

Let's first briefly explore how the blazing light of the church in American society has grown dim.

DRIFT AND DESTINY

Drift can determine destiny. If the satellite trajectory of America's first moon shot had drifted off course by even one degree, we might never have heard the historic words, "One small step for man; one giant leap for mankind." Yet, somehow, we fail to rendezvous with reality when it comes to the spiritual dimension of our lives. We have convinced ourselves that we can drift off course and still connect with our intended destination.

Drift is inevitable. It happens to all individuals, institutions, and nations. And it invariably frustrates and often redefines destiny. Robert H. Bork wrote in his book *Slouching Towards Gomorrah,*

With each new evidence of deterioration, we lament for a moment, and then become accustomed to it. . . . So unrelenting is the assault on our sensibilities that many of us grow numb, finding resignation to be the rational, adaptive response to our environment that is increasingly polluted and apparently beyond our control. . . . As behavior worsens, the community adjusts to that conduct once thought reprehensible but is no longer deemed to be so.[524]

In his book *Historical Drift*, Arnold L. Cook admits, "To concede that historical drift is inevitable sounds negative. In all other aspects of life, we expect and pay professionals to tell the truth, even if its terminal. Only in the church do people want just good news. Current popular evangelical leaders skillfully downplay anything potentially negative. To affirm the inevitability of the loss of spiritual vitality falls into the unsavory category."[525] It was not always so in the land of the free, but we have drifted far from our roots.

Historical drift, declares Cook, is the inherent tendency of humans and their organizations to depart over time from their original purposes.[526] It also is the tendency to depart from and diminish values, precepts, and convictions that were once held as foundational, yes, even fundamental. The Hebrews of the Old Testament experienced such drift in almost predictable cycles. After Moses led the Israelites out of Egyptian bondage, he turned over the reigns of leadership to Joshua to lead them to the Promised Land. But the book of Judges records the tragic pattern.

The people served the Lord all the days of Joshua, and all the days of the elders that outlived Joshua, who had seen all the great works of the Lord, that He had done for Israel. . . . And there arose another generation after them, which knew not the Lord, nor yet the works which he had done for Israel. And the children of Israel did evil in the sight of the Lord. . . and they forsook the Lord God of their fathers.[527]

This pattern, or cycle, of drift was repeated over and over, from godliness to godlessness. When they lived godly lives, they were blessed; when they drifted, they suffered increasingly severe consequences. After Joshua's wholehearted Godly leadership, when the people drifted to their own devices, Scripture records,

The anger of the Lord was hot against Israel, and he delivered them into the hands of spoilers . . . so that they could not any longer stand against their enemies. . . . And they were greatly distressed.[528]

Despite their drift, God raised up judges to deliver them, but they would not listen to the judges. When a given judge was dead, "they corrupted themselves more than their fathers." "And the anger of the Lord was hot against Israel; Because that this people hath transgressed my covenant."[529]

Someone said of that lengthy period of Jewish history, "every man did that which was right in his own eyes."[530] No phrase could better describe the recent pattern of modern America from the church house to the schoolhouse to the White House.

But patterns of spiritual drift persisted in the New Testament era as well, proving that Christians can drift rapidly from truth. The apostle Paul warned the early churches continually of deception and doctrinal drift. And the apostle John, delivering the "Revelation of Jesus" within just sixty years of the death and resurrection of Christ, warned the seven churches of Asia that if they did not repent—which means to admit and turn from hearts turned cold or lukewarm back to a heart of righteousness toward God—they faced judgment and removal from their place of favor in God's plan in history.[531] The church in America can claim no better position today. In fact, it might have drifted into even greater decadence. If so, our national destiny lies in the balance, and reasonable men ought both to contemplate and to fear divine judgment.

THE TESTIMONY AND THE EVIDENCE

Drift, by its very nature, dulls our perception of truth and reality. Having long since abandoned or lost sight of landmarks that once gave us a sense of place and security, and having pulled up anchor from the truth that once held us firmly, we—individually and as a society—then begin to measure ourselves by the standards of those who are drifting with and around us in the great sea of relativity. Eventually, we all can become lost at sea without someone or God's Spirit to guide us back to safe harbor.

For this reason, you might at this point have reservations about this blanket moral and spiritual assessment of America's lighthouse, the Christian church in our midst. A good trial lawyer, of which most of our countrymen are enamored, would present both testimonial and documentary evidence to support his case. In summary form, therefore, the experts shall speak, presenting an offer of proof in lieu of documents. The pages of an entire book could be filled with such evidence, but let us be brief so that we can, indeed, catch the drift. This exercise is painful, but we must see ourselves the way we are—not the way we want to think of ourselves or the way we see ourselves by comparison with some other group.

Opening Statement

Pollsters, pastors, and prognosticators agree within a few percentage points that the following national religious profile is broadly descriptive of *We the people:*

- 96 percent believe in God;

- 85 percent profess to be Christian, at least in moral precept;

- 45 percent claim to be born-again Christians, meaning that they are saved, confessing Jesus Christ as their personal Savior for forgiveness of sin and its eternal penalty; and

- 8 to 15 percent claim to be evangelical, meaning that they are not only born again but also believe the Bible to be the only inspired and authoritative Word of God that must be obeyed.

The question we must ask before looking further is this: "With all this widespread belief in Jesus, how can we as a nation be in the advanced steps of moral decline?" This, says the author of *Awakening the Giant,* "is the most persistent, perplexing, demanding question of all."[532] James Russell writes, "As I review the span of my lifetime, I find it almost incomprehensible to believe any nation, especially one with such previously idealistic and high moral character, could culturally degenerate as rapidly as has the United States."[533]

The answer, of course, is drift. Writes *Newsweek,* "Provocative new surveys reveal a nation where most claim to be religious but few take their faith seriously."[534]

The Evidence

What happens when people do not possess what they profess in terms of a truly biblical faith? Drift leads to decadence, as the following statistics testify.

- Ninety-one percent of us lie regularly, telling conscious, pre-meditated lies. This fact means that at least 75 percent of professing born-again Christians lie regularly so that lying is now called "a cultural trait in America."[535]

- Only 13 percent of us believe in all of the Ten Commandments. "There is absolutely no moral consensus in the country."

- Thirty-three percent of all of our children are born illegitimate.

- Eighty percent of our children in our larger cities are illegitimate. (Note: the illegitimacy rate for adults over age twenty far exceeds out-of-wedlock births to teens.)[536]

Rather than belabor these nauseating statistics or add pages of such statistics that portray the sheer hypocrisy of our current use of our national motto "In God We Trust," we must look closely at what may well be the most shocking set of statistics related specifically to professing born-again and evangelical believers. Spiritual drift is so decided among those of us who claim to believe the Scriptures from cover to cover that we have literally taken the lead in tearing down the American family. All of our protestations to the contrary, the facts speak for themselves. Gird yourself for the jolt of your life.

- The divorce rate among born-again Christians now exceeds the nation as a whole by 4 percent.

- The divorce rate among fundamentalist Christians now exceeds the national average by 7 percent.[537]

- The divorce rate in the Bible belt of America now exceeds the nation as a whole by 50 percent.[538]

These realities are profoundly painful to the sensibilities of those of us who profess to be Bible-believing Christians. So shocking were they to the governor of Arkansas that he declared a state of marital emergency. No state was more embarrassed than Oklahoma, whose governor hired a nationally known Christian couple to minister full time, giving direction to state government in an effort to rectify the devastation being wreaked upon the citizens of the state by divorce.[539]

Divorce has become to the church what abortion is to the nation. As a point of perspective, abortion kills a child, but divorce kills the whole family and spews its venomous toxin through subsequent generations. Just as many within the nation will do almost anything to protect the right to abortion, so the evangelical church and its conservative allies will do almost anything to protect divorce as a sacrosanct right untouchable by God or man. So strongly do cultural conservatives and Christians protect the practice of divorce that it drew editorial fire from *USA Today* in a headline that asked, "Values? What about divorce?" The writer probingly asks, "If . . . the Christian Coalition is worried about family values, shouldn't they put divorce at the top of the list? How come that's not in the Contract with America?"[540]

Interestingly, Baptists have the highest incidence of divorce among denominational Christians. But the highest rate among all Christians can be found among nondenominational Protestants. The lowest divorce incidence is among Catholics and Lutherans. Divorce is much less likely in the Northeast than in other regions of the nation.[541]

Dr. Popenoe, codirector of the National Marriage Project at Rutgers University, noted in explaining these differences that "the lowest divorce rates are in the northeastern states with large numbers of Roman Catholics whose church doesn't recognize divorce. Southern states, in contrast, are dominated by fundamentalist Protestant denominations that proclaim the sanctity of marriage but generally do not want to estrange churchgoers who do divorce." The shocking truth is that whereas marriage is to be the earthly model of the beauty and dependability of the relationship of Christ to His church, "Christians are more likely to experience divorce than non-Christians."[542]

Because the scriptures that evangelical, fundamentalist, and born-again Christians purport to believe clearly declare that God "hates" divorce and considers it "treachery,"[543] the dramatic extent of spiritual drift for those who claim to be the spiritual strength among us reveals how the unbelievers among us could have likewise drifted. It becomes increasingly obvious that the true battle in our midst is not a culture war but a spiritual war in which we cultural and Christian conservatives have abandoned our own moral post. Now we, in the name of God, export our model of family faithlessness across the seas to our friends in Israel, where Rabbi Ben-Dahan voiced regret that families in Israel are "becoming similarly dysfunctional to those of the U.S."[544]

Our pastors now have joined their flocks in the moral and spiritual slide. A Hartford Seminary study confirmed that pastors now divorce their covenant partners as often as do their parishioners[545] and that pastors now have the second highest divorce rate of all professions.[546] It is "cause for alarm," warned an editorial in *Charisma* in its first issue for the new millennium. Discussing the proliferation of pastoral divorces, Jack Hayford, veteran pastor of pastors, declared, "There simply is no way to describe the present situation in lesser terms: "We are at a point of crisis." "Neither grace nor love," says Hayford, "should ever be a label used to bandage over our neglect or self-indulgence."[547]

Pornography also has become a plague to pastors and people alike. A recent survey reveals the somber statistics that "twenty percent of all ministers are involved in the behavior,"[548] one-third of all pastors confess some inappropriate sexual behavior with someone in the church," and twenty percent "admit to having an affair in the ministry."[549] Truly, like ancient Israel just before God's judgment was poured out upon her, it is now "like people, like priest" in modern America. And this is just "the tip of the iceberg."

Abortion, homosexuality, and divorce, now sacrosanct practices in sanctimonious America, all stem from the same root. Each is a defiant deviancy from the creation ordinance of the Creator, each is purportedly made "holy" by a people who are hell-bent on the pursuit of personal happiness. Each is a mortal blow to marriage, family, and faith. The God who "hath made and preserved us a nation" declared, "Be ye holy," which we have redefined as "be ye happy," and now we are neither happy nor holy. We have normalized the abnormal and defiled the desirable to protect that which our own laws have historically deplored. Indeed, "If therefore the light that is in us be darkness, how great is that darkness!"[550]

Will the God we purport to serve gloss over this gross display of godlessness with a glib grace? To what persons who profess His name will He extend mercy and on what terms? The psalmist makes clear that the Lord is merciful and gracious . . .

- toward them that fear Him,
- to such as keep His covenant, and
- to those that do His commandments.[551]

WHAT MUST WE DO?

What should God do? What should we do? Could it really be that we have become a decadent people on the verge of destruction notwithstanding our good and Godly heritage? Can we really save ourselves by electing to government offices "Christian" representatives like us or by advancing well-meaning social programs to be run by "Christians" who currently live and think as we obviously do?

Do you find yourself practicing self-justification by comparing yourself with someone else or a group whom you think is more decadent or whom you believe has drifted farther away than you have? Who sets the standards? And who resets them? Is it the Creator God who "made and preserved us a nation," or is it His creatures who now, in our American pride, deign to preempt His authority in His own house? What can bring us back to our spiritual senses?

We Must Admit Drift

A dying patient who denies the disease that consumes him will not seek a physician to heal him. A nation that, with positive thinking, believes it can ignore the moral and spiritual cancer that ravages her citizens will soon awake to the chaos that ravages her streets and schools. And Christians who continue to measure their own decline by the more advanced decadence of surrounding society will soon find that they have become the society they formerly despised. If the light and the glory are to be restored to America, God's light and glory must be restored to those who profess to be His children. We—individually and collectively, as professing Christians—must confess the prevailing absence of God's purity in our own lives.

An entire generation has resisted just such admission and confession. We have decried the moral drift in the White House, but we have refused to see the same shift in the church house. And the light in America's lighthouse now flickers faintly, barely visible through the soot of sin that shrouds the windows of our own souls.

Since our nation's bicentennial, we have pleaded with the pagans to repent; yet, we have failed to heed the words of the God we claim to serve, who lovingly promised, "If my people, which are called by my name, shall humble themselves, and pray, and seek my face, and turn from their wicked ways; then I will hear from heaven, and will forgive their sin, and heal their land."[552] The Word of God must again become "the sword of the Spirit," piercing our hearts, before it becomes a salve promoting our healing. Peace in the land will follow purity in our lives. We are reminded, "Righteousness exalteth a nation: but sin is a reproach to any people."[553] Admission of personal and collective spiritual drift will take us across the threshold of truth into a place of hope and healing. But there must also arise a profound and holy fear of divine judgment.

We Must Fear Judgment

A prominent Christian leader recently lamented, "If God does not judge America, He will have to apologize to Sodom and Gomorrah."[554] Another Christian leader writes, "Our nation has become like Sodom and Gomorrah, only worse because we, as the most powerful nation on earth, export our . . . filth and corruption to the rest of the world. We are not only destroying ourselves but are playing a major role in helping to destroy the moral and spiritual values of the rest of the world as well."[555]

Rather than exporting the good news, or true gospel, we—individually, collectively, and as professing Christians—are exporting lifeways and thinking that are diametrically contrary to the gospel that lies at the very root of our reason for being as a nation. If you were the God who both "made and preserved us a nation," how would *you* respond to such a rebellious people or to such a sinful nation?

The words of Jefferson have never been more appropriate to define the attitude that we need for such a time as this:

> Can the liberties of a nation be thought secure when we have removed their only firm basis, a conviction in the minds of the people that these liberties are the Gift of God? *That they are to be violated but with His wrath?* "Indeed I tremble for my country," said Jefferson, "when I reflect that God is just; that His justice cannot sleep forever"[556] (emphasis added).

These words are engraved on the Jefferson Memorial in Washington, D.C., and they remind us that God is not only a God of love but also a God of justice and judgment. John Adams, our second president, writing to Jefferson on June 20, 1815, made clear then, and it is clear now, "The question before the human race is, whether the God of nature shall govern the world by His own laws. . . ."[557] Amos, the great prophet of justice, put it simply: "Can two walk together, except they be agreed?"[558] We cannot be "under God" and out from under Him at the same time.

We Americans tend to see ourselves as the exception to every rule—even God's rule. In our power and prosperity, we have become proud and pompous before God and the nations of the earth. We have convinced ourselves, in the smugness of our hearts, that we are not to be concerned about divine judgment from a holy God for our unholy ways because, after all, we are Americans. Yet, we stand in awesome danger of the fullest expression of God's judgment even as we revel in the hope of a Godly heritage.

We are in massive breach of covenant with the God who "hath made and preserved us a nation." God is holding us collectively as a people—*We the people*—to the terms of that covenant. And, as John Winthrop so aptly warned, "If we deal falsely with our God in this work, . . . we shall be made a story and a byword throughout the world, . . . and He will make us to know the price of the breach of such covenant."[559]

What might such a price be? Internal civil war? Terrorist assault by nuclear or biological agents? A missile attack from a foreign aggressor? Famine and pestilence? Devastating weather and natural disasters? Loss of freedom and tyrannical government? What will it take for God to get America's attention? What will it take for Him to regain our hearts' obedience? What must I do to avert the further corrective hand of a God before whose only begotten Son every knee will ultimately bow?[560]

The Scriptures record that "judgment must begin at the house of God."[561] God will order it to "begin at my sanctuary."[562] The lighthouse of our land—the church of Jesus Christ, professing Christians—will become God's focal point of disciplining judgment. To whom much has been given, much shall be required.[563] If God would renew the soul of America, His church must turn from her wicked ways.[564] That includes pastors and people alike. "Let the priests, the ministers of the Lord, weep. . . ."[565]

We Must Weep

"The First Great Awakening had largely missed Virginia in the 1740s and left her one of the most materialistic of all the colonies."[566] When Devereux Jarratt, an Anglican, became rector in Dinwiddie County in 1762, he stood alone, "not knowing of one clergyman in Virginia like-minded." To his hearers, his preaching was both "strange and wonderful." They flocked from far and near. In the spring of 1774, as the tension rose in the colonies just before the Revolutionary War, Jarratt's preaching was "attended with such energy, that many were pierced to the heart. Tears fell plentifully from the eyes of the hearers, and some were constrained to cry out."[567]

America has again forgotten how to cry. Tears flow as we lament the anguish of parents who lose children in the wake of school shootings. Tears wash the marble corridors of America's divorce courts, and silent cries tear the souls of children torn from their own flesh and blood. Tears filter through the rubble of disintegrated symbols of America's trust and power as hateful terrorists draw tears from long-dry wells of self-encrusted hearts. The collective pain of a distressed nation is palpable. Yet, despite the agony, hubris has hardened our hearts to the horrible truth—we have sinned against a holy God whose justice demands judgment unless we repent.

Truly it is time to weep. We have sown to the wind and are reaping the whirlwind. "Crying out to God with holy tears has a way of cleansing our spiritual eyes,"[568] writes Stephen Hill. But they must be tears of remorse for our offense against God, not tears for the pain that flows to us from the consequences of our spiritual rebellion. Brokenness in our hearts will lead to wholeness in our homes. "Weeping may endure for a night, but joy cometh in the morning."[569]

Spiritual revival in the nation will depend upon tears of personal repentance in the lighthouse. "It's time to stop criticizing America and our leaders," declares Dr. Paul Cedar, president of Mission America, sponsor of the recent "Lighthouse" movement. "It's time to sit down in the presence of God and each other, to repent and weep over our sins."[570]

WILL AMERICA BE GIVEN
ANOTHER CHANCE?

The apostasy of a nation and her people does not happen overnight. It happens with each compromise, with every accommodation by those who man the *lighthouse* to the subtle lure of popular culture, with the inexorable shift of priorities from pleasing God to pleasing the people for political or private gain or even religious promotion.

In 1949, just four years after the conclusion of World War II, *LIFE* magazine declared, "For all of our churches and church-goers, we have become a secular and god-less civilization."[571]

How did this happen? Perhaps no person was better qualified to answer that question than Dr. Richard C. Halverson, veteran Presbyterian pastor, deeply respected former Chaplain of the United States Senate for fourteen years, and a leader in the national prayer breakfast movement.

On October 15, 1995, Dr. Halverson mustered all of his remaining strength and climbed out of what proved to be his deathbed to make what may well have been his last public appearance on *Viewpoint*, the author's daily radio broadcast. It was his final plea. It was his closing prayer, a living memorial to the church and her leaders, a speaking legacy to the nation. Following are a few excerpts.

CRISMIER: Dr. Halverson, do you feel that the church is in danger of forfeiting its soul today?

HALVERSON: I do.

CRISMIER: Why is that?

HALVERSON: Well, I think the church is becoming more and more like the world around it.

CRISMIER: That is a pretty serious indictment.

HALVERSON: Well, I think that the church has adopted the secular way, the secular spirit, secular methods. Even the most evangelical tend to be very secular in their approach to life.

Secularism takes many forms. It morphs to mask its real identity. It even presents itself as an angel of light. But it invariably consumes the spiritual oxygen from the environment, extinguishing both the flame of true faith and the flame of freedom.

"Secularism is . . . the result of a vacuum of God-centered Christianity in the culture," writes Michael Horton in *Beyond Culture Wars*. "Having trusted too much in the idols of nation, pragmatism, ideology, and secular power, whether the carved image is in the shape of a donkey or an elephant, the stage is perhaps set for a return to the main message and mission of the church."[572] "In the Culture Wars, the Gospel has been a casualty—not from the shells of the secularist but from the 'friendly fire' of its own soldiers."[573]

"We have," continues Horton, "turned the one true God of history and Father of our Lord Jesus Christ into a tribal deity of the American experience."[574] "The world would instantly be attentive if it saw a church on its knees in repentance for its own sins."[575]

Erwin Lutzer, pastor of Moody Memorial Church in Chicago asks, "Will America be given another chance?" His answer returns our gaze to the lighthouse. "Whether America has another chance is up to God; whether we are faithful is up to us."[576] "Revived Christians beget revival. It must begin with us, in our own homes where our true character is revealed and in our churches where our burning hearts can ignite others."[577]

"We may glibly proclaim that we want this nation to have another chance to capture the meaning of 'In God We Trust.' But if we knew what such a transformation would personally demand, we might just prefer to leave things as they are. We may have become too comfortable to pay the price."[578] Have you?

CHURCH'S REVIVAL—NATION'S SURVIVAL

"A spiritual revival is not important to the Church and to America. It is *imperative!*" This moment is "the darkest in our nation's history and, for that matter, in world history," warns Leonard Ravenhill.[579] "We need a baptism of honesty in the courts of the Lord. Honesty means truth, and truth can be painful."[580]

The painful truth is that the nation's survival depends upon the church's revival, and the church's revival depends upon you and me. Without God, we can do nothing; without us, God will do nothing. We must repent!

For a generation, we have exhorted sinners to repent while the saints persisted in their sins. We are now beginning to get the message that if pagans are to repent, the saints must first turn from their own wicked ways so that light can shine in national darkness.

"Our nation is standing at the brink of judgment," writes Cindy Jacobs. "Our spiritual crisis requires a desperate response."[581]

"There must be deep, genuine repentance," declares Billy Graham. "What good does it do to become the wealthiest nation in the world if we are spiritually bankrupt?"[582]

"No matter how fervently we pray," warns Chuck Colson, "the Lord will not grant renewal to a nation that does not honor Him. First, we must repent."[583]

"One of the most striking aspects of true revival is the degree to which massive and often totally unexpected repentance takes place," writes David Aikman, twenty-three-year veteran correspondent for *Time*.[584]

We have not yet witnessed the kind of profound anguish of soul-revealing deep conviction of heart leading to massive personal and societal change characteristic of true revival. For that reason, pollster George Barna, in response to the well-meaning but glib rhetoric of prevailing revival floated so freely around the country by pastors and parachurch leaders, reports that "no statistical evidence" supports the claims that revival has or is taking place. In spite of the much characteristically American positive talk of revival, little true walk has occurred, and we have seen no net increase in born-again Christians since 1992.[585]

We desire the results of revival, but we still largely despise its conditions. Peter Marshall, author of *The Light and the Glory*, makes plain the reason: "A revival is a lasting and permanent change in society. We haven't seen nationwide revival because there has been no serious teaching on daily repentance as a way of life." "Nationwide repentance and revival," says Marshall, is "America's only hope." "We may have only five years left before American society will become too sick, too decadent, too self-destroyed to reverse the destruction."[586]

"Whatever happened to repentance?" asks the pastor of the Times Square Church in New York City. "You rarely hear the word even in Baptist, Pentecostal or evangelical circles."[587] The reason was succinctly stated to me by a national leader at a gathering of thousands for fasting and prayer for revival: "It's too negative!" Yet, the entire message of the gospel is framed around repentance. Repentance no longer fits the marketing mantras for the new positively polite dogma of American Christianity. And that is one more reason we must repent.

Repentance means "turning around," but it also requires deep contrition or Godly sorrow. It requires unequivocal admission of sin and guilt before God. It drives one to his knees, crying out in pain for having grieved the Lord whom we purport to love and serve. It begins with conviction of the heart that leads to confession of the mouth and leads to a new cooperation with God on His terms. Repentance is always attitude and behavior specific. For the

Christian, no such thing exists as generic repentance (i.e. "Please, God, forgive me if I have done something wrong," or "Please forgive me for my sins.")—I cannot turn from that which I refuse to admit or articulate as sin without specificity.

Because the word *repent* accuses of guilt and calls for change, it seems challenging, unnerving, and intimidating. It proclaims that God is not pleased; therefore, it is unpopular, particularly in the American church of almost any brand or description at this critical moment of our history. "The man who says *repent* sets himself against his age, and will for the time being be battered mercilessly by the age whose moral tone he challenges."[588]

Yet, without repentance, there can be no revival. Repent is, in reality, the most positive and hope-filled word we can utter in our generation. Without it, we will see the end of the American gospel enterprise[589] and the ultimate demise of our country.

POWER IN THE PULPIT

"The best way to revive the church is to build a fire in the pulpit,"[590] declared Dwight L. Moody, a great preacher in America's past. Yet, many of the people who are most resistant to true revival have been pastors who fear losing power, perks, and position if they rock the boat. For this reason, we need a "shaking in the pulpit."

Pastor Ken Hutchinson of Kirkland, Washington, writes, "We are afraid to upset our congregations or our substantial givers. What we excuse as diplomacy has actually become compromise." "There are hot potato issues," he says, that we know will cause difficulty in our ministries, "so we avoid them like the plague." "The greatest problems in the church lie in the fearful hearts of those who stand in the pulpits."[591]

"Fearless preaching is all the more necessary in dangerous times," exhorts John MacArthur. "When people will not tolerate the truth, that's when courageous, outspoken preachers are most desperately needed to speak it." "Sound preaching," he says, "confronts and rebukes sin, and people in love with sinful lifestyles will not tolerate such teaching. They want to have their ears tickled."[592] "Churches are so engrossed in trying to please non-Christians that many have forgotten their first duty is to please God."[593]

"The church suffers not so much from the sins of the world as the world is suffering from the sins of the church," observes Jim Russell. "Individual blatant and subtle sin," he states, must be "defined, identified and dealt with according to biblical truth."[594]

Our national destiny will be determined by rekindling the fire of the Spirit in America's preachers whose flame will ignite the people. Let those manning the lighthouse blaze once again with holy fire that the glory of the Lord may shine forth from these shores across the seven seas and the seven continents. May those visiting from afar once again declare, "Not until I went into the churches of America and heard her pulpits aflame with righteousness did I understand the secret of her genius and power."[595]

BY THE DAWN'S EARLY LIGHT

A lighthouse is prophetic. It stands as a sentinel, wooing and warning the unwary of danger. But if its light has gone out or if it emits only a faint flicker, it not only fails to fulfill its purpose but also lures into dangerous shoals the unsuspecting souls who depended upon its radiant beam. So it is with the church in America, with pastors and people alike, with you and with me.

Dr. Henry Blackaby, co-author of the much-celebrated *Experiencing God* studies, made us painfully aware of God's viewpoint on America's dramatic decay. "The problem of America is not the unbelieving world," declared Blackaby. "The problem of America is the people of God."

Speaking at the Billy Graham Training Center on May 22, 1999, Blackaby minced no words. "If things get darker in America, the problem is not with the darkness—it's acting just like its nature. The problem's with the light." "All the way through the Bible," he noted, "judgment came on a nation when God's people would not return unto Him." "The tragedy," said Blackaby, "is that God's people (the lighthouse) and their leaders are totally unaware of the ways of God," so that when God says "return to Me," we respond as Israel did to the prophet Malachi; we ask innocently, "Wherein have we departed."

"If you didn't hear anything else," Dr. Blackaby concludes, "understand that it is God's people who hold the destiny of America. The future of America rests in our hands."[596]

Has your heart been touched as you have read these difficult pages? In their book *Heal Our Land*, Jimmy and Carol Owens encourage us, observing, "There's no time like the present to take care of neglected housecleaning. Look deep inside. Ask the Holy Spirit to begin the convicting process, then listen."[597] Confess, repent, and allow yourself to be "crucified with Christ."[598] A church that again glories in the Cross will have the light to lead America through her moral and spiritual crossroad.

"Now is the time to challenge the deepening darkness and begin to penetrate the night with the light of a new dawn,"[599] encourages Joseph Stowell. But we must dare to challenge the night with lives committed to righteousness. Will hope arise again in America by the dawn's early light? It will all depend upon whether the light from the lighthouse can guide her through the night.

SOUL-STIRRING QUESTIONS FOR PERSONAL AND GROUP REFLECTION

1. A fundamental rule of politics is to "go to strength." What was the undergirding strength of America? Was it political or spiritual? What is our strength today?

2. How has the light from the church, America's lighthouse, grown so dim?

3. How does drift determine destiny?

4. What happened to ancient Israel when they drifted spiritually?

5. Do you believe that our nation and the church within our land has drifted into decadence? Have you?

6. How can you explain that 96 percent of Americans believe in God, but 91 percent of Americans consciously and regularly lie?

7. Can you explain how 80 percent of the children in America's larger cities are born illegitimate, yet 86 percent of Americans claim to be Christian in moral precept?

8. What explanation do you have for why the divorce rate among those who claim to be born-again Christians is slightly higher than that of the nation as a whole? Is your life part of the problem? How did it happen? Do you think that God is pleased with this situation?

9. If you were God, what would you do with a nation where the church of His so-called "called-out ones" refuses to obey His voice?

10. Can we really save ourselves by merely electing government representatives from the general cross section of professing Christians, or is something more drastic required?

11. Do you think that God will give America another chance? Why, or why not?

12. Do you believe that spiritual revival in the church is necessary for America's survival? Why, or why not?

13. Do you believe that your spirit needs to be revived and your soul renewed? Why, or why not?

14. What will it take to renew the soul of America?

15. Will the light from the lighthouse of your life be sufficient to guide that portion of America in your sphere of influence through the darkening night?

16. Will you repent?

Chapter 22

AN AMERICAN PARABLE

THERE WAS A "ROAR LIKE THUNDER." It was the most infamous disaster in American history.

On June 1, 1889, Americans awoke to the news that Johnstown, Pennsylvania, had been devastated by the worst inland flood in the nation's history. More than twenty-two hundred people were dead. Many more were homeless. Many people believed that if this was a "natural disaster," then man was an accomplice—and God allowed it.

The doomed city was built in the Conemaugh Valley at the joining of two rivers: the Little Conemaugh and Stony Creek. It was a steel company town. Founded in 1794, just after the birth of the nation, it began to prosper with the building of the Pennsylvania Mainline Canal in 1834 and the arrival of the Pennsylvania Railroad, known by most Americans today only from their Monopoly playing board.

PITTSBURGH AND AMERICAN PROSPERITY

Everyone was beholden to Cambria Iron and Steel. Thirty thousand people packed the little valley, all fueling America's Industrial Age by the steel they produced. Conservation was irrelevant in the face of progress. Capitalism and commerce slashed at the earth with impunity in the name of profits and power. The valley throbbed to the pulse of molten metal. Two-thirds of America's iron and steel were produced in the region. Through the smoke and odors, living was comfortable for the wealthy and attractive to the ambitious.

Fourteen miles upstream from the Little Conemaugh was Lake Conemaugh, a two-mile lake held on the side of a mountain 450 feet above Johnstown by the Old South Fork Dam. It had been poorly maintained. Every spring, the townspeople talked about how the dam might not hold. Yet it always had, and the threat became somewhat of a casual joke in town.

The South Fork Fishing and Hunting Club was an exclusive resort for the wealthy people of Pittsburgh. They bought the abandoned reservoir, raised the level of the lake, and built a clubhouse surrounded by great cottages. Locals called it "The Bosses' Club." Capitalist moguls Andrew Carnegie and Andrew Mellon and their friends frolicked there in their private haven. The dam level was lowered to provide passage for their carriages to the sumptuous cottages. The charter of the Club was noble—protection of game and fish. Some critics said that they should have been more concerned about people. Some people said that the dam was then the world's largest. The Club had carelessly repaired and maintained it, and they had not consulted any engineer.

At first, the 72-foot-high, 931-foot-long mass of earth and stone frightened the residents below. People wondered why the dam was not reinforced. But nothing was done. Business went on as usual as the trains lurched up and down the mountain. Telegraph wires linked the people below the dam to the people above. Gradually, people talked less and less of the impending threat. The hustle and bustle of daily life filled the air.

IT BEGAN TO RAIN

The morning of May 31 was fresh and delightful. The city was in its gayest mood. The day before, they had celebrated life by honoring the dead servicemen on Memorial Day. Few people noticed how dark and threatening the clouds had become.

Heavy snows had fallen in April and May. Rain had drenched the land for eleven days. The river was riding high. But folks were used to spring floods, and they didn't pay attention any more. It was business as usual. One more storm was hardly noticed.

It began to rain. People rushed hurriedly home for shelter, not realizing that their homes would no longer provide protection from the gathering forces about them. The river had been rising eighteen inches an hour. Johnstown was again under water. Many people moved to higher ground. But most of them thought, *We've seen floods and troubles before.* And after seeking a dry corner, they stood gazing at the events around them, disengaged as though they were mere observers in a theater. For many people, it became a holiday from school and work.

Railroad tracks were swept away by the raging Conemaugh, and the trains were stopped. Telegraph messages warned of rapidly rising water: "Higher than ever known," "South Fork Dam liable to break," "The dam is becoming dangerous," "Water over breast of dam," "Prepare for worst." But the warnings went unheeded. Even in the face of the mounting evidence of imminent danger, a quiet smugness of self-sufficiency prevailed. It will never happen here.

A Roar Like Thunder

A few people knew immediately what had happened. There was a low rumble, then a roar like thunder. As the water began to spill over the top of the dam, it began to slice like a knife through the middle. Suddenly, the water seemed to push out all at once. It was not a break; it was just one big push. A massive maelstrom of water, mud, and stone exploded.

The people of South Fork were first to flee the deadly wall of water. The power was unimaginable! A tidal wave forty feet high plunged down the mountain at forty miles per hour. It was like standing directly under Niagara Falls. The wave hit a massive seventy-foot-high stone viaduct. The giant structure held momentarily, but then it just disappeared. Nothing could stop the water now.

The hideous wall of water plunged toward Johnstown. Woodvale was swept away in five minutes—woolen mill, barns, and hundreds of homes. The great boilers of the Gautier Wire Works exploded in geysers of steam. An eerie pallor of darkness hovered over the advancing wave.

Now all of the telegraph lines were down. No more messages could be sent. More than twenty-two hundred townsfolk were tragically unaware that death was moving down the valley.

Twenty million tons of water took its natural course. One observer commented that it "roared like a mighty battle."

Most people never saw a thing until the mighty wall engulfed them, consuming everything in its path. Those who saw from safety said that it "snapped off trees like pipestems," "crushed houses like eggshells," and "threw locomotives like so much chaff."

Thousands of people tried desperately to escape but were slowed, as if in a nightmare, by the two to seven feet of water already covering parts of town. A few people pulled themselves to safety seconds before the water overtook them.

From the moment the dam broke, it took one hour before judgment leveled Johnstown fourteen miles away. They did not have a prayer. Their chances had passed them by. Homes were instantly crushed. In some homes, people climbed to the upper stories just as the tidal wave tore the structure from its foundations. People clinging to rafters, rooftops, and rail cars were swept downstream.

The crushing torrent spared nothing. The pent-up power was no respecter of persons. Pride, power, and poverty were devoured equally. One person said that the streets "grew black with people running for their lives."

Thousands of tons of debris piled against the old stone bridge. Darkness fell. Machinery, hundreds of freight cars, fifty miles of track, bridge sections, boilers, telephone poles, trees, animals, and hundreds of townspeople were jammed together in the oil-soaked mass. They had no escape as the frightful current held them, bound together by barbed wire, against the bridge.

THE FURY OF FIRE

Then the oil caught fire. Flames spread throughout the whole mass. The Johnstown newspaper recorded the burning to be "with all the fury of hell." The screams, the burning, the crashing water—the horror was indescribable.

I've seen the pictures of the twisted steel and devastation, but what gnaws at my soul are the pictures taken *before* the flood—all of those unsuspecting faces looking contentedly at the camera, never imagining the horrors that lay ahead of them.

When they could, they did nothing. When the dam broke and the waters descended, those in control of the media ignored the telegraph warnings. The messages were not passed on. Their final notice was the shrill whistle of the Cambria Iron Works and the frantic clang of the church bell because even their pastors had been silenced by prosperity.

DO WE HAVE A PRAYER?

They did not have a prayer. But America still does have a prayer before the dam breaks.

We must pray! Join me and thousands of your countrymen in humility and prayer. It is our only hope if it is followed by heart-rending repentance. Give America a prayer. It's serious, folks! A nation is in the balance—and so is the future of our children.

This nation we love dwells in the Valley of Decision. The river of mounting anger, anxiety, and frustration has overflowed the banks. Our cities are under the water of crime, racism, rebellion, alienation, loneliness, family breakdown, and sexual perversion. Some people have sought higher ground, but most people dwell aloof, numbed to the true magnitude of the situation.

It could never happen—not in America, most people seem to think. Yet, the pent-up power of pride and moral decay is perched precipitously over us. The moral and spiritual substance of *We the people* is severely weakened. If and when the dam breaks, both rich and poor will be devoured together in the horrendous wave of evil, corruption, and chaos that will engulf us. As though they were modern-day prophets, *Newsweek* and *U.S. News and World Report* emblazoned the word *chaos* across front-cover backdrops of the U.S. Constitution and a banner reading "We the people" in their December 18, 2000, issues.

We might seem to be already under water. Some people have already thrown up their hands in despair. But we haven't seen anything yet. This is the last hour of hope! Let's act—and repent—while we have a prayer. We face not only chaos from within but also the impending hand of judgment from the God who "hath made and preserved us a nation." Today, if you will hear His voice, harden not your heart. Pastor, president, and people alike—none of us is exempt.

DUE PROCESS: INTERPRETING THE PARABLE OF JOHNSTOWN AND YOUR TOWN

"Due process of law" is a phrase with which most Americans are familiar as a characteristic of a "nation of laws and not of men." Due process is the threshold requirement for providing "liberty and justice for all." It is also God's threshold requirement because He is a God of justice.

Conditions for Preservation

The God who "hath made and preserved us a nation" is "a God of truth and without iniquity." He is "just and right."[600] Because the character of our Creator is truth and He is just and right, He expects the same of those whom He has created in His image (you and me), and He acts toward us accordingly. He expects us to walk in His ways and to keep His commandments. This expectation is true for the Jew as seen in the "Sh'ma": "Hear O Israel"[601]—of the ancient Torah, and for Gentiles as restated in the New Testament, voiced by both Christ and His disciples. Our love of and favor with God are revealed by our loving obedience to His commands.[602]

"The Lord commanded us to do all these statutes, to fear the Lord our God, for our good always, that He might *preserve us* alive . . ,"[603] that it may go well with us, and that we may possess the land which the Lord has provided to and through our forefathers.[604] But what happens if *We the people* rebel and refuse to align our will individually and corporately with that of the God who "hath made and preserved us a nation"?

Although God is patient and of great mercy, He declares, "My Spirit will not always strive with man."[605] A time comes when the just nature of God requires that He bring judgment upon a people—even upon America. If He spared not Israel, the chosen people, from such Divine judgment and correction, why should we think that He will do otherwise with America? He must act consistent with His just, holy, and righteous character. But before the God of love becomes the refining God of judgment, He always, without exception, gives a lengthy and fair warning of His impending intentions through prophetic voices. We Americans call this warning period "due process."

Classic Justice

One of the classic demonstrations of God's due process of sending His messengers to woo and warn the people to turn from their increasingly wicked ways is the message of the prophet Isaiah concerning Judah and Jerusalem. Never have truer or more applicable words been spoken to twenty-first-century America and her spiritual and political leaders.

> *The Lord hath spoken, I have nourished and brought up children, and they have rebelled against me. . . . Ah sinful nation. . .they have forsaken the Lord. . .they are gone away backward. Why should ye be stricken any more? . . . the whole head is sick, and the whole heart faint. . . . Your country is desolate, your cities are burned with fire: your land, strangers devour it. . . . Except the Lord. . .had left unto us a very small remnant, we should have been as Sodom, and we should have been like unto Gomorrah?*[606]

Isaiah then spoke to the spiritual leaders of the ancient Jewish people, who were walking in rebellion while reveling in their religious practices and even purporting to be gathering in solemn assemblies seeking spiritual revival:

> *Hear the word of the Lord, ye rulers of Sodom; . . . To what purpose is the multitude of your sacrifices unto me? . . . Bring no more vain oblations . . . the calling of assemblies . . . it is iniquity, even the solemn meeting. Your appointed feasts my soul hateth . . . I am weary to bear them. And when ye spread forth your hands, I will hide mine eyes from you: yea, when ye make many prayers, I will not hear.*[607]

What, then, does the God who "hath made and preserved us a nation" expect? What response does He require when a people are under His due-process warning? Isaiah again makes the answer clear in general terms. Each of us must respond in accordance with the nature of our own personal and corporate offense against a holy God. Listen carefully, with an open heart, to God's wooing:

> Wash you, make you clean; put away the evil of your doings . . . ; cease to do evil; Learn to do well; seek judgment (justice), relieve the oppressed, judge the fatherless, plead for the widow. Come now, and let us reason together, saith the Lord: though your sins be as scarlet, they shall be as white as snow. . . .[608]

Then comes the warning, something that few people want to hear but what all must hear. This warning is implicit in our "American parable," a parable for Johnstown and your town:

> If ye be willing and obedient (meaning that we fully repent), ye shall eat the good of the land: But if ye refuse and rebel, ye shall be devoured with the sword: for the mouth of the Lord hath spoken it."[609]

Due Process in Our Time

God speaks in our time just as He did through Isaiah. His character never changes. He is a God of justice and due process. Therefore, in 1993, He stirred the heart of Willard Bickers, a young man in his twenties, to put up a sixty-foot billboard on one of the busiest Southern California freeways declaring for sixty consecutive days, "The SWORD of the LORD coming soon." So profoundly did this young man sense both God's call and urgency that he invested his entire savings in two such billboards. He issued a small book titled *Your Country Is Desolate*,[610] translating the words of the ancient prophets to the hardening American heart.

Since our nation's bicentennial, the God who "hath made and preserved us a nation" has been warning us with increasing urgency to amend our ways. He has even co-opted the services of secular media for fifty years to deliver the warning when He found it increasingly difficult to speak through the mouths of pastors and prophets who were becoming like the people. Consider the following examples of such warnings in secular media.

In 1949, *LIFE* magazine warned,

"For all of our churches and church-goers, we have become a secular and God-less civilization."[611]

In 1960, *Look* magazine warned,

"Christianity is in retreat," despite "the outward evidence that seems to indicate otherwise."[612]

In 1992, *Forbes* magazine lamented,

". . . we could tell (in 1939) we were beginning to lose God—banishing Him from the scene. . . . And it is a terrible thing when people lose God."[613]

In 1992, *Time* magazine noted on its front cover,

"The Generation That Forgot God."[614]

In 1993, *Newsweek* reported,

"New surveys reveal a nation where most claim to be religious but few take their faith seriously."[615]

In 1993, *Time* declared America to be

"One Nation Under Gods."[616]

In 1994, a cover of *Newsweek* boldly declared,

America is in "SEARCH for the SACRED" because "A lot has changed in the last half century." "We've stripped away . . . the importance of religion and family . . . it has left a gaping hole."[617]

In 1995, *Time* observed,

"In So Many Gods We Trust."[618]

Our Opportunity

Dr. Henry Blackaby, co-author of the phenomenally popular *Experiencing God* series that has crossed most denominational lines, spoke on May 22, 1999, at the Billy Graham Training Center at the Cove in North Carolina. Someone asked him, "What do you see as the future for the United States?"

He answered, "If you put the U.S. up against the Scriptures, we're in trouble. I think we're very close to the judgment of God."[619]

What do you think?

Time is short. Destiny knocks at the door. America's future lies finally in your hands, your heart, and your home. The God who "hath made and preserved us a nation" declares, "This is a nation that obeyeth not the voice of the Lord their God, nor receiveth correction: truth is perished, and is cut off from their mouth."[620] Thus saith the Lord, "Shall not my soul be avenged on such a nation as this?"[621]

The door of opportunity is yet open. A day of grace is yet extended. Perhaps today is the propitious moment to pray as we have never prayed, to obey as we have never obeyed. If you confess your sin, God is faithful and just to forgive your sin and to cleanse you from all unrighteousness.[622] Don't delay. Do it today. Perhaps the words of Lincoln can again lead us in this desperate moment as they did on April 30, 1863, in calling an unrepentant people to "fasting, humiliation, and prayer." Lincoln stated,

> We have been the recipients of the choicest bounties of Heaven. We have been preserved, these many years, in peace and prosperity. We have grown in numbers, wealth and power, as no other nation has ever grown. But we have forgotten God. We have forgotten the gracious hand which preserved us; and we have vainly imagined, in the deceitfulness of our hearts, that all these blessings were produced by some superior virtue and wisdom of our own. Intoxicated with unbroken success, we have become too self-sufficient to feel the necessity of redeeming and preserving grace, too proud to pray to the God that made us! It behooves us, then to humble ourselves before the offended power, to confess our national sins, and pray for clemency and forgiveness.[623]

May God, by His grace and through our humble repentance, preserve us a nation by renewing the soul of America.

POSTSCRIPT

Victor Heisner was sixteen when the Johnstown flood struck. He watched in horror as his home—with his parents in it—was swept away. Clinging to the barn roof, he had a wild ride down the Conemaugh River. Then he was swept up Stony Creek in the backwash when the wave hit the side of the mountain. Later he recalled that "the townspeople, like those who lived in the shadow of Vesuvius, grew calloused to the possibility of danger."

Is history doomed to repeat itself? Will that be the memory of America's youth? Will we cruise on in bliss, oblivious to the fact that the dam is about the break? What further evidence do we need?

To repeat the facts of the great threat that looms above our nation would seem to insult our intelligence. We have heard about the 600 percent increase in violent crime and the 500 percent jump in illegitimate births. We see a generation of fatherless and valueless children growing up around us. We have not taught them right from wrong because we seem ourselves to have forgotten the difference.

What can you and I do? First we must pray. To pray implies that we cannot do it all ourselves. Yes, get involved in the governmental process. Fulfill your civic responsibilities. Use your phone and fax. But do not place your trust there. Our problems are moral and spiritual, and they will be resolved with only moral and spiritual remedies. That outcome will require personal repentance, returning in humble obedience to the God of our Fathers.

Let us pray now while we can still pray in faith and not in panic. Let us ask the Lord of Nations to reveal the wickedness lurking in our own hearts and the manner in which we have strayed in our own lives from His ways. What He reveals might be shocking. And it must bring us to our knees again before we can stand up for our country.[624]

SOUL-STIRRING QUESTIONS FOR PERSONAL AND GROUP REFLECTION

1. How were the ways and attitudes of the citizens of Johnstown like those of America's citizens today?

2. How did prosperity affect the thinking of the people of Johnstown?

3. Why did urgent warnings go unheeded? Certainly it was not lack of information or technology, so what was lacking?

4. When the dam broke, did status, power, wealth, or church membership save the people of Johnstown from destruction? Why, or why not?

5. "When they could, they did nothing," someone said of the people of Johnstown. How does that assessment differ from the people of your town today? How does it differ from you?

6. When the dam broke, Johnstown did not have a prayer. Does America still have a prayer? If so, who must pray? What should we pray? Why should we pray? What must we do? What must you do?

7. What does "due process" mean?

8. Why does God provide due process before He judges a nation or a person?

9. How does God provide due process? Is it possible that this book, along with the messages of countless others, may be fulfilling the requirement of due process that justice may be served?

10. Why shouldn't God bring judgment on America? Should God give better treatment to our nation than He gave to Israel when they, as His covenant people, refused to obey Him?

11. What do you think of the numerous warnings even from our nation's secular magazines?

12. Have you sinned in displeasing and even rebelling against the God "who hath made and preserved us a nation"?

13. Are you willing to humble yourself, to seek God's forgiveness, and to turn from your independent ways that God might preserve us a nation by renewing the soul of America—beginning with you?

Chapter 23

CAN AMERICA COUNT ON YOU?

AN ASTOUNDING NEWSWEEK EDITORIAL IS titled "The Future Be Damned." It is a piercing, if not scathing, observation of the growing propensity of Americans to live for today without consideration for tomorrow and the generations to follow. The author concludes, "We won't endure small hurts today to avoid larger hurts tomorrow, and we know it. Self-deception has become a way of life."[625]

I pray that this will not be America's epitaph. You and I are writing the script of America's future today. With every word, every decision, every thought, every act—for good or ill—we are either rebuilding our foundations or bringing further decay. Each one of us plays a part and bears the consequences.

History is now rolling up like a scroll, and we must reassess our moments of destiny. Did we, as a nation, recognize and respond to the divine hand in history? Did you and I grasp the moment of grace extended to us?

This is the greatest opportunity that you and I have ever had personally to make a difference. I hope that you will begin today, if you have not already begun. The seriousness of our nation's dilemma will not permit delay. Every day is critical. Your life counts!

Some people are intent on undermining and destroying the principles that have made America great and that have allowed the hand of God to prosper us. Other people have contributed to our national deterioration through benign neglect, also causing God to withhold His hand of blessing. Many people have rebelled even in God's own house against His authority, subjecting this nation to deserved divine judgment.

Together, however, with repentant hearts and God's help, we must now cast ourselves on the mercy of the God "that hath made and preserved us a nation." I trust that we can count on you. Can we? Can God count on you?

If this book has been helpful and of encouragement to you, please write and express your thoughts. I know that this message has been direct, but the time for political correctness, polite word mincing, and the avoidance of offense is long past. A battle is raging for the mind, heart, and soul of America. If you share my concern for our nation, obtain further copies of this book for your friends, relatives, coworkers, pastor, club members, elected representatives, and others.

Do not let discouragement tie your hands or close your mouth. Now is the time for all good and godly men and women to come to the aid of their country. A national revival will begin only when we are on our knees.

Remember these words:

I am only one, but I am one.
I cannot do everything, but I can do something.
What I can do, I should do,
And by the grace of God, I will do.

—Everett Hale

Portrait of a Covenant Community

JOHN WINTHROP

"A MODEL OF CHRISTIAN CHARITY"

Perhaps the best expression of what
America was to be and become.

A Prescription for Healing America's Broken Heart

Presented by

Save America Ministries

APPENDIX

A Voice from the Past
A Vision for the Future
John Winthrop,
a Godly attorney and governor

HIS WORDS REMAIN A MODEL of what life in America was meant to be.

> "We must delight in each other, make others conditions our own, rejoice together, mourn together, labor and suffer together, always having before our eyes, our community, as members of the same body."[626]

One of the most distinguished members of the Massachusetts Bay Colony was the Puritan John Winthrop, who left England with his followers in four ships on March 22, 1630, and, after a delay of several weeks in Yarborough, arrived in Salem on June 12. Winthrop had given much thought to not only his personal decision to leave England but also the goals, both religious and civic, that he thought the Puritans should pursue in their new community. Before debarking from his flagship, the Arabella, he wrote a statement of the working principles upon which the colony would be built. Titled "A Model of Christian Charity," it is perhaps the best expression of the Puritan ideal of what America was to be and become. It reveals the seed from which America was conceived, the spiritual womb from which the nation was born. It is, in short, the American Vision—a vision for a covenant community.

God Almighty, in His most holy and wise providence, has so disposed of the condition of mankind, as in all times some must be rich; some poor; some high and eminent in power and dignity; others mean and in subjection.

The Reason Hereof: first, to hold conformity with the rest of His works, being delighted to show forth the glory of His wisdom in the variety and difference of the creatures and the glory of His power, in ordering all these differences for the preservation and good of the whole; and the glory of His greatness in that, as it is the glory of princes to have many officers, so this Great King will have many stewards, counting Himself more honored in dispensing His gifts to man by man than if He did it by His own immediate hand.

Second, that He might have the more occasion to manifest the work of His spirit; first, upon the wicked in moderating and restraining them, so that the rich and mighty should not eat up the poor, nor the poor and despised rise up against their superiors and shake off their yoke; second, in the regenerate in exercising His graces in them, as in the great ones their love, mercy, gentleness, temperance, etc.; in the poor and inferior sort, their faith, patience, obedience, etc.

Third, that every man might have need of others, and from hence they might be all knit more nearly together in the bond of brotherly affection. From hence it appears plainly that no man is made more honorable than another or more wealthy, etc., out of any particular or singular respect to himself, but for the glory of his Creator and the common good of the creature, man. Therefore, God still reserves the property of these gifts to Himself, as [in] Ezekiel 16:17; He there calls wealth His gold and His silver, etc; [in] Proverbs 3:9 He claims their service as His due: "Honor the Lord with thy riches," etc. All men are thus (by Divine Providence) ranked into two sorts, rich and poor; under the first are included all men such as are able to live comfortably by their own means duly improved; and all others are poor according to the former distribution.

There are two rules whereby we are to walk one toward another: justice and mercy. These are always distinguished by their act and in their object, yet may they both concur in the same subject in each respect, as sometimes there may be an occasion of showing mercy to a rich man in some sudden danger of distress; and also doing of mere justice to a poor man in regard of some particular contract, etc. There is likewise a double law of grace, or the moral law or the law of the gospel (we may omit the law of justice as not properly belonging to this purpose otherwise than it may fall into consideration in some particular case). By the first of these laws, man . . . is commanded to love his neighbor as himself. Upon this ground stand all the precepts of the moral law which concerns our dealings with men. To apply this to the works of mercy, this law requires two things: first, that every man afford his help to another in every want or distress; second, that he perform this out of the same affection which makes him careful of his own good, according to that of our Savior (Matthew 7:12) "Whatsoever ye would that men should do to you. . . ."

The law of grace or the gospel has some difference from the former as in these respects: First, the law of nature was given to man in the estate of innocence; the law of the gospel in the estate of regeneracy. Second, the law of nature propounds one man to another, as the same flesh and image of God, the law of the gospel as a brother in Christ also, and in the communion of the same spirit, teaches us to put a difference between Christians and others. . . . The law of nature could give no rules for dealing with enemies, for all are considered as friends in the state of innocence, but the gospel commands love to an enemy. . . . "If thine enemy hunger, feed him; love your enemies; do good to them that hate you" (Matthew 5:44).

This law of the gospel propounds, likewise, a difference of seasons and occasions. There is a time when a Christian must sell all and give to the poor as they did in the apostles' times. There is a time also when Christians (though they give not all yet) must give beyond their ability. . . . Likewise, community of perils calls for extraordinary liberality and so does community in some special service for the Church. Lastly, when there is no other means whereby our Christian brother may be relieved in this distress, we must help him beyond our ability, rather than tempt God in putting him upon help by miraculous or extraordinary means.

This duty of mercy is exercised in . . . giving, lending, and forgiving.

Question: What rule shall a man observe in giving in respect to the measure?

Answer: If the time and occasion be ordinary, he is to give out of his abundance—let him lay aside, as God has blessed him. If the time and occasion be extraordinary, he must be ruled by them. . . . Then a man cannot likely do too much, especially if he may leave himself and his family under . . . means of comfortable subsistence.

Objection: A man must lay up for posterity; the fathers lay up for posterity and children, and he is worse than an infidel that provides not for his own.

Answer: For the first, it is plain that the statement is made by way of comparison and must be meant for the ordinary and usual course of fathers and cannot extend to times and occasions extraordinary, for in another place the apostle speaks against those who walk inordinately, and it is without question that he is worse than an infidel who through his own sloth and voluptuousness shall neglect to provide for his family.

Objection: "The wise man's eyes are in his head," says Solomon (Ecclesiastes 2:14), "and foreseeth the plague," therefore we must forecast and lay up against evil times when he or his may stand in need of all he can gather.

Answer: Solomon uses this very argument to persuade to liberality. Ecclesiastes 2:1: "Cast thy bread upon the waters . . . for thou knowest not what evil may come upon the land"; Luke 16 "Make you friends of the riches of iniquity." You will ask how this shall be? Very well. First, he that gives to the poor lends to the Lord, who will repay him even in this life and a hundredfold to him or his. The righteous man is ever merciful and lends, and his seed enjoy the blessing; and besides we know what advantage it will be to us in the day of accounting, when many such witnesses shall stand forth for us to witness the improvement of our talent. And I would know of those who plead so much for laying up for time to come, whether they hold Matthew 6:19 to be gospel: "Lay not up for yourselves treasures upon earth." If they acknowledge it, what extent will they allow it? If only to those primitive times, let them consider the reason whereupon our Savior grounds it. The first is that treasures are subject to the moth, rust, and the thief; the second is that they will steal away the heart; where the treasure is, there will the heart be also.

The reasons are of like force at all times; therefore, the exhortation must be general and perpetual, which applies always in respect of the love and affection for riches and in regard to the things themselves, when any special service for the church or particular distress of our brother call for the use of riches; otherwise it is not only lawful but necessary to lay up as Joseph did, to have ready upon such occasions as the Lord (whose stewards we are) shall call for them from us.

Christ gave us an instance of the first when He sent His disciples for the ass and bade them answer the owner thus: "The Lord hath need for him" (Matthew 21:2–3). The Lord expects that when He is pleased to call for anything we have, our own interest must stand aside till His turn is served. For the other instance, we need look no further than John 1 "He who hath this world's goods and seeth his brother in need, and shuts up his compassion from him, how dwelleth the love of God in him?" Which comes punctually to this conclusion: If your brother is in want and you can help him, you can have no doubt as to what you should do. If you love God, you must help Him.

Question: What rule must we observe in lending?

Answer: You must observe whether your brother has present or probable or possible means of repaying you, or if none of these, you must give to him according to his necessity, rather than lend to him as he asks. If he has present means of repaying, you are to look at him not as the recipient of mercy but by way of commerce, wherein you are to walk by the rule of justice. But if his means of repaying you are only probable or possible, then he is an object of mercy and you must lend to him though there is danger of losing it. Deuteronomy 15:7-8: "If any of thy brethren be poor. . .thou shalt lend him sufficient." That men might not shift off his duty because of the apparent hazard, he tells them that though the Year of Jubilee were at hand (when he must remit it, if he could not repay it before), yet he must lend, and that cheerfully. Deuteronomy 15:10: "It may not grieve thee to give him," and because some might object, why so I should impoverish myself and my family, he adds: "With all thy work." Matthew 5:42: "From him that would borrow of thee turn not away."

Question: What rule must we observe in forgiving?

Answer: Whether you lend by way of commerce or in mercy. If he has nothing to repay, you must forgive him (unless you have a surety or a lawful pledge). Every seventh year the creditor was to quit that which he lent to his brother if his brother was as poor as he appeared. . . . In all these and like cases Christ gave a general rule in Matthew 7:12: "Whatsoever ye would that men should do to you, do ye the same to them also."

Question: What rule must we observe and walk by in the case of a community of peril?

Answer: The same as before, but with more enlargement toward others and less respect toward ourselves and our own right. Hence, in the primitive church they sold all and had all things in common, nor did any man say that what he possessed was his own. Likewise, in their return from captivity, because the work was great for the restoring of the church and the danger of enemies was common to all, Nehemiah exhorted the Jews to liberality and readiness in remitting their debts to their brethren, and disposed liberally of his own goods to those that wanted, standing not upon what was due him, which he might have demanded of them. Some of our forefathers did the same in times of persecution in England, and so did many of the faithful in other churches, and so we keep an honorable remembrance of them.

It is also to be observed both in the Scriptures and later stories of the church, that those who have been most bountiful to the poor saints—especially in . . . extraordinary times and occasions—God has left highly commended to posterity. . . . Observe again that the Scripture gives no caution to restrain any from being overly liberal in this way, but recommends all men to the liberal and cheerful practice hereof by the sweetest promises. . . . Isaiah 58:10-12:

If thou pour out thy soul to the hungry, then shall thy light spring out in darkness, and the Lord shall guide thee continually, and satisfy thy soul in drought, and make fat thy bones; thou shalt

*be like a watered garden, and they shall be of thee that shall build the
old waste places.*

On the contrary, most heavy curses are laid upon those who are
illiberal toward the Lord and His people. . . .

Having already set forth the practice of mercy according to the
rule of God's law, it will be useful to lay open the grounds of it;
also being the other part of the commandment, and that is the
affection from which this exercise of mercy must arise. The apostle
tells us that this love is the fulfilling of the law (Romans 13:10). Not
that it is enough to love our brother and no more. . . . Just as, when
we bid a man to make the clock strike, he does not lay his hand on
the hammer, which is the immediate instrument of the sound, but
sets to work the first manner or main wheel, knowing that it will
certainly produce the sound which he intends, so the way to draw
men to the works of mercy is not by force of argument on the
goodness or necessity of the work, for though this course may persuade a rational mind to some present act of mercy (as is frequent
in experience), yet it cannot work the habit of mercy into a soul so
that it will be prompt on all accessions to produce the same effect
except by framing the affections of love in the heart, which will as
natively bring forth mercy as any cause produces an effect.

The definition which the Scripture gives us of love is this: love
is the bond of perfection (Colossians 3:14). First, it is a bond, or lig-
ament. Second, it makes the work perfect. There is no body that
does not consist of parts, and that which knits these parts together
gives the body its perfection, because it makes each part so con-
tiguous to the others that they mutually participate with each
other, both in strength and infirmity, in pleasure and in pain. To
instance the most perfect of all bodies: Christ and His church make
one body. The several parts of this body considered apart before
they were united were as disproportionate and as much disor-
dered as so many contrary qualities or elements, but when Christ

came and by His spirit and love knit all these parts to Himself and to each other, it became the most perfect and best proportioned body in the world. . . .

For patterns we have first our Savior, who out of His goodwill and in obedience to His Father became a part of this body, and, being knit with it in the bond of love, found such a native sensitivity to our infirmities and sorrows that He willingly yielded Himself to death to ease the infirmities of the rest of His body and so heal their sorrows. From like sympathy of parts did the apostles and many thousands of saints lay down their lives for Christ again, as we may see in the members of this body among themselves, and as we shall find in the history of the church in all ages: the sweet sympathy of affections in the members of this body, one toward another, their cheerfulness in serving and suffering together. How liberal they were without repining, harborers without grudging, helpful without reproaching, and all from this, that they had fervent love among them, which only makes the practice of mercy constant and easy.

The next consideration is how this love comes to be wrought. Adam in his first estimate was a perfect model of mankind in all generations, and in him this love was perfected. . . . But Adam rent himself from his Creator, rent all his posterity also one from another; whence it comes that every man is born with this principle in him, to love and seek himself only. And thus a man continues till Christ comes and takes possession of his soul, and infuses another principle—love to God and our brother. . . .

The third consideration concerns the exercise of this love, which is twofold—inward or outward. The outward has been handled in the former preface of this discourse; for unfolding the other we must take . . . that maxim of philosophy, *simile simili guadet*, or, like will to like. . . . The ground of love is recognition of some resemblance in the things loved to that which affects it. This is the reason why the Lord loves the creature to the extent that it has any of His image in it; He loves His elect because they are like Him; He beholds them in His beloved Son. So a mother loves her child, because she thoroughly conceives a resemblance of herself in it. Thus it is between the members of Christ. Each discerns by the work of the spirit his own image and resemblance in another, and therefore cannot but love him as he loves himself. . . .

If any shall object that it is not possible that love should be bred or upheld without hope of requital, it is granted. But that is not our cause, for this love is always under reward; it never gives but always receives with advantage. . . . Among members of the same body, love and affection are reciprocal in a most equal and sweet kind of commerce. . . . In regard to the pleasure and content that the exercise of love carries with it, we may see in the natural body that the mouth receives and minces the food which serves to nourish all the other parts of the body, yet it has no cause to complain. For first, the other parts send back by secret passages a due proportion of the same nourishment in a better form for the strengthening and comforting of the mouth. Second, the labor of the mouth is accompanied by pleasure and content that far exceed the pains it takes, so it is all a labor of love.

Among Christians, the party loving reaps love again, as was shown before, which the soul covets more than all the wealth in the world. Nothing yields more pleasure and content to the soul than when it finds that which it may love fervently, for to love and be loved is the soul's paradise, both here and in heaven. In the state of wedlock there are many comforts to bear out the troubles of that condition, but let those who have tried the most say whether there is any sweetness . . . comparable to the exercise of mutual love. . . .

Now make some application of this discourse to the situation which gave the occasion of writing it. **Herein are four things to be propounded: the persons, the work, the end, the means.**

First, for the persons, **we are a company professing ourselves fellow members of Christ.** . . . Though we are absent from each other by many miles, and have our employments at far distance, **we ought to account ourselves knitted together by this bond of love, and live in the exercise of it,** if we would have the comfort of our being in Christ. This was common in the practice of Christians in former times; they used to love any of their own religion even before they were acquainted with them.

Second, **the work we have in hand is by mutual consent with a special overruling Providence, with a** more than ordinary **mandate from the churches of Christ to seek out a place to live and associate under a due form of government both civil and ecclesiastical.** In such cases as this the care of the public must hold sway over all private interests. To this not only conscience but mere civil policy binds us, for true rule that private estates cannot exist to the detriment of the public.

Third, **the end is to improve our lives to do more service to the Lord and to comfort and increase the body of Christ** of which we are members, so that ourselves and our posterity may be better preserved from common corruptions of this evil world in order to serve the Lord and work out our salvation under the power and purity of holy ordinances.

Fourth, the means whereby this must be effected are twofold. First, since the work and end we aim at are extraordinary, we must not content ourselves with usual ordinary means. Whatsoever we did or ought to have done when we lived in England, we must do that and more also wherever we go. **That which most people in churches only profess as a truth, we bring into familiar and constant practice. We must love our brothers without pretense; we** must love one another with a pure heart and fervently; we must bear one another's burdens; we must not look on our own things but also on the things of our brethren. Nor must we think that the Lord will bear with such failings at our hands as He does from those among whom we have lived, for three reasons: (1) Because of the closer bonds of marriage between the Lord and us, wherein He has taken us to be His own in a most strict manner, which makes Him more jealous of our love and obedience, just as He told the people of Israel, "You only have I known of all the families of the Earth; therefore will I punish you for your transgressions" (Amos 3:2); (2) Because the Lord will be sanctified in those who come near Him. We know that there were many who interrupted the service of the Lord, some set up altars to other gods before Him, others offering both strange fires and sacrifices; yet no fire came from heaven, or other sudden judgment upon them. . . ; (3) When given a special commission He wants it strictly observed in every article. . . .

Thus stands the case between God and us. We are entered into covenant with Him for this work. We have taken out a commission. The Lord has given us leave to draw our own articles; we have promised to base our actions on these ends, and we have asked Him for favor and blessing. Now if the Lord shall please to hear us, and bring us in peace to the place we desire, then He has ratified this covenant and sealed our commission, and will expect strict performance of the articles contained in it. But if we neglect to observe these articles, which are the ends we have propounded, and—dissembling with our God—shall embrace this present world and prosecute our carnal intentions, seeking great things for ourselves and our posterity, the Lord will surely break out in wrath against us and be revenged of such a perjured people, and He will make us to know the price of the breach of such a covenant.

Now **the only way to avoid this shipwreck and to provide for our posterity is to follow the counsel of Micah: to do justly, to love mercy, to walk humbly with our God.** For this end, we must be knit together in this work as one man; we must hold each other in brotherly affection; we must be willing to rid ourselves of our excesses to supply others' necessities; we must uphold a familiar commerce together in all meekness, gentleness, patience, and liberality. **We must delight in each other, make others' conditions our own and rejoice together, mourn together, labor and suffer together, always having before our eyes our commission and common work, our community as members of the same body.**

So shall we keep the unity of the spirit in the bond of peace. The Lord will be our God and delight to dwell among us as His own people. He will command a blessing on us in all our ways, so that we shall see much more of His wisdom, power, goodness, and truth than we have formerly known. **We shall find that the God of Israel is among us, and ten of us shall be able to resist a thousand** of our enemies. **The Lord will make our name a praise and glory. For we must consider that we shall be like a City upon a Hill.**

If we deal falsely with our God in this work we have undertaken and so cause Him to withdraw His present help from us, we shall be made a story and a byword throughout the world; we shall open the mouths of enemies to speak evil of the ways of God and all believers in God; **we shall shame the faces of many of God's worthy servants and cause their prayers to be turned into curses upon us, till we are forced out of the new land where we are going.**

Now to end this discourse with the exhortation of Moses, that faithful servant of the Lord, in his last farewell to Israel (Deuteronomy 30:14-20).

Beloved, there is now set before us life and good, death and evil, in that we are commanded this day to love the Lord our

God, and to love one another; to walk in His ways and to keep His commandments and His ordinance, and His laws, and the articles of our covenant with Him, that we may live and be multiplied, and that the Lord our God may bless us in the Land whither we go to possess it. But if our hearts shall turn away so that we will not obey, but shall be seduced and worship other gods, our pleasures and profits, and serve them; it is propounded unto us this day, we shall surely perish out of the good land whither we pass over this vast sea to possess it. Therefore, let us choose life that we and our seed may live; by obeying His voice, and cleaving to Him, for He is our life and our prosperity (emphasis added).

AMERICA'S ONLY HOPE: A RESTORED COVENANT COMMUNITY

It all began on the shores of the James River. God's covenant in America was born in 1607 under the Virginia Charter by the planting of a cross at the "Falls" at Richmond.

Later, in 1620, the Pilgrim fathers declared in the *Mayflower Compact* their intent to plant a colony in the northern parts of Virginia "for the glory of God and advancement of the Christian faith. . . ."

But it was John Winthrop, a godly attorney, who, in 1630, penned for posterity the clearest expression of God's design for America. Having sought for years to purify the church in England from corrupt practice and doctrine, the Puritans yearned to plant a "City set on a hill."

So Winthrop solemnly penned the vision that was to become America. It was a vision of the church, a vision that formed a nation used of God to bless the world with the Gospel. He called it "A Model of Christian Charity," declaring, "We are a company, professing ourselves fellow members of Christ, we ought to account ourselves knit together by this bond of love. . . ."

So was born our nation's covenant—that we would be a people who would love God with all our heart, mind, and strength . . . and as proof of that love, we would live in covenant community with one another. As we have fractured our covenant with God, we have splintered our covenant with our fellow citizens.

And now America lies in acute distress, gasping for the oxygen of faith and a flow of moral truth that will renew her soul and revive her heart.

Restoring faithfulness to Christ in covenant community is America's only hope.

ENDNOTES

Chapter 1

1   *The Bible,* II Corinthians 3:17.
2   *Church of the Holy Trinity v. U.S.*; 143 U.S. 457, 465, 470–471 (1892).
3   A. A. Montapert, ed., *Distilled Wisdom* (Edgewood Cliffs, NJ: Prentice-Hall Inc., 1964), p. 235.
4   Irving Berlin, *God Bless America.*
    Note: Much of the general information regarding the Statue of Liberty was taken from Sue Burchard, *Birth to Rebirth, Statue of Liberty* (New York: Harcourt Brace Jovanovich, Publishers, 1985).

Chapter 2

5   Gaillard Hunt and James B. Scott, ed., *The Debates in the Federal Convention of 1787 Which Framed the Constitution of the United States of America,* reported by James Madison (New York: Oxford University Press, 1920), pp. 181–182.
6   Attributed to James Madison, known as the Father of the Constitution.
7   As compiled by James D. Richardson, *Messages and Papers of the Presidents, 1789–1897* (Bureau of National Literature 1913, 1897), George Washington's Farewell Address, 1:205–216.
8   Alexis de Tocqueville, *Democracy in America* (first published in 1835 and 1840). *Note:* Alexis de Tocqueville arrived in the United States from France in May 1831 and returned to his native France in February 1832 after studying American society and forming his impressions, which he published in *Democracy in America.* That work has become a classic commentary on the American experiment in self-government and the American people.
9   Robert Flood, *The Rebirth of America* (Philadelphia: The Arthur S. De Moss Foundation, 1986), p. 12.
10 *Messages and Papers of the Presidents,* 1:205–216.
11 A congressional resolution in 1954 ratified by President Dwight D. Eisenhower.
12 Robert J. Samuelson, "How Our American Dream Unraveled," *Newsweek,* March 2, 1992, pp. 32–39.
13 Jerry Adler compiled a joint report of reporters from Washington, Chicago, Boston, Atlanta, and Detroit, "Down in the Dumps," *Newsweek,* January 13, 1992, pp. 18–22, with front-cover headline.
14 Samuelson, "How Our American Dream Unraveled," p. 32.
15 Robert Hughes, "The Fraying of America," *Time,* February 3, 1992, pp. 44–49, with front-cover headline.
16 Bart Ziegler, "Experts denounce Japan's comment on U. S. laziness" (Associated Press), as reported in *Star News,* Pasadena, California, January 21, 1992, p. 1.
17 Charles Krauthammer, "In Praise of Mass Hypocrisy," *Time,* April 27, 1992.
18 Samuelson, "How Our American Dream Unraveled," p. 38.
19 "First Lady Denies Psychic Overtones" and "Chats Called Role-Playing." Associated Press articles, *Richmond Times Dispatch,* June 25, 1996, p. A-2.
20 Maureen Dowd, "Hillary Hangs Out With Quack and the Dead," *Richmond Times Dispatch,* July 1, 1996, p. A-9.
21 William Safire, "Nothing Outrages? Just More Scandal From Scandalous Politicos," *Richmond Times Dispatch,* October 14, 1996, p. A-11.
22 Michael Kinsley, "Everybody Does It," *Time,* April 29, 1996, p. 108.
23 "Consulting the Oracle," *Time,* December 4, 1995, p. 52.
24 "Speak Up! You Can Be Heard!" *U.S. News and World Report,* February 19, 1986, p. 42.
25 A popularly quoted version of John 8:7 from the *King James Version* of the Bible, usually used improperly to sidestep taking corrective action for moral failure in both church and society.

26 George Gallup, *Emerging Trends*, March 1999, p. 3.
27 Jeff Grunfield, "The Looking Glass—Voter Anxiety: A Chronic Condition," *Time*, April 22, 1996, p. 58.
28 "The Generation That Forgot God," *Time*, April 5, 1993, front cover.
29 George Gallup, *Emerging Trends*, "Public More Concerned About Morals Than at Any Time in Last 60 Years," March 1997, p. 5.
30 Don Hodel and Randy Tate, "Priorities—Staying on the Road to Victory," *Christian American*, Jan./Feb. 1998, p. 46.

Chapter 3
31 James D. Richardson, *Messages and Papers of the Presidents* (1789–1897), Vol. VI, p. 164, March 30, 1863.
32 John Adams, *The Works of John Adams*, Charles Francis Adams, ed. (Boston: Little, Brown, 1854), Vol. IX, p. 229.
33 James Patterson and Peter Kim, *The Day America Told the Truth* (New York: Prentice Hall, 1991).
34 Ibid., p. 32.
35 Jefferson, *The Writings of Thomas Jefferson*, Vol. II, from Jefferson's "Notes on the State of Virginia," Query XVIII, 1781, p. 227.
36 Noah Webster, *The History of the United States* (New Haven: Durrie & Peck, 1832), p. 309.
37 Thomas Jefferson, *Writings of Thomas Jefferson*, Albert Bergh, ed. (Washington, D.C.: Thomas Jefferson Memorial Assoc., 1904), Vol. II, p. 227, from "Jefferson's Notes on the State of Virginia," Query XVIII, pp. 289, 1781.
38 *The Bible*, Psalm 11:3, *King James Version* (1611).

Chapter 4
39 James Madison, *The Papers of James Madison*, Robert Rutland, ed. (Chicago: University of Chicago Press, 1973), 8:299, 304, June 20, 1785.
40 *The Bible*. Philippians 2:8-10, *King James Version* (1611).
41 *The Bible*. Matthew 23:12, *King James Version* (1611).
42 *The Bible*, Matthew 23:11, *King James Version* (1611).
43 Gorton Carruth & Eugene Ehrlich, ed., *American Quotations* (Avenil, NJ: Wings Books 1992), pp. 461–463, John F. Kennedy Inaugural Address, January 20, 1961.
44 A. A. Montapert, ed., *Distilled Wisdom* (Englewood Cliffs, NJ: Prentice-Hall Inc., 1965), p. 137.
45 Ibid.
46 Ibid.
47 Charles Krauthammer, "In Praise of Mass Hypocrisy," *Time*, April 27, 1992.
48 *The Bible*, Song of Solomon 2:15, *King James Version* (1611).

Chapter 5
49 James Patterson and Peter Kim, *The Day America Told the Truth* (New York: Prentice-Hall Inc., 1991), p. 5.
50 Ibid., p. 6.
51 *The Bible*, Proverbs 29:18, *King James Version* (1611).
52 James D. Richardson, *Messages and Papers of the Presidents* (1789–1897). 5: Insert of Abraham Lincoln's Gettysburg Address between pp. 3371 and 3372.
53 Daniel L. Marsh, *Unto the Generations* (Buena Park, CA: ARC, 1968), p. 51; Tim LaHaye, *Faith of Our Founding Fathers* (Brentwood, TN: Wolgemuth & Hyatt 1987), p. 48.
54 Peter Marshall and David Manuel, *The Light and the Glory* (Grand Rapids, MI: Fleming H. Revell, 1977), p. 31. Quoting Isaiah 49:1,6 from *The Bible, King James Version* (1611).
55 Ibid., p. 111.
56 Ibid., p. 120. (From a photograph of the original in Kate Caffrey's *The Mayflower*, p. 115. Also, William Bradford, *The Plymouth Settlement* (Portland, OR: American Heritage Ministries, 1988), pp. 75–76.

[57] Bradford, ibid., p. 226; Marshall, ibid., p. 144.
[58] Marshall, ibid., p. 161–162.
[59] Ibid., p. 162.
[60] Ibid., p. 185.
[61] Robert N. Bellah, et al., *Habits of the Heart* (Regents of the University of California, 1985; reprinted in 1986 by Harper and Row), pp. 284–285,303.
[62] James D. Richardson, *Messages and Papers of the Presidents* 1789–1897 (printing authorized by Congress), Washington's Inaugural Address, 1:44.
[63] John F. Schroeder, ed., *Maxims of Washington* (Mt. Vernon: Mt. Vernon Ladies Assoc., 1942), p. 287.
[64] James D. Richardson, *Messages and Papers of the Presidents*, 1:212.
[65] Ibid.
[66] Gaillard Hunt and James B. Scott, ed., *The Debates in the Federal Convention of 1787 Which Framed the Constitution of the United States of America*, reported by James Madison (New York: Oxford Univ. Press, 1920), pp. 181–182.
[67] Benjamin Franklin, *The Writings of Benjamin Franklin*, Albert Henry Smyth, ed., 1907 (reprinted New York: Haskell House Publishers, 1970), 9:569, from letter on April 17, 1787.
[68] John Adams, *The Works of John Adams*, Second President of the United States, Charles Francis Adams, ed. (Boston: Little, Brown, 1854), 9:229.
[69] Thomas Jefferson, *Writings of Thomas Jefferson*, Albert Bergh, ed. (Washington, D.C.: Thomas Jefferson Memorial Assoc., 1904), 2:227, from Jefferson's "Notes on the State of Virginia," Query XVIII, pp. 289, 1781.
[70] James D. Richardson, *Messages and Papers of the Presidents* (1787–1897), Gettysburg Address, 5: Insert between pp. 3371 and 3372.
[71] James W. Michaels, "Oh, Our Aching Angst," *Forbes*, September 14, 1992, p. 54.
[72] Peggy Noonan, "You'd Cry Too If It Happened to You," *Forbes*, September 14, 1992, p. 69.
[73] Ibid.
[74] Ibid.
[75] Ibid.
[76] Ibid., p. 65.
[77] Ibid.
[78] Ibid.
[79] *The Bible*, Psalm 33:12.

Chapter 6
[80] A. A. Montapert, ed., *Distilled Wisdom* (Englewood Cliffs, NJ: Prentice Hall, Inc., 1964), p. 235.
[81] Ibid., p. 259.
[82] Ibid.
[83] Ibid.
[84] H. Jackson Brown, Jr., *A Father's Book of Wisdom* (Nashville, TN: Rutledge Press, 1988), p. 131.
[85] James D. Richardson, *Messages and Papers of the Presidents*, 1789–1897 (printing authorized by Congress), Washington's Inaugural Address, 1:212.
[86] John Adams, *The Works of John Adams*, Second President of the United States, Charles Francis Adams, ed. (Boston: Little, Brown, 1854), 9:229.
[87] Ibid.
[88] Nancy Leigh De Moss, ed., *The Rebirth of America* (Philadelphia: Arthur S. De Moss Foundation, 1986), p. 33.
[89] Author unknown.
[90] H. Jackson Brown, Jr., ed., *A Father's Book of Wisdom*, p. 23.
[91] Lewis C. Henry, ed., *Five Thousand Quotations for All Occasions*, p. 219.

Chapter 7

92 George Washington, *Maxims of George Washington*, John Frederick Schroeder, ed. (Mount Vernon, Virginia: The Mount Vernon Ladies' Assoc. 1989), p. 141, from a letter to Alexander Hamilton, August 28, 1788, as taken from "Writings," 30:67.

93 Paul Gray, "Lies, Lies, Lies," *Time*, October 5, 1992, pp. 32–38.

94 John Barry and Roger Charles, "Sea of Lies," *Newsweek*, July 13, 1992, pp. 29–37.

95 Paul Gray, "Lies, Lies, Lies," p. 34.

96 Ibid., p. 32.

97 James Patterson and Peter Kim, *The Day America Told the Truth* (New York:Prentice-Hall Press, 1991), p. 45.

98 Ibid., p. 49.

99 George Barna, *What Americans Believe—The Barna Report* (Ventura, Calif.: Regal Books, 1991), p. 36.

100 Ibid., p. 83.

101 George Barna, *The Barna Report*, January–March 2000, p. 3.

102 Ibid.

103 Ibid.

104 Patterson and Kim, *The Day America Told the Truth*, p. 31.

105 *The Bible*, John 18:38.

106 A. A. Montapert, ed., *Distilled Wisdom* (Englewood Cliffs, NJ: Prentice-Hall, Inc., 1964, 1965), p. 201.

107 H. Jackson Brown Jr., ed., *A Father's Book of Wisdom* (Nashville, Tenn.: Rutledge Hill Press, 1988), p. 62.

108 Peter Marshall and David Manuel, *The Light and the Glory* (NJ: Fleming H. Revell Co., 1977) p. 370, n. 10.

109 *The Bible*, John 8:31–32.

Chapter 8

110 David H. Appel, *An Album for Americans* (New York: Triangle Publications/ Crown Publishers, Inc., 1983), p. 87.

111 Alexis de Tocqueville, *Democracy in America*.

112 Gertrude Himmelfarb, "A De-moralized Society," *Forbes*, September 14, 1992, pp. 120–128.

113 Simon and Garfunkel, *The Sounds of Silence*.

114 James Patterson and Peter Kim, *The Day America Told the Truth* (New York: Prentice-Hall Press, 1991), excerpts compiled from throughout book.

115 Ibid., p. 238.

116 Ibid., p. 55.

117 Gertrude Himmelfarb, "A De-Moralized Society," *Forbes*, September 14, 1992, p. 128.

118 Ibid.

119 Ibid.

120 Kenneth L. Woodward, "What is Virtue?" *Newsweek*, June 13, 1994, pp. 38–39.

121 A. A. Montapert, ed., *Distilled Wisdom* (Englewood Cliffs, NJ: Prentice-Hall, Inc., 1964, 1965), p. 332.

122. James D. Richardson, *Messages and Papers of the Presidents*, 1789-1897 (printing authorized by Congress), Washington's Farewell Address, 1:212.

123 William J. Federer, *America's God and Country* (Coppell, TX: Fame Publishing Inc., 1994), p. 204.

124 Nancy Leigh De Moss, ed., *The Rebirth of America* (The Arthur S. De Moss Foundation, 1986), p. 33.

125 Charles Krauthammer, "In Praise of Mass Hypocrisy," *Time*, April 27, 1992, p. 74.

126 Gertrude Himmelfarb, *The De-Moralization of Society*, as quoted by Os Guinness in *The Great Experiment* (Colorado Springs: NAVPRESS, 2001), pp. 223–224

127 *Newsweek* cover, "The Politics of VIRTUE," June 13, 1994.

[128] Melissa Healy, "Fighting to Fill the Values Gap," *Los Angeles Times*, May 26, 1996, pp. A-1, A-20–21.

[129] Howard Fineman, "The Virtuecrats," *Newsweek*, June 13, 1944.

Chapter 9

[130] A. A. Montapert, ed., *Distilled Wisdom* (Englewood Cliffs, NJ: Prentice-Hall, Inc., 1964, 1965), p. 201.

[131] Nancy Leigh De Moss, ed., *The Rebirth of America* (Philadelphia, PN: Arthur De Moss Foundation, 1986), p. 15.

[132] Ibid., pp. 15–16.

[133] Ibid., p. 16.

[134] Ibid.

[135] Ibid., p. 24.

[136] A. A. Montapert, ed., *Distilled Wisdom*, p. 235.

[137] *The Bible*, I Samuel 15:22.

[138] James Patterson and Peter Kim, *The Day America Told the Truth* (New York: Prentice-Hall Press, 1991), p. 56.

[139] Ibid., p. 94.

[140] Ibid.

[141] Ibid., p. 95.

[142] Ibid., p. 207.

[143] Ibid., pp. 207–210.

[144] Paul Johnson, "An Awakened Conscience," *Forbes*, September 14, 1992, p. 188.

[145] James D. Richardson, ed., *Messages and Papers of the Presidents* (printing authorized by Congress, 1897), p. 212.

[146] Ibid.

[147] Nancy Leigh De Moss, ed., *The Rebirth of America*, p. 33.

[148] Ibid., p. 37.

[149] Ibid.

[150] *The Bible*, I Samuel 2:30.

[151] *The Bible*, Proverbs 18:12.

[152] Ibid.

[153] *The Bible*, I Peter 5:6.

[154] *The Bible*, Isaiah 60:12.

[155] Frank S. Mead, ed., *12,000 Religious Quotations* (Grand Rapids, MI: Baker Book House, 1989), p. 391.

[156] Ibid.

[157] J. C. Penney, *Fifty Years With the Golden Rule* (New York: Harper & Brothers Publishers, 1950), p. 239.

[158] Ibid., p. 242.

[159] Ibid., p. 243.

[160] Ibid., pp. 244–245.

Chapter 10

[161] David H. Appel, ed., *An Album for Americans* (New York: Crown Publishers, Inc., 1983), p. 40.

[162] Fred Cook, *The American Revolution* (New York: Golden Press, 1963), pp. 128–130.

[163] Lewis C. Henry, ed., *Five Thousand Quotations for All Occasions* (Garden City: Doubleday & Co., Inc., 1945), p. 46.

[164] *The Bible*, Song of Solomon 2:15.

[165] A. A. Montapert, ed., *Distilled Wisdom* (Englewood Cliffs, NJ: Prentice-Hall, Inc., 1965), p. 154.

[166] Ibid.

[167] George Gallup Jr., *Forecast 2000* (New York: William Morrow and Company, Inc., 1984), p. 113.

[168] Ibid., p. 114.

169 Ibid.
170 Ibid., pp. 114–123.
171 James Patterson and Peter Kim, *The Day America Told the Truth* (New York: Prentice-Hall Press, 1991), p. 94.
172 Ibid., p. 95.
173 Ibid., p. 100.
174 Ibid., p. 101.
175 *Newsweek*, January 18, 1993 (front cover). Feature article, pp. 16-23.
176 George Barna, *The Future of the American Family* (Chicago: Moody Press, 1993), p. 26.
177 Ibid., p. 27.
178 Ibid., p. 28.
179 Ibid., p. 35.
180 Dr. James C. Dobson, *Straight Talk to Men* (Waco, TX: Word Books, 1980), p. 21.
181 Ibid.
182 Ibid.
183 Ibid., p. 22.
184 Ibid.
185 Ibid. (quoting Derek Prince).
186 Author unknown.
187 Farai Chideya, et al., "Endangered Family," *Newsweek* cover story, August 30, 1993, with cover headline, "A World Without Fathers," pp. 17–27.
188 Ken R. Canfield, "Dads in the 90s," *Today's Father*, Vol. 3, No. 2–3, 1995.
189 George Barna, *The Future of the American Family*, p. 110.
190 *The Bible*, Romans 1:21–32 (specifically v. 30); II Timothy 3:1–7 (specifically v. 2).
191 *The Bible*, Malachi 4:6.
192 A. A. Montapert, ed., *Distilled Wisdom*, p. 117.
193 E. C. McKenzie, ed., *14,000 Quips and Quotes* (Grand Rapids, MI: Baker Book House, 1980), pp. 143–144.
194 Gorton Carruth and Eugene Ehrlich, eds., *American Quotations* (New York: Wings Books, 1988), p. 198.
195 Ibid., p. 200.
196 A. A. Montapert, ed., *Distilled Wisdom*, p. 118.
197 *The Bible*, I Corinthians 4:2.
198 *The Bible*, Ecclesiastes 12:13.
199 Peter Marshall and David Manuel, *The Light and the Glory* (Grand Rapids, MI: Fleming H. Revell, 1977), p. 120.
200 Ibid., pp. 161–162.
201 Ibid., p. 162.
202 Anthony T. Evans, *America's Only Hope* (Chicago: Moody Press, 1990), p. 62.
203 Ibid.
204 *The Bible*, I Peter 4:17.
205 George Gallup Jr., *Wallstreet Journal*, p. 153.
206 Alexis de Tocqueville, *Democracy in America*.
207 Anthony T. Evans, *America's Only Hope*, p. 75.
208 Ibid.
209 Ibid., p. 76.
210 Ibid., p. 77.
211 Ibid.
212 Ibid.
213 Ibid.
214 Ibid., p. 78.
215 Ibid.
216 Ibid.
217 Peggy Noonan, "You'd Cry Too If It Happened to You," *Forbes*, September 14, 1992, p. 68.

[218] Jon Mohr, "Find Us Faithful" (Birdwing Music/Jonathan Mark Music, 1987).

Chapter 11

[219] David H. Appel, ed., *An Album for Americans* (New York: Triangle Publications, Inc./Crown Publishers, Inc., 1983), p. 40.

[220] Ibid., p. 12.

[221] Ibid., p. 77.

[222] Ibid., p. 102.

[223] William Bradford, *Of Plymouth Plantation*, Wright and Potter edition, pp. 34–35.

[224] David H. Appel, ed., *An Album for Americans*, p. 33.

[225] Ibid., pp. 15–16.

[226] Gorton Carruth and Eugene Ehrlich, eds., *American Quotations* (Avenel, NJ: Wings Books, 1988), p. 164.

[227] Ibid., p. 399.

[228] David H. Appel, ed., *An Album for Americans*, p. 74.

[229] James Patterson and Peter Kim, *The Day America Told the Truth* (New York: Prentice Hall Press, 1991), p. 25.

[230] Richard Halverson, *Perspective,* April 22, 1992.

[231] Patterson and Kim, *The Day America Told the Truth*, p. 28.

[232] Ibid.

[233] Ibid., p. 32.

[234] A. A. Montapert, ed., *Distilled Wisdom* (Englewood Cliffs, NJ: Prentice Hall, Inc., 1964), p. 80.

[235] James Michaels, "Oh, Our Aching Angst," *Forbes*, September 14, 1992, p. 54.

[236] A. A. Montapert, ed., *Distilled Wisdom*, p. 74.

[237] Lewis C. Henry, ed., *Five Thousand Quotations for All Occasions* (Garden City: Doubleday & Company, Inc., 1945), p. 49.

[238] William Bentley Bell, ed., *In Search of a National Morality* (Grand Rapids, MI: Baker Book House, 1992), p. 12.

[239] Ibid., p. 43.

[240] Saxe Cummings, ed., *The Basic Writings of George Washington* (New York: Random House, 1948), p. 637.

[241] Abraham Lincoln, "The Gettysburg Address."

[242] Nancy Leigh De Moss, ed., *The Rebirth of America* (Philadelphia: The Arthur S. De Moss Foundation, 1986), p. 16.

[243] A. A. Montapert, ed., *Distilled Wisdom*, p. 80.

[244] Ibid.

[245] E. C. McKenzie, ed., *14,000 Quips & Quotes* (Grand Rapids, MI: Baker Book House, 1980), p. 114.

[246] Ibid.

[247] *The Bible*, Luke 18:1.

[248] A. A. Montapert, ed., *Distilled Wisdom*, p. 80.

[249] Quoted by Os Guinness in *The Great Experiment* (Colorado Springs: NAVPRESS, 2001), p. 224.

[250] *The Bible*, Joshua 1:8–9.

Chapter 12

[251] Fred Cook, *The American Revolution* (New York: Golden Press, 1963), p. 105.

[252] *The Story of America* (Pleasantville, NY: The Reader's Digest Assoc., Inc., 1975), p. 36.

[253] David H. Appel, ed., *An Album for Americans* (New York: Triangle Publications/ Crown Publishers, 1983), p. 43.

[254] Gorton Carruth and Eugene Ehrlich, eds., *American Quotations* (Avenil, NJ: Wings Books, 1988), p. 583.

[255] John Frederick Schroeder, ed., *Maxims of George Washington* (Mount Vernon, VA: The Mount Vernon Ladies' Assoc., 1989), p. 202.

[256] Ibid., p. 203.

257 James Richardson, ed., *Messages and Papers of the Presidents* (printing authorized by Congress, 1897), p. 44.
258 Charles Colson, *The Body* (Dallas: Word Publishing, 1992), p. 41.
259 George Barna, *What Americans Believe* (Ventura, CA: Regal Books, 1991), p. 176.
260 Ibid., p. 77.
261 George Gallup Jr., *Emerging Trends*, February 2001, p.2.
262 George Gallup Jr., *Emerging Trends*, June 2000, p.2.
263 George Gallup Jr., *Emerging Trends*, April 1997, p. 1; September 2001, p. 1.
264 James Patterson and Peter Kim, *The Day America Told the Truth* (New York: Prentice Hall Press, 1991), p. 199.
265 Nancy Leigh De Moss, ed., *The Rebirth of America* (Philadelphia, PA: The Arthur S. De Moss Foundation, 1986), p. 32.
266 Mark Collette, "Pang of Consciousness," *WORLD*, January 17, 1998, p. 18.
267 George Barna, *The Barna Report*, January–March 2000, p. 3.
268 Billy Graham, "Speaking Out—Our Right to Require Belief," *The Saturday Evening Post*, February 17, 1962.
269 George Gallup Jr., *Emerging Trends*, June 1997, p. 2.
270 Patterson and Kim, *The Day America Told the Truth*, p. 3.
271 Ibid., pp. 31–32.
272 *Time*, January 13, 1992, p. 34.
273 *Newsweek*, January 13, 1992, front cover and p. 18.
274 *Newsweek*, March 2, 1992, p. 32.
275 *The Bible*, John 8:31–32.
276 William Bradford, *The Plymouth Settlement* (Portland, OR: American Heritage Ministries, 1988), pp. 75–76.
277 Alexis de Tocqueville, *Democracy in America*.
278 George Gallup Jr., *Forecast 2000* (New York: William Morrow and Company, Inc., 1984), p. 151.
279 Ibid., p. 153.
280 Richard N. Ostling, "The Church Search," *Time*, April 5, 1993, p. 46.
281 Ibid., p. 47.
282 Ibid., p. 48.
283 Ibid.
284 Ibid.
285 Ibid., p. 49.
286 Nancy Leigh De Moss, ed., *The Rebirth of America*, p. 32.
287 Patterson and Kim, *The Day America Told the Truth*, p. 201.
288 Ibid.
289 Ibid.
290 Ibid., p. 202.
291 Ibid.
292 Ibid.
293 Ibid.
294 *The Bible*, Acts 16:25–34.
295 Katherine Lee Bates, "America the Beautiful."

Chapter 13
296 David H. Appel, *An Album for Americans* (New York: Triangle Publications, Inc., 1983), p. 13.
297 Ibid.
298 Dumas Malone, *The Story of the Declaration of Independence* (New York: Oxford University Press, 1954), p. 109.
299 Robert Flood, *America, God Shed His Grace on Thee* (Chicago: The Moody Bible Institute, 1975), p. 62.
300 Ibid., p. 63.
301 Dumas Malone, *The Story of the Declaration of Independence*, pp. 109–111.

302 Ibid., p. 109.
303 Ibid., pp. 110–111.
304 David H. Appel, *An Album for Americans*, p. 61.

Chapter 14
305 *The Bible*, II Timothy 1:7.
306 Gorton Carruth and Eugene Ehrlich, *American Quotations* (Avenil, NJ: Wings Books, 1988), p. 179.
307 Ibid., p. 185, from *Democracy in America*.
308 Steven Waldman, "Ask Not—'90s Style," *Newsweek*, September 20, 1993, p. 46.
309 Peter Marshall and David Manuel, *The Light and the Glory* (Grand Rapids, MI: Fleming H. Revell, 1977), p. 162.
310 Brian Heckmann. A California attorney.
311 John Dawson. International speaker, author—*Healing America's Wounds* (Regal Books, 1994) and *Taking Our Cities for God* (Creation House, 1989).
312 Bob Hunt. A California pastor.
313 Dr. John Perkins. Founder and president of John M. Perkins Foundation for Reconciliation and Development; author.
314 Debra Cruel. A Pennsylvania attorney.
315 Charles Colson. Former White House counsel under Richard Nixon, author, founder of Prison Fellowship.
316 Virgil Gulker. Founder of Love, Inc.
317 Bart Pierce, *Seeking Our Brothers* (Shippensburg, PA: Destiny Image, 2000), Front Cover Byline.

Chapter 15
318 Peter Marshall and David Manuel, *The Light and the Glory* (Grand Rapids, MI: Fleming H. Revell, 1977), p. 120.
319 Ibid., *(The Mayflower Compact)*.
320 Gorton Carruth and Eugene Ehrlich, *American Quotations* (Avenil, NJ: Wings Books, 1988), p. 183. Quoting James Russell Lowell in "New England Two Centuries Ago," *Among My Books*, 1870.
321 Peter Marshall, et al., *The Light and the Glory*, pp. 161–164, 180.
322 William J. Federer, *America's God and Country* (Coppell, TX: Fame Publishing, Inc., 1994), pp. 247–248.
323 Francis Scott Key, "The Star Spangled Banner" (second stanza).
324 *The Bible*, II Chronicles 7:14.
325 *The Bible*, I Peter 4:17.
326 James D. Richardson, ed., *Messages and Papers of the Presidents* (publication authorized by Congress, 1897), p. 212.
327 Adams, *The Works of John Adams*, 9:229.
328 *The Bible*, Deuteronomy 30:19–20.
329 Nancy Leigh De Moss, ed., *The Rebirth of America* (Philadelphia, PA: The Arthur S. De Moss Foundation, 1986), p. 32.
330 *The Bible*, Joshua 24:15.
331 David Barton, *The Myth of Separation* (Aledo, TX: Wall Builders Press, 1992), p. 246.
332 Dumas Malone, *The Story of the Declaration of Independence* (New York: Oxford University Press, 1954), p. 78.
333 David Barton, *The Myth of Separation*, pp. 41–46.
334 Marlin Maddoux, *A Christian Agenda* (Dallas: International Christian Media, 1993), p 63.
335 Ibid.
336 Ibid.
337 Ibid., p. 64.
338 *The Bible*, Isaiah 59:1–4.
339 Ibid.

[340] *The Bible,* Ephesians 5:27.

[341] *The Bible,* Acts 2:1.

[342] Harriet Beecher Stowe, *Uncle Tom's Cabin* (1852); William Federer, *America's God and Country,* (Coppell, TX: Fame Publishing, Inc., 1996).

[343] Alexis de Tocqueville, *Democracy in America.*

Chapter 16

[344] David H. Appel, ed., *An Album for Americans* (New York: Triangle Publications, Inc., 1983), p. 252.

[345] Carroll C. Calkins, ed., *The Story of America* (Pleasantville, NY: The Reader's Digest Assoc., 1975), p. 49.

[346] Eloise Salholz, et al., "Caught in the Act," *Newsweek,* March 23, 1992.

[347] Eleanor Cliff, "Running Against the Past," *Newsweek,* April 13, 1992, p. 30. George V. Church, "Questions, Questions, Questions," *Time,* April 20, 1992, p. 38.

[348] Associated Press, "Clinton discusses equality with garp," *Richmond Times Dispatch,* November 9, 1997.

[349] Gorton Carruth and Eugene Ehrlich, *American Quotations* (Avenil, NJ: Wings Books, 1988), p. 52 (from *The Autobiography of Will Rogers,* 1949).

[350] Ibid., p. 47. From the First Inaugural Address of Dwight D. Eisenhower, January 20, 1953.

[351] Charles Krauthammer, "In Praise of Mass Hypocrisy," *Time,* April 27, 1992, p. 74.

[352] George Barna, *The Barna Report—Absolute Confusion* (Ventura, CA: Regal Books, 1993).

[353] *The Bible,* John 14:15, 21, 23-24.

[354] James Patterson and Peter Kim, *The Day America Told the Truth* (New York: Prentice Hall Press, 1991), p. 8.

[355] Cal Thomas, *The Death of Ethics in America* (Dallas: Word Publishing, 1988), p. 20.

[356] Ibid., p. 21.

[357] Ibid., pp. 33–34.

[358] Clyde M. Narramore, "Character: Public or Private," *Psychology for Living,* July–August 1992, p. 2.

[359] G. Frederick Owen, *Abraham Lincoln—the Man & His Faith* (Wheaton, IL: Tyndale House, 1976), p. 73.

[360] Ibid., p. 18.

[361] Ibid.

[362] Peggy Noonan, "You'd Cry Too If It Happened to You," *Forbes,* September 14, 1992, p. 69.

[363] Michael Medved,"Hollywood's Poison Factory—Making It the Dream Factory Again," *Imprimis,* (Hillsdale, MI: Hillsdale College), November 1992, Vol. 21, No. 11.

[364] Michael Medved, *Hollywood vs. America* (San Francisco: Harper Collins/Zondervan, 1992).

[365] Patterson and Kim, *The Day America Told the Truth,* p. 25.

[366] Allan Bloom, *The Closing of the American Mind* (New York: Simon & Schuster, Inc., 1987).

[367] *The Bible,* Matthew 16:18.

[368] Richard N. Ostling, "A Refinement of Evil," *Time,* October 4, 1993, p. 75.

[369] Richard N. Ostling, "The Church Search," *Time,* April 5, 1993, pp. 44–48.

[370] Ibid., p. 46.

[371] Ibid., p. 47.

[372] George Barna, *What Americans Believe* (Ventura, CA: Regal Books, 1991), p. 36.

[373] Richard N. Ostling, "The Church Search," p. 48.

[374] David F. Wells, *No Place For Truth* (Grand Rapids, MI: Eerdmans Publishing Co., 1993), p. 300.

[375] Ibid., p. 48.

[376] Ibid., p. 295.

377 Richard N. Ostling, "The Church Search," p. 49.
378 Os Guinness, *Dining With the Devil* (Grand Rapids, MI: Baker Book House, 1993).
379 Warren W. Wiersbe, *The Integrity Crisis* (Nashville, TN: Thomas Nelson Publishers, 1991), p. 134.
380 Ibid., p. 136.
381 Ibid., p. 135.
382 Ibid., p. 61.
383 Anthony T. Evans, *America's Only Hope* (Chicago: Moody Press, 1990), p. 42.
384 Ibid., p. 39.
385 *The Bible*, II Chronicles 7:14.
386 *The Bible*, Psalm 25:21.
387 Chuck Colson, "Challenge to a Vital Faith," *The War Cry* (published by the Salvation Army), July 4, 1992, pp. 4–6.
388 Nancy Leigh De Moss, ed., *The Rebirth of America* (Philadelphia, PA: The Arthur S. De Moss Foundation, 1986), p. 37.
389 Ibid., p. 69, from the "Gettysburg Address."
390 James D. Richardson, ed., *Messages and Papers of the Presidents*, p. 212.
391 Carruth and Ehrlich, eds., *American Quotations*, p. 65.
392 Peggy Noonan, "You'd Cry Too If It Happened to You," *Forbes*, September 14, 1992, p. 65.
393 Os Guinness, *The American Hour* (New York: The Free Press, 1993), p. 4.
394 Ibid.
395 Ibid., p. 49.

Chapter 17
396 Source unknown.
397 Gorton Carruth and Eugene Ehrlich, ed., *American Quotations*, (Avenil, NJ: Wing Books, 1992), p. 107.
398 Ibid., p. 109.
399 *The Bible*, Proverbs 22:28.
400 From the final stanza of "The Star-Spangled Banner," our national anthem.
401 From our *Declaration of Independence*.
402 Ibid.
403 Associated Press, "Nation, it seems, is split in half," *Richmond Times Dispatch*, November 11, 2000, p. A-8.
404 *The Bible*, Mark 3:25.
405 *The Bible*, Matthew 12:25.
406 Associated Press, "Nation it seems, is split in half," p. A-8.
407 Ibid.
408 Attributed to artist Walt Kelly's cartoon strip character "Pogo."
409 A good overview of the pursuit of this "new god made in man's image" can be found in the cover story "The Church Search" by Richard N. Ostling, *Time*, pp. 44–49. The cover is titled "The Generation That Forgot God."
410 The Associated Press, "Clinton Discusses Equality with Gays," *Richmond Times Dispatch*, November 9, 1997.
411 Peter Marshall and David Manuel, *The Light and the Glory*, (Old Tappan, NJ: Fleming H. Revel Co., 1977).
412 Verna M. Hall, *Christian History of the Constitution of the United States of America* (San Francisco, CA: The American Christian Constitution Press, 1960).
413 Verna M. Hall, *Self-Government with Union* (San Francisco, CA: The American Constitution Press, 1962).
414 Verna M. Hall, *The Christian History of the American Revolution* (San Francisco, CA: The Foundation of American Christian Education, 1975).
415 Marshall Foster and Marry-Elaine Swanson, *The American Covenant–The Untold Story* (Thousand Oaks, CA, 1981).

[416] Mark A. Beliles and Stephen K. McDowell, *America's Providential History* (Charlottesville, VA: Providence Foundation, 1989).

[417] David Barton, *America: To Pray or Not to Pray* (Aledo, TX: Wall Builder Press, 1988, 1991).

[418] David Barton, *America's Godly Heritage*. Video production. (Aledo, TX: Wall Builders Inc., 1990, 1992).

[419] Pat Robertson, *America's Date with Destiny* (Nashville, TN: Thomas Nelson Inc., 1986).

[420] William J. Bennett, *The Book of Virtues*, (New York: Simon & Schuster, 1993).

[421] William J. Bennett, *The Moral Compass*, (New York: Simon & Schuster, 1995).

[422] M. Stanton Evans, *The Theme Is Freedom* (Washington, D.C.: Regnery Publishing, Inc, 1994).

[423] William J. Federer, *America's God and Country* (Coppell, TX: Fame Publishing, Inc., 1994).

[424] Ibid., back cover quote from George Washington's inaugural address in 1789.

[425] *The Bible*, Daniel 5 (specifically v. 5).

[426] *The Bible*, Daniel 5:27.

[427] *The Bible*, John 3:3–7.

[428] *In the Spirit of '76* (Washington, D.C.: Third Century Publishers Inc., 1975) *Note:* no author or editor is identified in the book. Copyright was issued to Third Century Publishers Inc.

[429] *The Bible*, Proverbs 29:2.

[430] *In the Spirit of '76*, cover quote.

[431] *The Bible*, II Corinthians 6:14.

[432] William J. Bennett, *The Index of Leading Cultural Indicators*, (New York: Touchstone / Simon & Schuster, 1994).

[433] George Gallup Jr., *Emerging Trends*, (Princeton, NJ: Princeton Religion Research Center, March 1999), pp. 2–3, *Note:* results taken from a CNN/Gallup Survey, February 1999.

[434] *The Bible*, Psalm 16:6.

[435] *The Bible*, Exodus 20:3.

[436] *The Bible*, Isaiah 40:15,17.

[437] President Abraham Lincoln's Proclamation for a Day of National Humiliation, Fasting, and Prayer, Washington, D.C., March 30, 1863.

[438] Cal Thomas and Ed Dobson, *Blinded by Might* (Grand Rapids, MI: Zondervan Publishing House, 1999).

[439] Don Hodel and Randy Tate, "Staying on the Road to Victory," *Christian American*, January–February 1998, p. 46.

Chapter 18

[440] *The Bible*, Proverbs 29:18, "Where there is no vision, the people perish."

[441] *The Bible*, Matthew 28:19–20.

[442] *The Bible*, Matthew 24:14. *Note:* only the first half of this passage is actually engraved over CBN headquarters.

[443] Peter Marshall and David Manuel, *The Light and the Glory* (Grand Rapids, MI: Fleming H. Revell, 1977), p. 31 (quoting Isaiah 49:1,6 from the Bible, *Revised Standard Version*).

[444] *The Charters of Virginia*. *Note:* names of editors and/or authors not contained in book. (Virginia Beach, VA: Patriot Prints, 1994), The First Virginia Charter, April 10, 1606, no pagination given.

[445] Ibid.

[446] Virginius Dabney, *Richmond, The Story of A City*, (Charlottesville, VA: The University Press of Virginia, 1976, 1990), p. 1.

[447] *The Bible*, Psalm 2:8.

[448] Will Durant, *The Story of Civilization*, Part III, *Caesar and Christ* (New York: Simon & Schuster, 1944).

[449] *The Bible*, II Timothy 2:3.

[450] *The Bible*, II Corinthians 4:7.

[451] Peter Marshall and David Manuel, *The Light and the Glory*, pp. 119–120.

[452] Herbert W. Titus, J. D., "The First Charter of Virginia: Seedbed for the Nation," (Virginia Beach, VA: *The Forecast*, April 15, 1994).

[453] Ibid.

[454] Peter Marshall and David Manuel, *The Light and the Glory*, p. 146.

[455] Robert N. Bellah, et al., *Habits of the Heart*, "Culture and Character" (New York: Harper and Row, 1984), p. 29.

[456] Peter Marshall and David Manuel, *The Light and the Glory*, p. 146.

[457] William Benton, *The Annals of America* (Chicago, IL: Encyclopedia Britannica, Inc., 1968), pp. 114–115.

[458] *The Bible*, Ecclesiastes 5:4–5; Genesis 28:20; Numbers 21:2.

[459] William Benton, *The Annals of America*, p. 115. Taken from John Winthrop's "A Model of Christian Charity."

[460] William J. Bennett, *The Index of Leading Cultural Indicators* (Colorado Springs, CO: Waterbrook Press, 1999), pp. 3–6.

[461] *The Bible*, Psalm 111:10.

[462] *The Bible*, Jeremiah 51:51.

[463] *The Bible*, John 15:2.

[464] *The Bible*, Luke 12:48 (*Note:* written as generally quoted in common parlance rather than verbatim.).

[465] *The Bible*, Isaiah 40:15.

[466] Francis Scott Key, "The Star-Spangled Banner," last stanza.

[467] George Gallup Jr., *Emerging Trends* (Princeton, NJ: Princeton Religion Research Center, Vol. 21, No. 3, March 1999), pp. 2–3.

[468] Michael L. Brown, *The End of the American Gospel Enterprise* (Shippensburg, PA: Destiny Image Publishers, 1993), p. 3.

[469] James Russell, *Awakening the Giant* (Grand Rapids, MI: Zondervan Publishing House, 1996), p. 27.

[470] Ibid.

[471] *The Bible*, John 14:15. Also confirmed in other passages, including John 14:21,23-24; I John 5:2–3; Revelation 14:12.

[472] James Russell, *Awakening the Giant*, p. 5.

[473] Ibid., p. 105.

[474] George Barna, *The Barna Report* (Ventura, CA: Barna Research Group, Ltd., January–March 2000), p. 4.

[475] James Russell, *Awakening the Giant*, pp. 163–164.

[476] *The Bible*, Daniel 9:8–11.

[477] Phillip Yancey, "A State of Ungrace," *Christianity Today*, February 3, 1997, p. 35.

[478] Richard N. Ostling, "The Church Search," *Time*, April 5, 1993, p. 45.

[479] Lauren F. Winner, "The Spiritual Sampler," *New Age*, January–February 2001, p. 67.

[480] George Gallup Jr., *Emerging Trends*, March 1999, p. 4.

[481] Bill Bright and John N. Damoose, *Red Sky in the Morning*, (Orlando, FL: New Life Publications, 1998), pp. 244–245).

Chapter 19

[482] Leonard Ravenhill, *America Is Too Young to Die* (Minneapolis, MI: Bethany House Publishers, 1979), p. 3 and cover title.

[483] Ibid., p. 30.

[484] Winkie Pratney, *Revival—Principles to Change the World* (Lindale, TX: Agape Force, 1983, 1984), p. 127, quoting Basil Miller's biography, *Charles Finney*.

[485] Ibid., quoting Perry Miller's biography, *Finney, The Heart of Truth*.

[486] James D. Richardson, *Messages and Papers of the Presidents* 1779–1897 (published by authority of Congress 1899), 1:52–53. George Washington's Inaugural Address April 30, 1789.

[487] Gaillard Hunt and James B. Scott, ed., *The Debates in the Federal Convention of 1787 Which Framed the Constitution of the United States of America*, reported by James Madison (New York: Oxford University Press, 1920) pp. 181–182.

[488] William J. Federer, *America's God and Country* (Coppell, TX: Fame Publishing, Inc. 1994), p. 656.

[489] Ibid., pp. 668–669.

[490] Winki Pratney, *Revival—Principles to Change the World*, p. 137.

[491] Basil Miller, *Charles Finney* (Minneapolis, MI: Bethany House Publishers, 1942), p. 18.

[492] Pat Robertson, *America's Dates with Destiny* (Nashville, TN: Thomas Nelson, Inc., 1986), p. 133.

[493] Iain H. Murray, *Revival and Revivalism* (Carlisle, PA: The Banner of Truth Trust, 1994), p. 225.

[494] Charles Finney, *Holy Spirit Revivals* (New Kensington, PA: Whitaker House, 1999), p. 195.

[495] Ibid., p. 189.

[496] Ibid., p. 190.

[497] Ibid., p. 194.

[498] Ibid., p. 195.

[499] John S. Tompkins, "Our Kindest City," *The Readers Digest*, July 1994, pp. 53–56.

[500] Ibid., p. 55.

[501] Basil Miller, *Charles Finney*, p. 52.

[502] Leonard Ravenhill, *America Is Too Young to Die*, p. 63 and cover title.

[503] Keith J. Hardman, *Charles Grandison Finney* (Grand Rapids, MI: Baker Book Company, 1990), p. 199.

[504] Ibid., p. 210.

[505] Charles Finney, *Holy Spirit Revivals*, p. 197.

[506] Pat Robertson, *America's Dates with Destiny*, p. 136.

[507] Ibid., p. 139.

[508] William J. Federer, *America's God and Country*, p. 575.

[509] Pat Robertson, *America's Dates with Destiny*, p. 52.

[510] Ibid., pp. 50–51.

[511] *The Bible*, Matthew 16:1–3.

[512] *The Bible*, Hosea 4:6–9.

[513] Leonard Ravenhill, *Why Revival Tarries*, (Minneapolis, MI: Bethany House Publishers, 1991), unnumbered pages of the Foreword.

[514] Leonard Ravenhill, *America Is Too Young to Die*, p. 25.

[515] Dr. Bill Bright and John N. Damoose, *Red Sky in the Morning* (Orlando, FL: New Life Publications, 1998), pp. 23–25.

Chapter 20

[516] David A. Kaplan and Anne Underwood, "The Iceberg Cometh," *Newsweek*, November 25, 1996, p. 68.

[517] Ibid.

[518] Ibid., p. 69.

[519] *The Bible*, Matthew 5:14.

[520] *The Bible*, Matthew 6:23.

Chapter 21

[521] Robert H. Bellah, et al., *Habits of the Heart* (New York: Harper and Row, Publishers, 1985), preface, p. vii.

[522] Ibid., p. 28, from *Democracy in America* by Alexis de Tocqueville.

[523] W. Cleon Skousen, *The Making of America* (Washington, D.C.: National Center for Constitutional Studies, 1985), p. 679.

[524] Robert H. Bork, *Slouching Towards Gomorrah* (New York: Harper Collins, 1996), p. 2.

[525] Arnold L. Cook, *Historical Drift*, (Camp Hill, PA: Christian Publications, Inc., 2000), p. 56.

[526] Ibid., p. 11.

[527] *The Bible*, Judges 2:7,10–12.

[528] *The Bible*, Judges 2:14–15.

[529] *The Bible*, Judges 2:16–20.

[530] *The Bible*, Judges 21:25.

[531] *The Bible*, Revelation 2–3.

[532] Jim Russell, *Awakening the Giant* (Grand Rapids, MI: Zondervan, 1996), pp. 163–164.

[533] Ibid., p. 49.

[534] Kenneth L. Woodward, "The Rites of Americans," *Newsweek*, November 29, 1993, p. 80.

[535] James Patterson and Peter Kim, *The Day America Told the Truth* (New York: Prentice Hall Press, 1991), pp. 45–49.

[536] David Whitman, "The Trouble With Premarital Sex," *U.S. News and World Report*, May 19, 1997, cover story, pp. 57–64.

[537] George Barna, *The Barna Report*, premiere issue, pp. 5–6. Confirmed again October–December 1999.

[538] David Popenoe and Barbara Dafoe Whitehead, *The State of Our Unions*, a report of the National Marriage Project at Rutgers University, 1999.

[539] Michael Gartner, "Values? What About Divorce?" *USA Today*, June 6, 1995, p. 13-A.

[540] David Crasy, "Counterattack begun on the divorce rate," *Richmond Times Dispatch* (Associated Press article), November 12, 1999.

[541] David Crasy, "Counterattack begun on the divorce rate," p. A-2.

[542] George Barna, *The Barna Report*, "Christians Are More Likely to Experience Divorce Than Non-Christians," October–December 1999, pp. 9–10.

[543] *The Bible*, Malachi 2:13–17.

[544] *The Jerusalem Post*, "Divorce rate hits 30 percent," February 4, 2000.

[545] *Ministries Today*, "Divorced Ministers," September–October 1995, p. 18.

[546] Dennis Worden, "Partners in Prayer" report for Injoy Ministries, faxed to author August 20, 1998.

[547] Jack Hayford, "Don't Marriage Vows Matter Anymore?" *Charisma*, February 2001, pp. 60–68.

[548] Peter K. Johnson, "Assemblies of God Tackles Problems of Porn Addiction Among Ministers," *Charisma*, January 2001, p. 24.

[549] Dennis Worden, "Partners in Ministry."

[550] *The Bible*, Matthew 6:23.

[551] *The Bible*, Psalm 103:8–18; Jude 21; John 14:21–24.

[552] *The Bible*, II Chronicles 7:14.

[553] *The Bible*, Proverbs 14:34.

[554] Attributed to Ruth Graham, wife of Dr. Billy Graham.

[555] Bill Bright, *The Coming Revival* (Orlando, FL: New Life Publications, 1995), p. 23.

[556] William J. Federer, *America's God and Country* (Coppell, TX: Fame Publishing, Inc., 1994), p. 323.

[557] Ibid., p. 13.

[558] *The Bible*, Amos 3:3.

[559] Mortimer J. Adler, ed. *The Annals of America* (Chicago: Encyclopedia Britannica Inc., William Benton, 1968) p. 115.

[560] *The Bible*, Philippians 2:10–11.

[561] *The Bible*, I Peter 4:17.

[562] *The Bible*, Ezekiel 9:6.

[563] *The Bible*, Luke 12:48.

[564] *The Bible,* II Chronicles 7:14.
[565] *The Bible,* Joel 2:17.
[566] Iain H. Murray, *Revival and Revivalism* (Carlisle, PA: The Banner of Truth Trust, 1994), p. 87.
[567] Ibid., p. 64.
[568] Stephen Hill, *Time to Weep* (Lake Mary, FL: Creation House, 1995), p. 24.
[569] *The Bible,* Psalm 30:5.
[570] Bill Bright, *The Coming Revival,* p. 23.
[571] Richard C. Halverson, *The Living Body* (Gresham, OR: Vision House, 1994).
[572] Michael S. Horton, *Beyond Culture Wars* (Chicago: Moody Press, 1994), p. 39.
[573] Ibid., p. 107.
[574] Ibid., p. 116.
[575] Ibid., p. 220.
[576] Erwin W. Lutzer, *Will America Be Given Another Chance?* (Chicago: Moody Press, 1993), p. 42.
[577] Ibid., p. 44.
[578] Ibid., pp. 37–38.
[579] Leonard Ravenhill, *Revival God's Way* (Minneapolis: Bethany House Publishers, 1986), p. 55.
[580] Ibid., p. 30.
[581] Cindy Jacobs, "It's Time to Seek God's Face," *Ministries Today,* November/December 1996, p. 49.
[582] Billy Graham, "Speaking Out—Our Right to Require Belief," *The Saturday Evening Post,* February 17, 1962.
[583] Chuck Colson, "A Nation That Has Forgotten God," *Jubilee,* Summer 1996, p. 19.
[584] David Aikman, "Are You Ready for Revival," *Charisma,* May 1997, p. 86.
[585] George Barna, *The Barna Report,* April–June 1999, p. 2.
[586] Peter Marshall, "Marshall Sounds a Wake-up Call," *Charisma,* November 1994, p. 101.
[587] David Wilkerson, "Whatever Happened to Repentance?" *Times Square Church Pulpit Series,* August 2, 1999.
[588] Michael Brown, *The End of the American Gospel Enterprise* (Shippensburg, PA: Destiny Image Publishers, 1989), p. 29.
[589] Ibid., cover title.
[590] Dwight L. Moody quotation, *Charisma,* May 1997.
[591] Ken Hutchinson, "Shaking in the Pulpit," *Ministries Today,* November/December 1998.
[592] John F. MacArthur, *Ashamed of the Gospel,* (Wheaton, IL: Crossway Books, 1993), p. 35.
[593] Ibid., p. 102.
[594] Jim Russell, "Whatever Became of Shame," *Crosswinds,* November/December 1999, p. 4.
[595] Alexis de Tocqueville, *Democracy in America,* as quoted in *America's God and Country* by William J. Federer, p. 205.
[596] Dr. Henry Blackaby, "What Do You See As the Future of the United States?" address given at a conference at the Billy Graham Training Center at the Cove, North Carolina, on May 22, 1999; printed by Intercessors for America.
[597] Jimmy and Carol Owens, *Heal Our Land* (Grand Rapids, MI: Fleming H. Revel, 1997), p. 84.
[598] *The Bible,* Galatians 2:20.
[599] Joseph M. Stowell, *The Dawn's Early Light,* (Chicago: Moody Press, 1990), p. 17.

Chapter 22
[600] *The Bible,* Deuteronomy 32:4
[601] *The Bible,* Deuteronomy 6:3–18.
[602] *The Bible,* John 14:21–24; I John 5:2–3.

[603] *The Bible*, Deuteronomy 6:24.
[604] *The Bible*, Deuteronomy 6:18
[605] *The Bible*, Genesis 6:3
[606] *The Bible*, Isaiah 1:2–9.
[607] *The Bible*, Isaiah 1:10–15
[608] *The Bible*, Isaiah 1:16–18
[609] *The Bible*, Isaiah 1:19–20
[610] Williard Bickers, *Your Country Is Desolate* (New York: Vantage Press, 1996).
[611] Dr. Richard Halverson, *The Living Body* (Gresham, OR: Vision House 1994), p. 31.
[612] James A. Pike, "Christianity Is in Retreat," *Look*, December 20, 1960, front cover and pp. 23–26.
[613] Peggy Noonan, "You'd Cry Too If It Happened to You," *Forbes*, September 14, 1992, pp. 58–69, 65.
[614] "The Generation That Forgot Time," *Time*, cover title, April 5, 1992.
[615] Kenneth L. Woodward, "The Rites of Americans," *Newsweek*, November 29, 1993, pp. 80–81.
[616] Richard N. Ostling, "One Nation Under Gods," *Time*, fall special issue, 1993, pp. 62–63.
[617] Barbara Kantrowitz, et al., "In Search of the Sacred," *Newsweek*, November 28, 1994, pp. 53–55.
[618] "In So Many Gods We Trust," *Time*, January 30, 1995.
[619] Dr. Henry Blackaby, *What Do You See as the Future of the United States?* Address at the Cove, North Carolina, May 22, 1999.
[620] *The Bible*, Jeremiah 7:28.
[621] *The Bible*, Jeremiah 9:9.
[622] *The Bible*, I John 1.
[623] President Abraham Lincoln's "Proclamation for a National Day of Fasting, Humiliation and Prayer," April 30, 1863. James D. Richardson, *A Compilation of the Messages and Papers of the Presidents, 1789–1897* (published by authority of Congress, 1899), 6:164.
[624] The facts woven throughout this "American Parable" and upon which it is based were gleaned primarily from the following sources obtained at the Johnstown Flood National Memorial: National Park Service, U.S. Department of the Interior, an extensive brochure titled "Johnstown Flood," 1993. Script of the film of the Johnstown Flood National Memorial. Paula and Carl Degen, *The Johnstown Flood of 1889*. (Eastern Acorn Press for Eastern Park and Monument Association), 1984.

Chapter 23
[625] Robert J. Samuelson, "The Future Be Damned," *Newsweek*, January 16, 1992, p. 36.

Appendix A
[626] Robert Bellah, et. al., *Habits of the Heart*

ABOUT THE AUTHOR

FOR A VETERAN TRIAL ATTORNEY to be referred to as "a prophet for our time" is indeed unusual, but many people who have heard **Charles Crismier's** daily radio broadcast, *VIEWPOINT*, believe just that. Now, in *Renewing the Soul of America*, his words, "full of passion and conviction," provide a "road map for renewal" in our nation.

Crismier speaks from an unusual breadth of experience. After nine years as a public schoolteacher, he spent twenty years as a trial attorney, pleading causes before judge and jury. As a pastor's son, also serving in pastoral roles for 20 years, Crismier has been involved with ten distinct Protestant denominations—both mainline and otherwise, together with other independent and charismatic groups from coast to coast and from North to South—providing an enviable insider's view of American Christianity and life.

Deeply troubled by the direction of the nation he loves, this attorney left his lucrative Southern California law practice in 1992 to form SAVE AMERICA Ministries and was awarded the Valley Forge Freedom Foundation award for his contribution to the cause of "Rebuilding the Foundations of Faith and Freedom." Chuck probes the heart and conscience of our nation with both a rare combination of insight, directness, urgency, and compassion and a message that "desperately needs to be heard and heeded before it is too late."

From the birthplace of America—Richmond, Virginia—this attorney speaks provocatively and prophetically on daily national radio as "a Voice to the Church," declaring "Vision for the Nation" in America's greatest crisis hour.

Charles Crismier can be contacted by writing or calling:

P.O. Box 70879
Richmond, VA 23255
(804) 754-1822

or through his website at
www.saveus.org

Additional copies of this book
are available from your local bookstore or
through Elijah Books.

If you have enjoyed this book, or if it has impacted your life,
we would like to hear from you.

If you would like to help distribute the message of this book
either individually or through your church, ministry or other
organization, substanaial case-lot discounts are available.

Please contact us at
Elijah Books
P.O. Box 70879
Richmond, Virginia 23255
(804) 754-3000
or by e-mail at
elijahbooks@comcast.net

elijah books